WILLIAM CAREY

Building With Old Stones: Collected sermons of Rev. William H. Carey

Dedication

This book is dedicated to the memory of Bro. and Sis. Hanby, two of the most godly people I ever met. They loved me, taught me, and nurtured me, and now both have gone on to their eternal reward.

Contents

Called to Minister

I'm reading from the book of Matthew, chapter 23, and verses 11 and 12:

But he that is greatest among you shall be your servant and whosoever shall exalt himself shall be abased and he that shall humble himself shall be exalted.

The word minister is much misunderstood in the Christian world today. Many people hear the word minister and think of priests. They think of pastor, preacher, teacher, master. All of these things associated with the word minister: Leader, governor, elder.

But what does the word minister mean? The word minister can be both a noun and a verb. And the meaning is basically the same, whether used as a noun or a verb, and it has only one meaning: The word minister means servant. The verb minister means serve.

I can remember when I first entered Bible School to prepare for the ministry. I had pretty much the same attitude that many ministerial students have: *I'm called to the ministry! I'm called to the ministry!* There's a certain amount of pride in that statement. *I have a call to the ministry! I'm going to stand in the Pulpit! I'm going to preach! God is going to use me! Great things are going to happen! Miracles are going to be done! I'm called to the ministry!*

I was in for a bit of a rude awakening. Among the things that I was given to do were take the trash out, clean the bathrooms in the school and the church, mop floors, fill the paper towel dispensers, do dishes, straighten out the hymnals in the church...

Wait a minute! Somebody must have made a mistake! I'm called to the ministry! There are people in the church who can do those other things. I mean, the church janitor can bring the garbage out. The church cleaning committee can take care of the bathrooms. I'm called to the ministry! I don't take out the garbage. I don't clean the bathrooms. I was ready to jump up into the pulpit. I'm called to preach. I'm called to the ministry.

What I didn't realize was, they were trying to teach me a very important lesson, and I was very slow to learn this like so many others in the Bible school. I thought my ministry began in the pulpit, or at least on a street corner with a Bible in my hand. *That is where my ministry begins!* No, this is not where the ministry begins. The ministry does not begin in the pulpit, does not begin on the street corner, doesn't begin with a Bible in your hand. That's not where the ministry begins. It may eventually end up there, only God knows, but that's not where the ministry begins.

They were trying to teach me what it means to be a minister, so they told me to take the trash out. They were trying to teach me what it means to be a minister, so they handed me a toilet bowl brush and told me to go scrub, to go clean the urinals. There's probably nothing more degrading in the world than cleaning urinals. They were trying to teach me what it means to be a minister. *I don't understand! What's the connection? God called me to preach! God called me to minister! What am I doing in the bathroom? What am I doing lugging heavy trash cans down the hallway to put them out front on trash day? I don't understand!*

I was called to minister. I was called to serve. My ministry didn't begin in the pulpit. My ministry didn't begin on the street corner. My ministry didn't begin with a Bible in my hand. My ministry began with a toilet bowl brush in the men's room at the church, scrubbing out urinals. That's where the ministry begins.

Oh, not me, I'm called to preach! I can bypass all that. No, you can't bypass that. You can't. You've **got** to start there. That's where your ministry begins: Serving.

The one among you who wants to be the greatest of all must be the servant of all. They asked Jesus who's going to be the greatest in the Kingdom. Well, they thought He would choose one of them, or maybe mention the names of one of the prophets, or some great leader. But Jesus took a little child and put him in the middle of the group and said, "Whoever does not become like a little child will not enter into the kingdom of heaven." What's childlike? Humble, trusting. And they tend to do an awful lot of work that their parents give them to do. Maybe not always willingly, but then neither do we.

You want to be a minister? Then you want to be a servant. You want to someday stand in the pulpit? Start in the bathroom. You want to someday preach to a crowd of 1500? Take the trash out. This is where Ministry begins, because a minister is a servant.

Above all else, a minister is a servant, and that never changes. That never changes. The minister is a servant from the day he first received the call from heaven to go and preach the word. He is a servant until the day that God calls him home. He is a servant. The man or woman who is called by God to minister must know how to serve.

Jesus and His disciples sat down for dinner one time. And Jesus poured some water in a basin and began to wash the feet of the disciples. And I understand exactly what Peter was thinking: *What in heaven's name are you doing? Lord, You are our master! You're the minister! What are You doing? Washing our feet?* I understand what he felt. That's my own initial reaction. That's my own natural thought. *What are you doing? You're the minister.*

Pastor, why are you shoveling the snow? Pastor, why are you vacuuming the sanctuary? Pastor, why are you taking out the trash? Pastor, why are you getting up at three o'clock in the morning to go over to somebody's house? Because the minister is a servant.

The minister was not called to be the greatest in the congregation, the greatest in the Kingdom. The minister was called to be the servant. The minister was not called to be first. The minister was called to be last. The minister was not called to be great and powerful or noble. The minister was called to be humble, to be a servant, to clean the bathrooms, to take out the trash. The minister was called to do these things. And from there, the ministry can grow.

Well, you want a plant to grow? You put a seed in the ground. This is the natural order of things. You put a seed in the ground. It works best this way. That's God's way of doing things: You start small and let it grow to something big.

Your ministry can't start off as a fully mature plant. It has to start as a seed. It starts as the call, and then it goes to service, and it continues with service throughout the entire span of your ministry. Service. Service to others, always being the servant, always putting yourself last.

One of my teachers, probably the greatest example I had in preparing for the ministry, was old Brother Hanby. And I can still remember when they would have ministers' conferences, and all the UPC [United Pentecostal Church] ministers from the state of New York would gather at our church. Brother Hanby was the senior minister. Bro. Hanby was the District Superintendent for all of New York State. Brother Hanby was one of the pioneers of the Pentecostal Church. There might have been no UPC if it wasn't for Bro. Hanby because he was instrumental in forming the UPC. There would have been no merger to form the UPC without Bro. Hanby. Bro. Hanby was on the General Board of the UPC. Bro. Hanby was an important minister. But you wouldn't have known it to watch Brother Hanby in that group of ministers. Bro. Hanby didn't take any position of honor. Bro. Hanby didn't call any attention to himself. Bro. Hanby wasn't standing there in a $300 suit. Bro. Hanby took a place, right with the other ministers; sat right with them as one of them. Not in any position of honor, but right with them. Bro. Hanby saw to it that they had enough to eat, that they had places to stay, that they were comfortable. He did these things himself. He made sure. He was a servant to them.

Once a year, we used to have foot washing service at the church. Well, you would think that surely the pastor of the church, Bro. Hanby, as important a minister as he was, surely, Bro. Hanby didn't need to go around washing anybody else's feet. Bro. Hanby did. And there I was, just just a novice in the Bible school, trying to make some sense out of what it means to be called a minister, and Bro. Hanby washed my feet. And my thoughts were those of Peter, when Jesus washed his: *No, you're not going to wash my feet; you're above me!* But Bro. Hanby was teaching me something once again, just as when he told me to take out the trash, just as when he told me to go clean the bathrooms. Bro. Hanby was telling me that being a minister means being the servant of all. It means being the lowest. It means being the last. It means having the least.

Beware of the ministers in [very expensive] suits, with huge cars, expensive houses and expensive jewelry on all their fingers, and around their neck! Beware of them; there's something not quite right.

The man of God doesn't need a three-piece suit. It's okay to have one, but a man of God doesn't need one that costs more than some of the people in his congregation are living on. It's okay for the man or woman of God to have a car. But it doesn't have to be the best one available that money can buy.

A minister is content with little; he's a servant. Remember, a servant is not greater than the master. We are put here to minister to the flock of the Lord. That means we're put here to serve them, and if we are here to serve them, then we cannot be greater than they are.

What kinds of minister are there? Today, churches have tried to invent many different kinds of ministers. Some churches, they go around ordaining half the congregation. Ordain the organist and the music minister. And ordain the deacons. Ordain everybody! Ordain the secretary! Next week we're going to ordain the janitor!

But these are not ministers. Yes, they minister. Their work is important. The music ministry would surely suffer without a good organist or pianist. The church administration would surely suffer without a good secretary. These people do minister, but not as ministers, not as the kind of ministers the Bible teaches us are placed in the church.

The Bible tells us of five types of ministers. These are found in the book of Ephesians chapter 4, verses 11 through 15.

And he gave some apostles, and some prophets, and some evangelists, and some pastors and teachers, for the perfecting of the saints for the work of the ministry, for the edifying of the body of Christ, till we all come in the unity of the faith and of the knowledge of the Son of God, unto a perfect man, unto the measure of the stature of the fullness of Christ, that we henceforth be no more children, tossed to and fro and carried about with every wind of doctrine, by the sleight of men and cunning craftiness whereby they lie in wait to deceive, but speaking the truth in love, may grow up into Him in all things, which is the head, even Christ.

Five kinds of ministers: Apostles, prophets, evangelists, pastors and teachers. Those are the five kinds of ministers, and even some churches that know this still confuse these ministries. They are separate and distinct. A person may have more than one ministry, but these ministries are separate and distinct.

And some churches try to force people into ministries for which they were not called. In some churches, it's understood that when a young person graduates from Bible school, they will evangelize for one or two years before becoming a pastor. They have been forced into this mold. But it's wrong. Because of this, there are only two or three types of ministers that function. In churches like that, it is very difficult for people to find the ministry for which they are called, because the church is telling them this is the ministry you will do. But you can't force someone into the wrong ministry; the people will suffer. Nothing in the world to me is more dangerous than an evangelist trying to pastor. Nothing so dangerous. You see, a pastor, for me, is a very special kind of ministry, very special. Now, it is not the most important. None of these ministries is more important than the others. All five are necessary for the functioning of the church. All five are equally important. Each of the five has its purpose, its ministry, its work.

A pastor is a Shepherd. That's what the word pastor means, many people don't know that. In fact, in some languages, there is no distinction between the two words. In Spanish, *pastor* is the word for Shepherd.

In Psalm 23, verse 1, in Spanish, it doesn't say the Lord is anything else other than *"mi pastor." "Jehová es mi pastor."* The Lord is my pastor. The Lord is my shepherd. A pastor is a shepherd. Okay, that much people can seem to understand. But there's something that a pastor must must have, and that is a pastor's heart, a shepherd's heart. What does that mean? Well, if you have any doubts about what it's like to be a shepherd, read about King David, because he was a wonderful shepherd. And read the parable of the good shepherd. Who is the good shepherd? He will leave the ninety-nine to go look for the one. Why? Because the Bible says so? No, because he *loves* the one. Because the good shepherd, the good pastor, loves *every* one of the sheep so much that he'd risk anything to help them, to rescue them.

The pastor always puts himself last. There's no other way around that: The pastor puts himself last, because the people have to come first. The pastor loves the congregation that's been given to him to lead to God, and never forgetting that he is their servant. He takes care of them, he meets their needs. He loves them.

An evangelist is an entirely different type of ministry. Now, certainly, an evangelist, as a Christian, must love the people, but not the way the pastor does. The proper role of an evangelist is part of the local church, to preach the good news, which is what the name means. But unfortunately, the churches have redefined the ministry of evangelist to that of an itinerant preacher, someone who goes from church to church preaching revival services. And those evangelists generally don't pull any punches. They preach about people being left behind at the Rapture. They preach about sin. They preach about hell. They preach heavy. They preach hard. That's the modern concept of an evangelist.

And people do need to hear good preaching, but after hearing the modern evangelist, they may well need their pastor to bind up their emotional and spiritual wounds when it's all over. They need the pastor to love them and nurture them. But the modern evangelist doesn't do that. If a modern evangelist, accustomed to preaching only hard-hitting sermons and then moving on to another church, should become a pastor, can you see what might happen? Can you see that all of their sermons would be these hard-hitting sermons that can hurt, but there is no true pastor to bind up the wounds? There's nobody to pour in the oil and wine afterwards. There's nobody to really love them. The modern evangelist cannot love them the way a pastor can.

Now, this doesn't mean that a person can't actually be called to both ministries, but if they are called to the ministry of pastor, they will love the people the way only a pastor can. Too often, I've seen people who have functioned as a modern evangelist, but who then try to be a pastor, because they've been taught by their church that that they **have** to pastor, that it's their responsibility to pastor. But it is NOT their responsibility to pastor. As a result, the people suffer. The people are hurt. The people are confused, and there is nobody to truly love them. There is nobody to nurture them. There is nobody to pastor them. There's nobody to shepherd them.

We need pastors and evangelists in every local church, and we need the teachers. Now, certainly, every minister needs to be able to teach. Certainly. This is one of the requirements for ministers that he or she be willing to teach, apt to teach, able to teach. This is important. But there is a ministry of teacher. This is the man or woman who is called only to teach, to teach the saints and to train new ministers.

We need someone who is called to teach in order to train new saints who've just come into the Way and who don't know all the things they need to know. Someone has to teach them, and who better than a teacher, somebody whose gift, who's calling, is teaching? This is necessary, because what happens without teaching? Well, read down in the 14th verse: ...*that we henceforth be no more children, tossed to and fro, and carried about with every wind of doctrine, by the sleight of men and cunning craftiness, whereby, they lie in wait to deceive, but speaking the truth in love, may grow up...* Speaking the truth! Well, how will they know the truth unless someone teaches it to them? If they don't know truth, they will fall for any lie that comes their way. All the saints must be thoroughly grounded in the truth, because there are many out there who would deceive them with false teachings. So we must have teachers among us who are firmly grounded in the truth of the word of God, who are full of the Spirit of God, and who know how to teach, who have been called to teach. We must have our teachers. There are too many people today, the Bible calls them people with itching ears. These people gather themselves teachers. They don't want to hear truth; they want to hear whatever makes them feel good people. They don't want to endure sound doctrine, but the church must endure sound doctrine. The church must be founded on proper doctrine, and we need our teachers for this.

What about apostles? What's an apostle? Well, many people think of apostle as some kind of a great leader. There are churches today that believe that they have to be governed by apostles and have a board of twelve apostles, always governing them. But that's not what an apostle is for. An apostle wasn't ordained to govern. They are not governors, they are not rulers. We have another word in English that means exactly the same thing as apostle and most people don't realize it. That word is missionary. An apostle is a missionary. Look at the twelve that Jesus chose: What was their job, what was their function? They were to go into all the world and preach the gospel. They were to go to places where the gospel had not yet been preached and preach it. They were the ground breakers. They were the pioneers. They were the ones who were called to begin the work.

Now, we may think that today we have no need for such things. After all, hasn't the whole world heard the Gospel of Jesus Christ. So what do we need, then, for people to go and preach, because everywhere it's been preached at one time or another? No, we must still have our Apostles because as much as we may like to think that this world has been evangelized, it has not. 99% of Christianity is still in total darkness, still preaching doctrines that have no connection whatsoever to the Bible. And in some countries, Christianity doesn't seem to exist at all, or it's illegal. How can we say our world has been evangelized, if this is the condition? *Well, we can't go to those countries where it's not allowed!* Oh, can't we? The original Apostles did. They didn't care. They had no regard for the rules of man if they contradicted the rules of God. Yes, we must obey the rules of man, but not when they contradict the rules of God. And if God says go into a particular country and preach the gospel, then we must do it. Even if the government of that country says no, if that means living underground, a secret of life, then that's what we must do. But even right here within the United States of America, we have a tremendous harvest that has never been tapped. Never been tapped! And the [LGBTQ] community especially has not been able to reach this harvest. We have not been able to do it. And so today, God is calling heterosexual men and women and is calling them and sending them into *our* harvest. Now, we must not resent them for doing this. God has called these people to do this. Some of them do not even have full truth yet, and God has sent them in because the harvest is so great. The need is so tremendous; the people are dying, and nobody has been sent with the Gospel. Nobody has brought the healing power of the Gospel to them.

This is where apostles come in. We must have people who are called as apostles, that is, people who are called as missionaries, people who are willing to go to a city or to a state were never before among the [LGBTQ] community has the Gospel been preached in its truth, and to go in there and make a stand for truth. To go, just like the apostles did, go to the people and begin to talk to them about the things of Jesus Christ, and begin to build a church. How long do you stay there? Until the church is able to support itself. The Apostle stays only until the church is self-supporting. Self-supporting not so much financially, but so that it is able to exist on its own, until there is someone there who can take over the work. And then, this apostle will appoint or ordain ministers to take over the work. Somebody to lead it. Somebody to teach, to take their place, and then the apostle will go on somewhere else. The apostle does not stay with a church forever. He or she stays only until the work is able to stand by itself, until they no longer need his or her services. And then the apostle moves on somewhere else, always moving, always beginning new works, always going where it has not yet been taken, where it has not yet been preached, where the people have never heard that Jesus loves us.

And what about the prophets? Well, we know that one of the Gifts of the Spirit is the Gift of Prophecy. Is anyone who has that Gift a prophet? To a certain extent, yes, anybody who prophesies is a prophet. But we're talking about a special kind of prophecy here. We're talking about the ministry of a prophet. We are talking about someone who is called as a prophet. We haven't seen this ministry very much. We haven't seen it operating in the church because people are afraid of the ministry of a prophet. Because surely enough, if there's something wrong in the church, or there is sin, it's the prophet who is going to stand up and say *thus saith the Lord.* And the sin is going to have to be taken out of the church, or the church will fold. We need the prophets. We need the man or woman of God, who isn't afraid to stand up and say *thus saith the Lord,* even if the message is unpopular. There were prophets who came from Jerusalem and they went to where Paul was preaching. They begged Paul not to go where he was going to go. They told him he was going to be arrested, and they were afraid that he would be killed. They knew! The Spirit of God told them how Paul was going to be arrested, and they begged him, *Don't go!* They weren't afraid to say this, even though this was not going to be a popular message. You don't want to go and tell someone, hey, God just told me you're going to die if you do what you're doing. You don't want to tell somebody that. That's a scary thing to tell somebody. People wonder if you start telling them that they're going to die, or or that they're going to be in trouble, if they do something.

Paul wasn't afraid. Paul went and did what he had to do anyway. But it was the ministry of the Prophet to come and tell him what God had said. God wasn't telling Paul that he shouldn't go. God was just saying this is what's going to happen. Be prepared. I want you to know ahead of time. You're going to be arrested. They're going to take you where you don't want to go. They're going to arrest you, they're going to tie you up.

Jesus warned Peter, he was going to die that way. Jesus told Peter, when you were young, you dressed yourself and went where you wanted, you tied on your own girdle. But when you're old, someone else is going to tie you up, and take you where you don't want to go.

Sometimes God will tell us ahead of time that things like that are going to happen. But it didn't stop Peter from doing what he had to do, and it didn't stop Paul from doing what he had to do. But thank God, there were prophets to tell them. Thank God, there were prophets. We don't see too much of the ministry of the Prophet. Every once in a while, it pops up in the Bible, and we see it. We see it mentioned from time to time. Philip had daughters who were prophets. They prophesied, and there was the prophet Agabus.

There were prophets in the New Testament church, and if they needed them, then we need them now.... perhaps even more. Perhaps even more, when the world has been exposed to so much false doctrine, as the church has, even more. We need a voice to say *Thus saith the Lord,* and to tell us what God wants us to do, to tell us what we're supposed to do. Hallelujah! We need all five of these ministers. We need the apostles to spread the word. We need the prophets to tell us what *thus saith the Lord.* We need the evangelist to preach the Good News to the lost and to help us feel the fire we felt when we were first filled with the Spirit.

We need the pastors to love us, to pray for us, to cry for us, to shepherd us. And we need the teachers to teach us the way, to teach us right from wrong.

The Bible tells us *"Stand in the ways and see, and ask for the old paths, where the good way is, and walk therein, and you will find rest for your souls."* We need those teachers to show us where those old paths are, to go the old way, the way of the apostles. I don't want to walk on any of the new paths. I don't want to walk on these yellow brick roads that these churches are building. I want to walk on a narrow trail. I want to go through a narrow strait gate on an old path because I know where that one's going. I know where that one's going.

We must have our five-fold ministry in the church, our five types of ministers.

I want to talk a little more about a pastor, because that's the type of minister we seem to see most often today. Sometimes we think that nobody ever really cared about us. But if you've ever had a pastor who was called to pastor, who *really* had the call to pastor, then there was someone who cared about you.

I think sometimes that the job of the pastor is one of the most difficult. Certainly, it's dangerous and it's difficult for the apostle to go to a country or to a state or to a city where they're not wanted, where they're doing something that's never been done there before. Certainly that's difficult. And certainly it takes courage for the prophet to stand up and say *thus saith the Lord.* Certainly, these things are difficult, and I'm sure the hardships on the evangelists are many.

Do you ever wonder why some pastors look so tired all the time? Why they look like they just don't seem to be getting enough sleep? If you only knew the things that they don't tell you, if you only knew the nights when the Spirit of God wakes them out of a sound sleep, and drives them out of their bed to their knees, when they cry.

I knew a man who was just walking down a hallway in the church late one night. He was the only person in the building, a man with a shepherd's heart. He was just passing one of the doors into the sanctuary when it happened: It was a sudden thing; he wasn't expecting it. He was driven from the hallway of the church into the sanctuary. The sanctuary was in total darkness. He was driven to his knees in the sanctuary, crying out to God and not even knowing why, because the burden came on him so suddenly, so powerfully.

And it must have been an hour that he laid there in mortal agony, on the floor, crying and groaning, not even knowing what the problem was. But somebody needed him, somebody needed prayer. Somebody was in desperate trouble and needed help. Somebody was in trouble... And how many times has the pastor been awakened in the middle of the night by the Spirit of God saying, Get up and pray! Get up and pray! Anybody else would say not now; I'll pray in the morning and go back to sleep. Not the pastor! Not the man or woman of God with a shepherd's heart. They get up out of the bed, they get down on the floor, and they cry and they pray for whatever it is.

It doesn't matter who it is. It could be someone in the church that they don't think is ever going to make it, somebody who just shows no signs of ever wanting to live for God. But it doesn't matter to the pastor, because they love them the same and the pastor will get up and the pastor will pray.

That man who was driven into the sanctuary lay there for an hour crying in mortal agony. It's what we call travail. It's a heavy, heavy spirit of prayer. And to hear it, you would think the person was literally dying. There is groaning and crying out loud in horrible agony. The pain isn't physical; the pain is emotional, the pain is spiritual, but it's every bit as real. Crying out! The Bible tells us that sometimes we don't know how we should pray as we ought, we don't know what the right thing is. Sometimes we don't even know what we're praying for when a burden comes on us. But the Bible tells us that the Spirit will make intercession for us with *"groanings that cannot be uttered."* Oh, for the days when the men and women of God used to travail! We don't see it in the church as much anymore. People are afraid to travail. It's so undignified. It's so scary to hear somebody in heavy travail, when someone is hit with a burden so strong that their native language fails them. And even sometimes beyond the point where speaking in tongues helps, when you're just driven down to the floor as if as if punched in the stomach, as if knocked unconscious, and laying there and groaning. Loud groaning and moaning as if in pain. We call it travail. What does that mean? Travail is the old word for when a woman was in labor.

I had a woman one time trying to describe travail to me, and she couldn't find the right words. I said, "It was like when you were in labor with your first child, except the pain isn't physical. It was every bit the same." And she said, "Yes, that's it! How did you know that?" That feeling is pretty common in the church. We feel that for a few different things, but this time it comes with such such force that all you can do is lay there and cry and groan and scream.

But that's important. And sometimes, you won't even know what you're praying for, who you're praying for. This man laid on the floor of the church and groaned for an hour, and cried and called out to God for mercy, not even knowing what the problem was. And then it was all over: The burden lifted as suddenly as it came. The pain was gone. The travail was gone, just as suddenly as it came. And then the phone rang, and he was told that a young man in the congregation had been in an automobile accident. He was in the hospital. The man was not seriously hurt, but this is what the travail was for, because even when we don't know what's wrong, the Spirit of God does, and the pastor, or sometimes even a saint, will be woken up, sometimes out of a sound sleep or taken away from some other activity that they're doing with no warning. The Bible tells us be instant in season and out of season. And certainly that applies to all the saints, but more so to the ministry. You must be willing to drop what you're doing at a second's notice and do the work of God.

Sometimes He doesn't give you a warning; sometimes you're needed right away. Sometimes instant prayer is needed. Sometimes you're called upon to pray when you're not ready to pray, when you're not in the mood to pray, when you're doing something else that you may think is very important. But the spirit of God says, Pray, Pray! Somebody needs you. Somebody needs you, and more so the pastor than any of the other ministers is going to get this. He or she is going to hear this and is going to respond to it, because the pastor loves the people. That love for them, Jesus says, is like the shepherd who will leave the ninety-nine and go after the one. The shepherd, the pastor, will get up out of bed at 3:00 in the morning, just for the one, just for the one lost sheep, the one who has gone astray, the one who keeps falling into sin and can't seem to live for God. It doesn't make the pastor reluctant, that he does those things: The pastor loves him the same, maybe even more, and was willing to do anything, to get up at three in the morning and go across town, to comfort somebody who is crying, and the pastor may not even know why, but is willing to get up and go because there is a need.

Because of their love, the pastors are willing to do without, so that the people can have things that they wouldn't ordinarily have. The pastor is willing, more-so than the other ministers, to put him or herself last. All ministers must remember to put themselves last, but the pastor is called upon to do it sometimes more than the others. But all this is necessary. All this that makes up our five fold Ministry his necessary.

Ephesians 4:12... Why is it necessary? ...*for the perfecting of the saints for the work of the ministry, for the edifying of the body of Christ.*

To what eventual goal? To what purpose? Verse 13: ...*till we all come in the unity of the faith and of the knowledge of the Son of God, unto a perfect man, unto the measure of the stature of the fullness of Christ.*

Why? Verse 14: ...*so that we will no more be children...* So that we won't be spiritual babies forever!

When we're born again, we start out as babies and we'll stay that way unless we're taken care of and that's what the ministry's for. Otherwise, we stay children, tossed to and fro, and carried about with every wind of doctrine, every new idea that comes up: swept away with it. What happens in congregations where there's no firm teaching? What happens when people are allowed to invent their own doctrines? I went to a meeting one time, a Charismatic meeting, where a man stood up and proclaimed that he had a revelation from heaven. These people had no teaching in the word of God, and they listened to his 'revelation.' And his revelation was not from God. His revelation involved doctrines of purgatory, and doctrines of praying to people other than God. These things are not biblical, but these people didn't know that. Nobody taught them. They had no teacher, and they had no pastor to guide them. They had no prophets to say *thus saith the Lord.* They had no ministers. No ministers. And they accepted this man's doctrine.

People need to be taught, and if they're not taught truth, they'll believe a lie. If they're not led by the five-fold ministry, then they'll be led by anybody. But Jesus said, "My sheep know my voice, and another they will not follow."

As we are His sheep and we follow Him. So then, we must be prepared to lead the others.

A minister: This is a servant. And a minister, like any servant, has a job to do, and it is that job he **must** do. Not someone else's job, but his own. The man or woman of God who feels a call, but isn't willing to be a servant cannot minister for the kingdom. The man or woman of God who has a call, but tries to follow another call cannot be a minister for the kingdom.

King Saul tried to offer a sacrifice one time. Samuel was supposed to do it, but Saul got impatient. He offered it instead, and he did all these things that he thought were so wonderful. Every single one of them in direct opposition to the word of God! When Samuel came along, he said to Saul, "What have you done?" And Saul said, "Oh, well, we took this and this and this, and we we did it all for sacrifice, all for God, all to the glory of God!" And Samuel said, "To obey is better than sacrifice, and to listen is better than the fat of rams."

Do you want to be a successful minister for the kingdom? Learn to obey the will of God. Learn to listen to what it is that God has called you to do and do it. We have no value to the kingdom if we cannot obey. We have no value to the kingdom if we cannot listen to the voice of God and obey it. No matter how noble our intentions might be, no matter how much good we may think we're doing, if we are not in obedience to the Spirit of God we're wasting our time... Our work is of no value.

To obey is better than sacrifice. To listen is better than the fat of rams.

Cause the Holy One of Israel to Cease From Before Us

I am turning to the book of Isaiah, Chapter 30. Now it's possible I might have used the same text in preaching to you before. Sometimes it's hard for me to remember that the Lord gives me something new from a particular verse of scripture. It's hard for me to remember if I've used that verse before. Doesn't matter. The word doesn't wear out. It can be used over and over and over again. You can read a verse of scripture a hundred times, in reading it for the hundred and first time, see something you never saw before. Thank the Lord! Thank the Lord for His word. He said His word will not return unto Him void, doesn't come back empty. It accomplishes what He sends it out to do. Thank the Lord!

Isaiah chapter 30. And I'm going to start at verse 8.

Now go, write it before them in a table, and note it in a book, that it may be for the time to come for ever and ever: That this is a rebellious people, lying children, children that will not hear the law of the Lord: Which say to the seers, See not; and to the prophets, Prophesy not unto us right things, speak unto us smooth things, prophesy deceits: Get you out of the way, turn aside out of the path, cause the Holy One of Israel to cease from before us.

A rebellious people. Lying children. Children that will not hear the law of the Lord. That was the way the Lord described the people of Israel to the prophet Isaiah. Now, I want to point out to you that he was not speaking of the Canaanites. He was not speaking of the Egyptians, or the Babylonians, or the Medes or the Persians. He wasn't speaking of the Syrians. He wasn't speaking of anybody but His own people, the chosen people.

He wasn't speaking of anyone but the descendants of Abraham and Sarah. He wasn't speaking to anyone, but the descendants of those who Moses led out of slavery. His people. His chosen people. The ones He told, "Your descendants will be as numerous as the sands in the sea, like the stars in the heaven, without number."

And He said this is a rebellious people. Rebellious. No, He wasn't speaking to Babylon, but He sure compared them. Remember Nimrod from Babylon? Nimrod means "he is in rebellion." Now, He's comparing his people to that. A rebellious people. Lying children. Children who will not hear the law of the Lord.

These words are not restricted by any means to the Jewish people. These words apply very much to our world today. Salvation came first to the Jewish people, because they were the chosen people. But when they rejected their Messiah, God turned to the Gentiles. And now every one of us has the opportunity to become part of his chosen people, his church.

But most of the people are rebellious. Most of the people do not want to hear the law of the Lord. And they will say to the prophets the same things that the people of ancient Israel said to their prophets. They said to the seers, *Don't see!* They said to the prophets, *Don't prophesy right things to us! Speak unto us smooth things. Tell us things that are easy on the ear. Prophesy deceits. Yeah, we know it's not the truth, but it's what we want to hear.*

We live in a world that doesn't place a very high value on truth. There are many people in this world who choose where they go to church by the wrong criteria. *"Well, I go to this church because they have such a wonderful choir." "Well, I go to my church because they let me believe anything I want and I don't have to believe anything if I don't want to. It's so easy and so convenient." "Well, I go to my church because it's the church I was raised in; my parents went to that church."* Truth doesn't seem to enter into it.

I spoke with someone not too long ago whose only criterion for choosing a church, her only criterion, was finding a church where she would be welcomed as a gay person, and she didn't care what they taught! She didn't care if there was truth taught or not. Didn't matter. They want an easy message.

Something that goes smoothly into the ear and can slip right out the other side.

And there are people, a dime-a-dozen, who will preach to you what you want to hear. And I'm not just talking about other churches. We've had this happen within our own organization. There was a man who held a position of authority in our organization and was a pastor in one of our earliest churches, who compromised truth even though he knew it. And when he left us, he went to another church, and denied ever having believed the truth. He was willing to say that he believed what that particular church taught, even though he knew it wasn't truth, because the love of truth was not in his heart.

And the people said to the prophets *Don't prophesy right things to us! Don't be telling us what we're supposed to do! Don't see the visions that God shows you. Close your eyes. Look the other way.*

They don't want to hear about what the prophets have seen. People in the church don't even want to know what God has shown the prophets for the church. Do you know, part of the five-fold ministry is the ministry of prophet, and you know, it's probably the one we see the least. I don't know too many off-hand with the ministry of a prophet. Is it because God is no longer calling people to that ministry? Oh no. No, it's because the people right in the pews of our churches don't want to hear what the prophets have to say. They don't want to know what *thus saith the Lord.* They don't want to hear what the prophets have seen. They don't want that vision, because that vision requires something of them, because we're part of that vision.

But the Bible says, *Where there is no vision, the people perish.* We'll die without the vision of the prophets. We will die without what they have seen for us, what they have seen us do, what they have seen that we are supposed to do. We'll die without it.

Don't see, they tell the prophets! Don't prophesy right things to us. Speak smooth things to us. Prophesy deceits. Go ahead and lie, doesn't matter, doesn't matter.

I'm reminded of the time when Israel and Judah were two separate kingdoms. The king of Israel was seriously backslidden; didn't worship the true God at all. But the king of Judah worshiped the true God. The king of

Israel said to the king of Judah, would you come with me? We're going to war, but I want you to come with me. We're going to go out to battle against these other people. I need your help. We're brothers! And they were brothers. Not not in the physical sense, but they were both Jewish. And it was customary for the kings to call the prophets, to see what the prophets had to say. Well the king of Israel didn't worship the true God, but he had hundreds of prophets: Prophets of the Babylonian religion. Prophets of the Canaanite religions. Plenty of them! Prophets were a dime-a-dozen, and every single one of them said exactly what the king wanted to hear. One picked up the horns of a bull and said, *This is how you're going to push the enemy.* And one said this, the other said that, but they all said the king is going to be victorious, go out and fight the battle.

The king of Judah said, *but isn't there a Prophet of the LORD left? Don't you have any prophets of the Lord here? I understand you don't worship the Lord, but see, I'm still a worshiper of the Lord, the Holy One of Israel, the one God. Don't you have any prophets of Him?* And the king of Israel said, *Yeah, I still got one, but I don't like him. He never says anything good about me!*

Notice how truth didn't enter into that? Notice how he didn't care what God had actually said. He just wanted a prophet who would tell him what he wanted to hear! The king of Judah insisted, and said *Now, don't be like that. Let's hear what he has to say.*

So they sent for this prophet, Micaiah. And the messenger said, *Now, look, all of the king of Israel's prophets have prophesied victory. Now, you better be as one of them. You better say what they say. You better go along with them. Don't rock the boat. Don't upset this. This is going very smoothly.*

Micaiah said *As the Lord my God lives, what He speaks, I will say.* But instead, he went out there and he made fun of the king of Israel. He said, *Oh yeah, go on out! Go ahead! You'll win, sure!* The king of Israel knew that Micaiah was making fun of him, so he decided to play holier-than-thou, and righteous, and say *How many times have I told you to only speak the truth in the name of the Lord?* Probably none. Could count the number of times on less than one hand.

The king of Israel wasn't interested in the truth. He was interested in hearing what he wanted to hear. And so Micaiah did what he was told: He spoke the truth. He said, *I see all of Israel scattered like sheep without a shepherd.* The king of Israel turned to the king of Judah said, *See, didn't I tell you he would only prophesy evil about me?* And he commanded that the prophet be thrown into prison and fed bread and water until he would return from the battle. And Micaiah looked at him and said, *If you return at all from the battle, then the Lord hasn't spoken by me.*

The king of Israel died in that battle. Micaiah alone of all the prophets spoke the truth. But they didn't want to hear it. They didn't want to hear it. Don't see. Don't prophesy truth; prophesy lies.

But you know, the real prophets, like Micaiah and Isaiah, they couldn't do that. And the real prophets of God still can't do that. They're still going to tell you what God says.

And the people of Israel realized that the prophets wouldn't stop what they were doing. And so finally, they said, *Get out of the way! Turn aside out of the path! Get away from us! And cause the Holy One of Israel to cease from before us! Stop confronting us with the Holy One of Israel! Every time we turn around, no matter what we're trying to do, there's the prophet of God saying, you can't do it that way. You can't do it that way. Cause the Holy One of Israel to cease from before us!*

And actually, that particular line is what I wanted to preach to you about today. They said, *Cause the Holy One of Israel to cease from before us.* Stop confronting us with the Holy One of Israel! There was never a more impossible request made than that: Cause the Holy One of Israel to cease from before us. You might as well say make the sun stopped shining. Make the moon disappear. Make the ocean stay away from the shore.

Make the Holy One of Israel stay away from us. They were the chosen people, and there was no way they could escape from the Holy One of Israel. No way. Why? Why wouldn't He just give up and leave them? The prophet Jeremiah explained it very well. The Lord spoke through Him. He spent half a chapter or more telling all the things the kingdom of Judah had done wrong, how she'd sinned worse than any of the heathen nations around her, and how she'd sinned worse than the Kingdom of Israel in the north. And God said, *You saw what I did to all those other nations because of their sin, and yet you're doing worse!*

And the natural conclusion one would draw logically is that God would say, *Forget it! I don't want anything to do with you. I'm going to destroy you like I destroyed all the others.* But he didn't. He said, *"Come back to me. I'm married to you."* So there's the answer. That's why they couldn't escape from the Holy One of Israel: Because He loved them and He would not let them go.

I have seen people leave the church, whether voluntarily or involuntarily. I have seen people taken out of the church. But you can't take the church out of them. I am constantly reminded of this.

I received a phone call a few months ago, and I may have told you the story already. A young man who was instrumental in trying to set up a church congregation here in Schenectady in 1985... Now, I never tried to drag this man into the church. In fact, I didn't even do a lot of heavy duty preaching to him. He knew I stood for the truth. He knew I was trying to build a church. And even though he expressed no interest in being part of it, he worked very hard and invested his time and money to help get it started.

One day while I was in Tucson, visiting the church there, this young man went to the United Pentecostal Church and asked them to baptize him in Jesus, name and pray for him so that he'd received the Holy Ghost. And when I came home, he said, "I've got it! I've got what you have!" He said, "You're right: It's everything you said it was." But then he didn't go to church. And he hasn't been to church in years.

But he called me a couple of months ago, and I was astonished at what he said. He started off by asking me if I could remember the name of the pastor of the United Pentecostal Church. I said, "Yes, but why?" He said, "I've been witnessing to a man at work." *You've been what?! You haven't been to church in years!* I didn't say that, but that's what was inside of me. *You haven't been to church in years. I don't understand. Why are you witnessing?* He said, "I'm a terrible one to be witnessing, but the man wants so much to know the truth." And he said, "I can't help it. I know the truth. I can't escape from it." He said, "I've told the man that I'm a terrible one to be telling him this, because I'm not living it, but I know the truth."

He took himself out of the church, but he can't get the church out of himself. He tried to take himself away from God, but God is still inside and God won't let him forget. And when somebody at work says to him *I'm looking for God,* or *I'm looking for truth,* he's confronted again with the Holy One of Israel, and he has no choice but to acknowledge: I know who God is. I know who God is.

What you and I are doing today is not religion in the usual sense of the word: go to church an hour a week and you've fulfilled your obligation. And it's not something nice to do until you grow up, and then you can just forget about it, and go maybe Christmas and Easter. This is a life commitment. It's a road that we have to walk down every day of our lives. And we may choose to stop walking, and to sit down on this road, but somehow we can't seem to get off this road. Somehow, no matter which way we turn, there's a reminder of the Holy One of Israel. There's a reminder of Jesus Christ, the Most High God. We can't escape from it.

When I left Houston, Texas in 1984 to come back to Schenectady, I was ready to resign from the ministry. There were a lot of years I put into it. I was called to the ministry when I was 7. I started teaching when I was 13. And I was ready to resign. I said, *I've had enough; I can't do this anymore. I can't do it anymore. I've put too much of myself into it. I've seen too little results. I feel like I'm banging my head against the wall. The people aren't listening. And the concept of Pentecostal churches in our community, it's never going to work. It's never going to work.*

And so I decided that I wouldn't preach in His name anymore. I wouldn't go to church anywhere. I wouldn't preach. I wouldn't try to build a kingdom for Him anymore. But you know, I couldn't get away from it, because every time I turned around, there He was, with the same call He gave me when I was a seven year old boy, sitting in the Catholic church, praying to I didn't know what. There He was.

Why? Why was it that every time I turned around, He was there? Was He trying to torment me? No, it was for the same reason He didn't destroy Judah. The same reason that the request that those people made of the prophet was impossible, that the prophet cause the Holy One of Israel to cease from before them, to stop putting the Holy One of Israel before their eyes. It's impossible, because he loves us.

Because He loves us, we cannot escape from Him. Because He loves us, He will be relentless.

We all know stories about someone who decided they were in love with someone who wasn't in love with them, but they chased them, they pursued them. We used to have a young couple in the United Pentecostal Church here in Schenectady, Dennis and Ruth. I met them when they had already been married a while, but they used to tell me the story of how they got together. Ruth had no interest in Dennis. He simply wasn't her type. She had no interest in him. First of all, Dennis was a hundred percent on fire for God, but Ruth was still kind of kind of lukewarm. I mean, she loved God and she came to church regularly, but she wasn't the power-house that Dennis was. But Brother Dennis, besides being head over heels in love with Jesus, was head over heels in love with Ruth. And Ruth kept trying to tell him, "I'm not interested. Go ask somebody else out to dinner. Go take someone else to lunch. I'm not interested."

But Dennis *was* interested. He loved Ruth and he would not let her go. And he loved her and loved her and loved her. And every time she turned around, there was Dennis. He loved her unconditionally.

That's why he won. That's what wore Sister Ruth down. The only weapon in the world that wins unconditional surrender is unconditional love. And Dennis loved Ruth persistently with that unconditional love until he won her heart. She saw that there was no way to defeat him, and no way to escape from him. She had no choice but to surrender to him.

God loves us with that same persistence. And He will pursue us and He will pursue us and pursue us. And every time we turn a corner, He'll be there waiting.

We've all played little games like that, where we've gone out of our way to be someplace so we could see somebody we were interested in, and you try and make it look like it was a coincidence that we just happen to be there. I've played the game. Don't tell me you haven't. We've all played it at some time or another, just to catch a glimpse of someone we were hung up on.

And there will be Jesus, every time we turn a corner. *You again!?* Oh, I just happened to be standing here! God is everywhere; He *did* just happen to be standing there. But He was waiting for you. He was waiting for me. We cannot escape from Him because He loves us too much to ever let go. And even those who have stopped going to church, who have tried to run away from Him, who've left Him... And that brother who called me... He's not the only one I've run into like that. I've run into so many people who were out of church for years, backslidden, and somebody asks them questions, and all of a sudden they just say, "I know the answers. I know what you're looking for. No, I'm not living it myself, but I know it's Jesus. Let me tell you about Him."

And that person who isn't living for God will direct the seeker to an Apostolic church. That's a wonderful place to be. They'll tell you who Jesus is; they told me. They will baptize you in Jesus' name; they baptized me. They'll pray you through to the Holy Ghost. They did it for me. And you'll never escape from Him again.

He loves you. He loves you too much to ever let go. So it was a pointless request that the people made. We won't stop seeing the visions. We won't stop prophesying what the Lord has told us to prophesy. We will not prophesy illusions, we will not prophesy deceits, we will not prophesy lies in the name of the Lord. And we couldn't cause the Holy One of Israel to cease before anybody, even if we tried, because He won't give up that easily. He's always going to be there right before us.

There was a time when I sort of resented that, especially in 1984 when I thought I could resign from the ministry. And I resented the fact that it seemed like every time I opened my mouth, the word of God was coming out when I didn't want it to. And I resented that. *God, You should look on Your desk. My letter of resignation is there somewhere. I know I wrote it. Don't you understand, God? I quit! Don't you understand, God? I don't want to do this anymore.*

And if I'd just stopped complaining long enough and listened, I would have heard Him saying, *Don't* **you** *understand? I love you! Don't you understand? I'm never going to let you go. You're mine. I bought you with My own blood and I* *love you. Don't you understand? Don't you get it? I love you. I love you.*

Confronted with that, I had no choice anymore. He loved me unconditionally. I had no choice but to surrender. Hallelujah! Thank the Lord! Thank you, Jesus!

Don't Lose The Vision

Don't Lose The Vision

I really like the Book of Proverbs. I don't always like the things that tells me, but I like the wisdom that's in there. Hallelujah!

Proverbs chapter 29, and I'm going to be reading verse 18. This is probably a verse that's familiar to us or at least part of it:

Where there is no vision, the people perish: but he that keepeth the law, happy is he.

I've got a poster that I put up the other day. It's one I made at work. It has a quote by Norman Vincent Peale, and I honestly couldn't even tell you who he is. I know I've heard the name since I was a little kid, but I have no idea who he is or was. I don't pay a lot of attention to things like that, but what he said showed a lot of wisdom. He said something to the effect, and I can't give an exact quote, that if you want to get somewhere, you have to know first where you're going. Then you have to start out on that journey and never, never, never quit.

That's simple, but it's wise at the same time. If you don't know where you're going, you're going to get lost. And if you don't start out on your journey, you'll never reach your destination. And if you quit, you don't get anywhere, do you?

It ties in a lot with this verse: *Where there is no vision, the people perish.*

In everything we do in our lives, if we want to be successful at it, we have to have a vision of what our goal is. When you buy something that needs assembly, it's not always easy to put it together if you don't know what it is, or at least have a picture of what it's supposed to look like when it's done. That's your vision of what you're aiming for, and without it you'll never get that thing together. Especially if you don't know what it's supposed to be, or what you're supposed to do.For many years, to a large extent, the church has floundered. Pretty much over the past 2,000 years, the church has floundered and tried to go in every direction at once. It kind of reminds me of somebody having an epileptic seizure, or somebody with very severe cerebral palsy. The brain may give an order, but it never makes it to the body. So, the body does whatever it pleases: One arm is going this way, one arm is going that way, one leg is going this way, and it really doesn't matter what the brain wants. And unfortunately, the body of Christ, the church, is in that kind of a state.

Jesus is supposed to be the head of the church. And what's in the head? The brain. Where do the orders to the body come from? The brain. But the body's not getting those orders and it's doing any old thing it wants. So the church fights against itself, runs into itself, defeats its own purpose.

I've always wondered what was the purpose of having five or six Apostolic churches in one city. They can't get along with each other. If you switch from one to the other, they act like you're backslidden. Something's not quite right there. I don't find that in the New Testament.

I think the problem is that the church has lost its vision of what it's supposed to be and what it's supposed to be doing. And without that vision, they defeat their own purpose, and they can perish. They can perish physically? Well, maybe. Spiritually? Definitely. Definitely.

There's so much confusion in the church about what it's supposed to be and what it's supposed to do. I had gone to a church conference one time a few years back in Dayton, and a minister who's a friend of mine did a teaching on what he felt was the main purpose of the church. *What was our main function here in the earth?* And as I sat there listening to him, I could see that he was very sincere in what he was teaching. He was also very wrong in what he was teaching.

Now, there was nothing wrong with what he said the church should be doing, because we should be doing that. But it was not the main function. He felt that the main purpose of the church, our main reason for existence, was to worship God. I don't think so. Now, yes, we are supposed to worship God; He's worthy of that. That's just something we do as part of our reasonable service, but that wasn't the Great Commission, was it? I don't even find that in the Great Commission.

You know, we use the words *Great Commission*. We throw them around. We don't stop to think about what that actually is. Something has been committed to us. Something has been given to us, a set of orders from the Captain. Or you can call it an electrical impulse from the brain for what the body is supposed to do. And I can't find any place where those orders have ever been changed or countermanded, which means until new orders are sent, those are the orders were supposed to be filling, fulfilling. That's what we're supposed to be doing. That's supposed to be our vision.

What is the goal that the church is trying to reach? What are we trying to do? Are we trying to build the largest building in the city? The best Sunday school program? The most successful denomination? Well, the answer is obviously no. And yet, in so many cases, the answer is yes, that we're more concerned with the things that don't matter that much, the things that won't matter a hundred years from now, and we forget about the things that we're supposed to be doing. We lose sight of the eternal, and we're hung up on the temporal.

The church has lost its vision, and we need to reclaim that vision. We'll find it in the Great Commission. The first word, if we take the Great Commission from Matthew, the first word is a verb. Go! Go! That right there precludes sitting in our buildings and having our services each week, and then going home and acting like nothing's different, nothing new, nothing is important. *Well, I go to church. I do my part. I go to church, I pay my tithes.* There was a song that I heard one time, about a man who had gone through his whole life, went to church regularly, and was considered a good man. But he was living for himself. And when he finally died, standing before the Lord, he says, "Well, You know, I went to church and I paid my tithes!" And God just

29

asked him one word: *Why? Why? Why did you bother?*

He never fulfilled the Great Commission, which started with go and teach. *"Well, I'm not a teacher!"* Well, I **am** a teacher, and I say to those people who say they're not teachers, "Everybody can teach something! Teach a little kid how to tie his shoes: You're teaching something."

No one's asking you to teach what you don't know. Teach what you *do* know. Teach people what you do know.

I love to talk about the old Schenectady Youth Group we had here years ago. Sister Wanda would take us kids out two by two to rural areas of this county, and we'd go door-to-door. These people like out in Esperance and Duanesburg, they didn't know what to make of this. They were used to an occasional Jehovah's Witness or Mormon at the door, to come and give them a memorized speech. *"Do you ever think about the kingdom of God?" "Here's a copy of Watchtower."* This was something entirely different. You've got a 14 year old girl at the door saying, "Can I take just a minute of your time to tell you what Jesus did in my life?" She wasn't teaching anything she didn't know. She didn't have a memorized speech. She was telling her own personal testimony, what God had done for her. Teaching what she knew.

Who do you teach? Let's see: I think the Great Commission said *all nations.* Everybody. Nobody is excluded. Well now, if you close your eyes and think about this for a minute: If the whole church went... past tense of go... and taught... past tense of teach... we might have something, wouldn't we? What can you picture? Maybe something like the day of Pentecost were several thousand were baptized in one day.

We're so excited when we convert by the single digits. *Oh, three people got the Holy Ghost at Sunday's service!* The first century Church did it by the thousands. We're not doing that good. Maybe it's because the first century church had a vision that they were aiming for. When they closed their eyes, they saw thousands saved. They had a vision of a harvest being reaped, and they wanted that harvest. So they went out and sowed the seed so they'd get it.

We've got a vision of having a bigger church than Brother So-and-so on the other side of town! No, that's the wrong vision. Change the channel!

Definitely the wrong channel. Try again.

We call ourselves an Apostolic church and that's an easy word to throw... well, no, it's not an easy word to throw around: Some people can't pronounce it, can't spell it, and don't know what it means. We call ourselves an Apostolic church because it means we want to be *like the apostles.* We want to teach what they taught. We want to believe what they believed. But it needs to go beyond that, into doing what they did.

The Acts of the Apostles is a fascinating book. They did an awful lot. And, you know, it's the only book in the New Testament that doesn't have a formal ending. All the others end with a blessing and an amen. Acts of the Apostles has no ending. Do you know why? It keeps going! It didn't end. It's supposed to be being written now. Not necessarily physically written, but written in our lives. We're supposed to be doing what the apostles did. But if we're not, we can't call ourselves in Apostolic Church.

We can't do that if we're not going to live in an Apostolic way, if we're not going to follow the pattern the apostles laid down, if we're not going to fulfill the Great Commission that Jesus gave to the apostles, which they in turn gave to us, if we've got the wrong vision. I want an Apostolic vision!

These signs shall follow them that believe. So when we're out, going, there are supposed to be signs and wonders following. We're so excited and thrilled when something happens, but it should be to the point where we're surprised when it doesn't happen! And I'm excited about the miracles, the reports we get from some of our churches, but they're not enough, you know? I'm excited to have Pastor Lewis call me and tell me that while counseling a couple, a deaf ear was opened! That's wonderful! That's great! We're *supposed* to see that!

But why don't I get that kind of call every week? Why don't I call down there every week to tell them the great thing that God has just done here? Because we haven't got the right vision.

Something's lacking. I want to close my eyes. and I want to see the lame walk. I want to see blind eyes opened and deaf ears opened. I want to see the dead raised. I want to see that. That's an Apostolic vision.

These are the signs that follow them that believe... and if they're not following us, maybe we don't believe! That's a different sermon, I preached that a couple of weeks ago.

Without that vision, an Apostolic vision in an Apostolic Church, a first century church at the end of the 20th century, the people perish. We, the people, perish without that vision. Yes, maybe physically, but definitely spiritually. Definitely spiritually!

Look at the history of Christianity. It's a sad, sad history. We talked a little earlier about how more people have probably been killed in the name of Jesus than for any other reason. But that really wasn't what Christianity was all about, was it?

But we see God restoring pieces of truth to the church, one at a time. He'll find somebody with an open heart and say, "Here is a piece of truth." And they get so excited! They've got something, a revelation, a restoration of a first-century truth, and that's great... And then they lose the vision. And instead of getting another piece of truth, they build a denomination around the first one, and they get nothing else, and spiritually, they're left behind. They perish, because when God's ready to restore another piece of truth, it has to go to somebody else.

And denominations today are a dime a dozen because of that very thing, because every time God wanted to restore another piece of truth, the people who got the last one don't want any more. They were satisfied. They'd lost the vision of the truth of the first century church, and they'd get no more, and so someone else had to get it.

Well, it's a terrible thing, but you would think that Apostolic people would know better than that. And yet it's a frightening thing that the Apostolic churches in this country and this world have not received a major revelation or restoration of truth since the second decade of the 20th century! Did God go out of the truth business?

Is it possible that our brains could contain every bit of truth that God knows? Or is it more likely that we just stopped receiving, that we lost the vision?

In the scripture, Jesus told the people, *"Remember how you heard..."* that's a phrase we overlook. What does that mean? Remember how you heard?

We don't have to remember how to hear; our ears work automatically, don't they? But not our spiritual ears: They **don't** work automatically. You have to remember how you heard, remember how you got that revelation of truth, and ask for more and more and more, and don't lose that vision of a first century Church, because without it we will perish; we won't be the church anymore.

You know, Paul told the Corinthians, he said, look, *"Look at your own calling."* He said, *Look among you: You don't have a whole bunch of noble people or wise or wealthy or anything.* Rather, they were the offscouring of the earth. They really were. They were the wrong side of the tracks. They were the bottom of the barrel, because those were the people who were willing to listen. And we look at ourselves and often we see the same thing: He's taken a despised group of people and used them. And yet we want to think, *Well, okay. We're the very bottom.* But I've got news: If we pass up on this, God will give it to someone else. He'll find someone even lower than we are, and He'll give it to them, somebody who *will* hold the vision.

You see, the word of God is forever settled in heaven, and the way it said it's going to happen, it's going to happen. There **will** be an Apostolic Church in the [end times]. There **will** be a full restoration of the first century Church. Whether or not we're part of it is entirely up to us. It's entirely up to us. If we don't want it, if we don't want that vision, if we don't hold that vision, and cherish that vision, there's someone, somewhere, who will.

We can't fall into the trap that the Jewish people fell into in the first century, telling Jesus, "Well, we're the children of Abraham. We've never been in bondage to any!" Wow, short memory, huh? How many years did they spend in slavery in Egypt? And then, how long were they in captivity in Babylon? Short memory? *We've never been in bondage to anybody!* Not only had they have been in bondage for hundreds of years, but they were still spiritually in bondage!

Well, we're the Apostolic Church! The same thing is true for us that was true for them back then: God can raise up descendants for Abraham, and He can raise up an Apostolic church, right out of the stones! We're not indispensable!

You know, it's nice to think that we can just sit in the pews, year after year, having what I call *Pentecost as usual,* and that God will just wait till we're good

33

and ready. It won't work that way. He did say He wouldn't always strive with a man, didn't He? He does have a limit to His patience. He will wait just so long for us to get our act together, and if we don't, He'll give it to somebody who will get their act together, somebody that we might be shocked to see. You know, I've shocked a few people, raised a few eyebrows in my time. But I'll bet you there are people who can raise my eyebrows, too.

I don't want to lose that vision. I don't want to lose that. That's too important. I don't want to perish spiritually. I don't want to be left behind. I want to see the Book of Acts continued. I want to see the dead raised. I want to see the lame walk. I've seen a little bit of these things. I want more.

All right, call me greedy. I'm not satisfied. ***I'm not satisfied!*** I'm not satisfied till they're converted by the thousands! I'm not satisfied until we're up all night baptizing! I can handle it! I can handle it!

I want to see that. And I won't settle for less. You've heard me say that here before, that's our heritage, that's our birthright. I will not settle for less! Don't you settle for less either! These things are promised to them that believe. If we don't see them, maybe we don't believe. Don't lose the vision! Don't lose the vision! If you can't see it when you close your eyes, pray about it. It's there somewhere. God, give me back the vision! Open my spiritual eyes! I want to see that church!

I want to see that Apostolic Church! Not the biggest denomination or the biggest building, not the best Sunday school program, not the highest numbers in church. I used to work for the New York District of the [United Pentecostal Church], and I used to have to publish every month the Sunday school figures from each church so that we could impress each other with how large we'd grown. What was hysterical was that what they were counting was bus kids, kids whose families didn't even come to church, but just sent their kids to Sunday School, and they're counting those as members of the church! I mean, what was that?! The Buffalo church was counting 300. Come on, their congregation was only 100! These were neighborhood kids who got sent by the parents who were looking for a few hours of free time on Sunday morning. But the Buffalo church was so impressed that they were the biggest in the state. Come on, that's not what matters. It isn't numbers.

That's the wrong vision! That's the wrong vision!

I'd rather have a church with one person living for God, than a cathedral full of people playing the game, with the wrong vision, trying to impress or outdo each other: Whose building is bigger, whose hairdo is higher? Sorry, that's the wrong vision.

Yes, Sister Thomas, big hair frightens me, too. There's a lot of truth in that button you're wearing. You know, big hair *does* frighten me, because they're trying to impress each other with the wrong things.

I don't care who's impressed with me; it doesn't matter. There's only one Person who decides my salvation, and I know there's nothing I can do in my flesh to impress Him. The best I can do is hope to please Him. That's the best I can do.

You know, I can't tell you how many times that when I've been praying and repenting of something I've done, that I've pointed out just what the prodigal son did: I'm not worthy to be called Your son. I'll settle for the position of a servant. I'm not even worthy for that, and I don't care if I get into the kingdom last, just let me in. Let me in! I don't want to lose out on this. I don't want to lose it.

I listen to a preacher for years who used to remind us that we had hold of the tail end of something like this world had never seen, and that was true at that point. But it's changed a little bit now, because we're no longer at the tail end. God has given us a very unique opportunity, and He's pushed us right up to the front of it.

We're a very small organization, with very little power and that's fine. I don't care. I don't want to be any different than that, but God is doing something with us right now that's affecting the other Apostolic churches. His prayer was that we would be one, and He's doing that now, and He's using a very unusual group of people. That puts a grave responsibility on us. If we lose the vision, that will mess up the whole plan; someone else will have to do it. It's a very heavy responsibility.

Don't lose the vision. The people perish when we lose the vision. I wonder if it's just the people who lose the vision who will perish, or if they all perish when the vision is lost? Somebody's got to have the vision! The Bible says

He's never left Himself without a witness. What's a witness? A witness tells what he's seen, what he's heard, what he's experienced. We can all do that! We can all do that! We can all say, *This is what I've seen. This is what I've experienced. This is what I've heard.* Firsthand experience! We can all teach that to anybody who's willing to listen.

Just presenting your own testimony in love works a whole lot better than trying to shove this corner of the Bible down their throat sideways. You won't get it in that way; It doesn't go in there. It goes in here, in the ears, and from there, into the heart.

Just by somebody saying, *Let me tell you what He did for me. I was lost now I'm found! I was blind; now, I see! In a very real sense, I was dead, and now I'm alive. And I've got a vision that I want to share.*

I've got a vision of a powerful church making a change in this world. Not that the world is going to be cured or healed or anything like that. The Jewish people have what they call *Tikkun HaOlam.* It means *repairing the world.* Trying to repair the world! I already know from [the Bible], it can't be repaired. But I'm planning to make an exit, and I'm going to take as many as I can with me!

I've got a vision! I've got a vision of an Apostolic Church, doing wonders in the land, and then being called Home, and I want to be part of that! People, don't lose the vision! Don't lose the vision! It's too important! It's too important!

Lord, plant that vision firmly in our hearts. Let it grow inside of us so that we never lose sight of it, So that when we close our eyes, we can see it, so that when we sit in silence, we can hear it, so that we can breathe it and taste it and feel it and believe it until it comes to pass. Let that vision become a part of us so that we can fulfill the work You've put before us. Don't let us fall by the wayside. Don't let us be crippled by our own pride, but let us surrender our will to Yours and take Your vision as our own, for the sake of Your kingdom. We ask this in the name of Jesus. Amen!

Thank the Lord!

Dry Bones

We're turning to the book of Ezekiel, the 37th chapter, starting at the first verse. This is the text of Ezekiel's dry bones.

The hand of the Lord was upon me, and carried me out in the spirit of the Lord, and set me down in the midst of the valley which was full of bones,

And caused me to pass by them round about: and, behold, there were very many in the open valley; and, lo, they were very dry.

And he said unto me, Son of man, can these bones live? And I answered, O Lord God, thou knowest.

Again he said unto me, Prophesy upon these bones, and say unto them, O ye dry bones, hear the word of the Lord.

Thus saith the Lord God unto these bones; Behold, I will cause breath to enter into you, and ye shall live:

And I will lay sinews upon you, and will bring up flesh upon you, and cover you with skin, and put breath in you, and ye shall live; and ye shall know that I am the Lord.

So I prophesied as I was commanded: and as I prophesied, there was a noise, and behold a shaking, and the bones came together, bone to his bone.

And when I beheld, lo, the sinews and the flesh came up upon them, and the skin covered them above: but there was no breath in them.

Then said he unto me, Prophesy unto the wind, prophesy, son of man, and say to the wind, Thus saith the Lord God; Come from the four winds, O breath, and breathe upon these slain, that they may live.

So I prophesied as he commanded me, and the breath came into them, and they lived, and stood up upon their feet, an exceeding great army.

Then he said unto me, Son of man, these bones are the whole house of Israel: behold, they say, Our bones are dried, and our hope is lost: we are cut off for our parts.

Therefore prophesy and say unto them, Thus saith the Lord God; Behold, O my people, I will open your graves, and cause you to come up out of your graves, and bring you into the land of Israel.

And ye shall know that I am the Lord, when I have opened your graves, O my people, and brought you up out of your graves,

And shall put my spirit in you, and ye shall live, and I shall place you in your own land: then shall ye know that I the Lord have spoken it, and performed it, saith the Lord.

Now, this was written to Israel, and we know from experience, and from the scripture, that many things in the Old Testament that were written to Israel apply to the church today. I want to submit to you that these dry bones are the church, what has become of the Christian church. Two weeks ago, we spoke about how in the history of the Christian church there was a great falling away that lasted almost two thousand years, when the church backslid and fell away from their original doctrine. They lost the power they once had, they lost the truth they once had, and it's this falling away that I think we're talking about here with the dry bones. Notice it said in the second verse *they were very dry.* These bones that Ezekiel prophesied to had been dead for a long time. It had been a long time since there had been flesh on those bones. It had been a long time since there had been breath, a spirit, in them. They were very dry.

And I want to mention something down in the ninth verse, where it said, *oh breath, breathe upon these slain that they may live.* These bones did not die a natural death. They were slain. They did not die of old age. It was murder of a sort. They were killed.

Now the Lord asked Ezekiel, He said, "Son of Man, can these bones live?" Is it possible for these dead bones to get up and live again? Well, the natural answer would have been no. What's dead is dead. The dead don't rise again. The bones are dry. There's no flesh left. There's no way the bones can live again. And some would look at the church world today, at all the mass of things called Christianity today and say, *Can it live? Can it be the way it once was? Can there be the power that there was in the early church? Can the Spirit be there again?* Looking at it today, we'd say *No, no.*

But Ezekiel didn't say no. He had a little more faith, not quite enough, but a little. He answered and said, "O Lord God, thou knowest!" I don't know, Lord. Only You know if these bones can live again. You tell me, can they live? Can it be that the church could have that power again? Could it be restored? Can the church be resurrected? Ezekiel didn't know. Many today don't know. Can the church once again be the way it once was? Can these dead bones rise?

The Lord said to prophesy to those bones. Prophesy to it: "Behold, I will cause breath to enter into you, and you will live." The Lord said the church would live again. It would be restored. So Ezekiel did prophesy to those bones, and the first thing that happened as he prophesied, verse 7, there was a noise. The first thing that happens when God's going to begin to move in the church: There's a noise.

A noise? What kind of a noise? It doesn't say what kind of a noise. Well, when you move dry bones, these going to be a rattling sound: bones rattling against each other, a sound that you cannot exactly describe. Perhaps the reason Ezekiel didn't describe the noise was because he couldn't tell exactly what it was. But I'll tell you, there's been a noise in the church ever since the day that Luther took his judgments against the Catholic Church and nailed them to the door.

From the day Luther first protested against the problems with Catholicism and there first began to be a reformation of the church, there's been a noise, a talking, a changing. You hear the murmuring: *God's doing something new here, God's doing something new there. Is this of God? Is that of God? This church is doing this. Why do they do that?* A changing, a noise... There's a noise in the church. And the next thing that happened, behold, there was a shaking, and the shaking is still going on.

You know, the way the bones fell, they couldn't go back together that way. You can't just put any bone to any bone. They have to be moved around so that the right end is joined to the right end. Notice that it said the bones came together, bone to his bone. A lot of times, we want to put the church back together the way we want the church to go together. And there are many in Christianity today saying, *This belongs in the church, but this doesn't. So we're going to put this next to this. This bone will go here.* But we can't always put the bones where we want to. God said the bones were going to go bone to his bone, where they belong, and this is the reason there's so much upheaval in the church world today, because God's moving the bones around. We've joined them where we wanted them. The church world has said, *This looks good here.* But it wasn't where it was supposed to be, and God's pulling it apart, and there's a shaking, shaking it loose, so that the bones can go where there were supposed to be, so they can be joined in the right place.

Many things that are where they are today are going to have to be moved. Almost everything that can be shaken, if it can be shaken, it *will* be shaken, because it's got to be moved around. We've got the church all in the wrong order, and God's got to straighten it out. The scripture tells us that the church is the body of Christ, but what good is a body if the parts don't work properly, if the brain gives an order and the body won't obey it?

Where I work, I work with the physically and mentally disabled, and lately, my coworkers and I have been discussing cerebral palsy. In this particular disorder, there is brain damage, so that if an order is given by the brain, the body is unable to carry it out. Somehow, these directions the brain is giving are not getting to the body parts, and so the body does not operate properly. And as a result, we see people who are contracted, whose limbs won't operate.

And the body of Christ is in this condition today. The church is in this condition. Jesus Christ is the head of the church. If He gives an order, the church should move in that direction, but it doesn't. It doesn't. It's got a mind of its own. Jesus gives an order, and the church does the exact opposite, or just sits there and does nothing. The bones are all put together wrong. That's why the message isn't getting through. The church is not in order. And so there is a shaking in the church world: The church is being shaken so that the bones will come loose, so bone can come to his bone.

And then there are some bones of the churches that say, *No, this doesn't belong in the church at all, and we won't let it in!* Do you know, there are denominations in the church world today that think the Book of Life in heaven has the name of their church engraved in gold on the front cover! But let me tell you, it doesn't. It doesn't matter what church organization you belong to. You know, I can't find any place in the scripture where it says only one particular denomination is going to heaven. Who's going to heaven are those people who obey the word of God. It doesn't matter what you call yourself. You can call yourself the First Church of Dishwater. It doesn't matter. The name is not important. It's not the name over the door, it's the Spirit that's inside. It's whether or not the church is obeying the word of God. And there are things that are being brought into the church today, being grafted in, and the church world says, No, it doesn't belong. This is what's happening with the [LGBTQ] church. God is grafting in a different kind of church, and putting it where it belongs in the body of Christ. And the rest of the body is violently reacting, and saying, No, that bone can't go here! But if God said the bone goes, the bone goes! And it doesn't matter what the rest of the body says.

You know, Paul talked about the body, the human body, and his point was that the eye can't say that because it's not the foot, it's not part of the body. And the foot can't say because I am not the hand, I am not part of the body. Each part of the body has its place and has its function, and each part is essential. If all of the body were one part, it wouldn't function properly. Paul said if all the body were, for example, the eye, where would the body hear, or if all the body were an ear, how would the body see? There are different parts to the body of Christ, and God is putting them together in the order that it pleases Him. So the bones are coming together. There's been a noise, and now there's a shaking, and bones are coming together, bone to his bone, bone to his bone.

A lot of moving is going to have to take place. We don't need to be alarmed at the shaking. It's God shaking the church. It's God shaking it. God is going to put the bones together where they belong. We can't do it. We are not creators of life. Only God can create life, and only God can restore life. And He promised to put His Spirit back in. He said, I will put breath in you. I will cause breath to enter into you, and you shall live. The Spirit of God will be restored to the church. Now, there are many that will say to me today, oh, the Spirit of

God never left the church. Well, let's look in the book of Acts, chapter 2 and verse 17:

It shall come to pass in the last days, saith God, I will pour out of My Spirit upon all flesh.

Well, why would God need to pour out his Spirit if the church already had it? The truth is that the Spirit was cut off from the church. Why? God didn't take His Spirit away from the church; the church pulled away from His Spirit. Church history shows us that there was a particular time in church history when they decided that the age of the apostles was over, the age of miracles was over, the age of receiving the Holy Ghost speaking in tongues was over. The church decided it was over, God didn't. The church said *We don't want the Spirit anymore.* It wasn't God.

So the true church that still had the Spirit went underground. All through history, we see little glimpses of them. You know, God has never left Himself without a witness. If he had left Himself without a witness, there would have been nobody to prophesy to those dry bones. But there was Ezekiel, there was still a witness. And all through history, we see glimpses of the true church. How do we know? Because we read the writings of the organized church and we read about what they called heresy. Every time they found a group of what they called heretics, we read what the so-called heretics preached, and we find that not all of these "heretics" were heretics. Some of them were preaching truth! So we know that God never left himself without a witness. All through history, there was a small group preaching the truth, waiting for the time when God would bring life to those dry bones again, and He promised He would put His Spirit back in them.

And so Ezekiel prophesied to the wind and told it to come and breathe upon the bones. The scripture says that they stood up as the spirit entered into them: They stood on their feet, a very great army. The church of God is going to be a very great army, and it will stand on its feet, and it will live, and it will have the same power that the early church had.

There are churches today that tell us that we can't have that kind of power. They say speaking in tongues is not for today, prophecy is not for today, miracles and healings are not for today. But, you know, they really can't find scripture to back that up. It wasn't the Bible nor was it the Spirit of God that said those things were all over; it was only the church. I'm here to tell you, these things are still happening. The Spirit of God is still being given to people. People still speak in tongues, people still prophesy, people still experience healings, people still see miracles happening.

I have so many testimonies that I could give you, personal testimonies of of miracles I've experienced, of healings I've experienced. I have testimonies of other people, countless testimonies of miraculous healings where there was no other explanation. I could tell you the story of a woman, right in the city of Schenectady, who was declared dead... not once, but if I'm not mistaken, three times this woman was declared dead. And today, she lives. She's not dead. God worked a miracle, because the age of miracles is not over.

God is putting His church back together and breathing His Spirit into them, And that great army is standing up. It's a difficult thing for many people to believe that the church could fall away, that there could be such a period of time where God was not in the midst of the church, where the church was operating on their own without any direction from God, when they had rejected God, and had fallen away and backslidden. People don't want to believe that. They say, *That can't be, because God said that the gates of hell would not prevail against his church!* Well, they won't. That's scripture. As I said earlier, all through history there was a small group of people still preaching the truth. We could always find little glimpses throughout history of people preaching the truth, but the vast majority of Christianity wasn't.

Why? How did we know this was going to happen? The prophets predicted it. Long before the church was even established, the prophets predicted that there was going to be a backsliding. They predicted that the church would no longer have the Spirit of God. I'd like to turn to the book of Joel, because it was Joel who predicted that the church would backslide. And he predicted the church would be restored. And it was, in fact, he who predicted that, in the last days, God would pour out His Spirit on all flesh. It was Joel who saw these things ahead of time.

Joel, chapter one, and the fourth verse:

That which the palmerworm hath left hath the locust eaten; and that which the locust hath left hath the cankerworm eaten; and that which the cankerworm hath left hath the caterpillar eaten. Awake, ye drunkards, and weep; and howl, all ye drinkers of wine, because of the new wine; for it is cut off from your mouth.

Now this might be a difficult thing to understand. Sometimes prophecy can be a little dark. Let me put a little light on it. New wine: New wine, in the New Testament, was a reference to the Holy Ghost. On the day of Pentecost, when the church was first filled with the Spirit of God, people mocked and said that they were full of new wine. And since that time, new wine has become symbolic of the Holy Ghost. Not just any wine, but new wine.

The drunkards who are spoken of by Joel, and the drinkers of wine, they're not people who get drunk on natural wine, but they were people who were drunk on the Spirit of God, who had experienced the Holy Ghost. These are the people who will howl and weep when the new wine is cut off. Why? Because what the palmerworm left behind, the locust ate. The church was being devoured bit by bit. The truth was being taken out of the church, not because God was taking it away, but because the people were throwing it away! The church was taking the truth, and bit by bit, throwing it away and replacing it with lies. And what was the eventual result? They didn't want the Holy Ghost anymore. It didn't fit in with their new doctrines and their new teachings. And so the new wine was cut off from their mouths, and they had good reason to weep and howl!

They were told to wake up: They were asleep. They didn't even know that they had lost anything! God told them to wake up and to cry and howl, because they no longer had the Holy Ghost. I don't think they ever did wake up: They just slept right on through, right on through the ages. The church just slept.

But we were promised a restoration! God promised He would restore. If we turn over to the second chapter of the book of Joel, beginning at the 23rd verse:

Be glad then, ye children of Zion, and rejoice in the Lord your God: for he hath given you the former rain moderately, and he will cause to come down for you the rain, the former rain, and the latter rain in the first month. And the floors shall be full of wheat, and the vats shall overflow with wine and oil. And I will restore to you the years that the locust hath eaten, the cankerworm, and the caterpillar, and the palmerworm...

God promised a restoration of all that was lost, all the things that these worms had eaten. This is speaking symbolically of the truth being eaten up, everything that made up the church being eaten up. He promised to restore it, and He spoke of the rain. You know, throughout the Old Testament, there are many symbols that are used to represent the Holy Ghost. One of these is rest, that is, the Sabbath. Other symbols of the Holy Ghost include oil, wine, new wine, and rain.

Rain is a symbol of the Holy Ghost. We speak here of the former rain and the latter rain, that is, two outpourings of the Holy Ghost. First, we had the outpouring on the day of Pentecost, but Joel had prophesied that in the last days God would pour out His Spirit again: The former rain and the latter rain. We are told that the former rain came down moderately, which suggests to us that the latter rain is not going to come down moderately, but that it will come down heavily.

In the book of Haggai, chapter 2 and verse 9, it speaks of the former house and the latter house:

The glory of this latter house shall be greater than of the former, saith the LORD of hosts: and in this place will I give peace, saith the LORD of hosts.

So God is going to restore His church, not only to its original glory, but even greater! Amen!

Hope Brokers

7-3-94

Lighthouse Apostolic Church

We're turning to the book of Jeremiah. We'll be using an assortment of different scriptures today, but I'm going to start in the 29th chapter of the book of Jeremiah. This is a particular verse that has meant a lot to me for a long time, that has often given me a lot of encouragement. In Jeremiah 29, and verse 11:

For I know the thoughts that I think toward you, saith the LORD, thoughts of peace, and not of evil, to give you an expected end.

Now, usually I stick to the King James Version, but with this particular verse, I prefer the way it sounds in the New International Version. In fact, I've got it up here on this poster:

For I know the plans I have for you declares, the LORD: plans to prosper you, and not to harm you, plans to give you hope and a future.

I thought, well, they're both worded a little differently from each other. So then I went to the Hebrew and read it in the Hebrew, and translated it directly from the Hebrew. And it's a combination of both. It says:

For I have known the thoughts that I think about you, says the LORD, thoughts of peace, and not of evil, to give you a future, and a hope.

Hope is what I want to talk about today. I'm going to be going to a few other verses from time to time, but you don't have to look them up unless you want to, especially since I'm not sure when I'm going to hit on any of them. But we're living in a world that doesn't seem to have a lot of hope. And it's not really a new situation; it's a situation that's been around for quite some time. There's a verse in Jeremiah 18, where the people said, the King James says, *there is no hope.* Actually, it was one Hebrew word that they said. It means hopeless. Hopeless! The situation is just hopeless. And because the people thought the situation was hopeless, that there was no longer any hope, anything to hope for, anything to hope in, they decided that they might as well live any way they wanted, and do anything they wanted. *We're going to go after our own ways, and everyone will do what is in his own evil heart.* They said, *because there's no hope.* There's no hope.

The world is without hope. The world is in despair. despair comes from Latin, meaning *without hope,* or *out of hope.* We're fresh out of hope. The world has lost its hope, and they have nothing to believe in, nothing to hope for, nothing to look forward to. The same thing every day. You pick up the newspaper and nothing but trouble. Nothing but turmoil. Every day, it seems there's a new war, a new calamity, a new earthquake, a new disaster, another country breathing out threatenings against former friends or neighbors. And everyday it's the same thing.

So many people I know tell me they don't bother to read the paper anymore. They don't bother to turn on the news, because it's the same thing every day. And they've lost their hope. There's nothing to look forward to. It's just the same thing. It's just the same thing: Hopeless, hopeless, pointless.

St. Francis of Assisi was trying to explain to somebody why he was living the way he was living. He was raised in one of the wealthiest families in the town of Assisi. And he went away to fight in the Crusades. He got very sick while he was there when he came home, for a time he wasn't able to speak. But a profound change had occurred to him during that illness. This man, who seemed to have everything to live for, who lived in a huge house, full of servants, who had everything money could buy, who had the respect of all the people of Assisi, and his family had an important place in the church... He had everything that you think he could want. And yet to him, life had become hopeless. There didn't seem to be any reason to continue with his daily routine. Something had to change. He found it all hopeless, all pointless. And what Francis did was, he gave away everything he owned to the poor.

And his parents were outraged, and dragged him to the to the bishop and to the governor of the city, and demanded some kind of action. And Francis gave back to his parents everything they'd given him, even his name. He gave back his clothes. And he dressed like a beggar from that day on. He no longer wore shoes, he shaved the top of his head. And he lived an entirely different life than what he been brought up to. And not only Francis, but almost every rich man and woman in the town of Assisi was converted by Francis, because they'd all come to the same conclusion, that the life they were living was hopeless.

That boggles the mind of people today, when you tell them something like that, because they think well, if I just had enough money, or if I just had this, or if I just had that... whatever possession it is they think will bring them happiness, then everything would be worthwhile. And yet, here were young people who had everything that money could buy, and they thought it was hopeless. And Francis tried to explain it. He said, "If the purpose of life is this loveless, hopeless toil we go through every day, then it's not for me." He said it's just not worth it. The things that really mattered were missing: Hope, love, faith.

These are things First Corinthians 13 talks about: *These three things remain: faith, hope, and love, but the greatest of these is love.* And those were the things that mattered. Not the house, not the servants, not the fancy clothes, or the jewelry. None of that stuff, not the position, the community. All those things he had, but it was still hopeless. Romans 8 tells us we're saved by hope. But hope that is seen is not hope. For if you see something, why do you yet hope for it? But if we hope for what we don't see, then we can wait for it with patience. We hope for the things we don't see. That's something else the world doesn't understand. They're hoping for things that they can hold in their hand, something tangible, the money, the position, the power. They want something tangible, and that's what they want to hope in. But if you can see those things, that's not much to hope for. But there's something that you can't see. And that's something to hope for something worth waiting for.

The Corinthian church had people in it who were preaching all kinds of different false doctrines. One of the doctrines they began to preach was that there was no resurrection of the dead, that once you died, that was it. That sort of doctrine baffled Paul, when he wrote to them, and he couldn't understand how they could believe something like that. And he said to them, "If the dead aren't raised, then Jesus wasn't raised, and we're still in our sins, and we have no more hope for the future. Now, if we only have hope in Christ in this life now, then we're more miserable than anybody out there," he said. But Christ *has* risen. And He was the first fruits of them that sleep, that is, the first of those who will rise, because we too shall rise. He straightened out the doctrine, but pointed out that we have a hope. We have a hope. In a world where there is no hope. We have a hope. We have a hope.

John said to the church, Beloved, we are now the children of God. That's what we are now. We don't even know yet what we will be. It doesn't appear; it's not seen yet. But we know that when He appears, we'll be like Him, for we'll see Him as He is, and everyone who has this hope.... There it is, again: A hope of something you can't see. ...he purifies himself, even as God is pure. Hope. The word hope is found 129 times in the Bible. And 60 of those are in the New Testament. Hope. And it's always the same thing, that we have a hope in a world that doesn't have a hope. We have a hope in a world that doesn't know what to believe. We have a faith. And in a world that's forgotten how to love, we still have love. It's beyond my comprehension, and probably beyond yours too, that there could actually be people who have no concept of love.

In American history, and in European history: When people reach their lowest, there was still some concept of love. Even in Nazi Germany, were terrible things went on in the concentration camps: In the German families, they still loved each other, they still had that concept of love. But for some people to totally lose the idea of love is beyond comprehension, and yet, it has apparent been known to happen. But the world is not far from that. It's not far from it. It doesn't take too many days in a row of reading the newspaper to find examples of parents who don't love their children, who don't take care of their children. The world has lost its capacity, it seems, to love and they've lost their capacity to believe. And above all, they've lost their hope.

Because without love and faith, what is there to hope in? What is there to hope for?

We've become a planet full of cynics, where nobody really believes anymore. There was a letter in the paper today from a man who was putting down Christianity pretty heavily, and referring to it as fairy tales. But unfortunately, to too many people in the world, even people who don't consider themselves to be atheists or agnostics, what we preach is just a fairy tale to them. Even people who call themselves Christians no longer have the hope, no longer have the faith. And it's just become a fairy tale. But we've got a hope. We've got a hope.

I saw the title of an audio tape the other day. It was the story of a couple who used to be insurance brokers, but that didn't work out for them. Instead, they found another business, and they began to sell something else, and that was hope. And the tape was called *Insurance Brokers to Hope Brokers*. And while I haven't even really had the chance to listen to the tape, I like the concept: Because that's what we are. We are called to be Hope Brokers. *We've got hope and it's available!*

If I knock on somebody's door, I'm not trying to sell them life insurance. I'm not trying to sell them stocks and bonds. I'm trying to sell them hope. I've got some hope. I've got something that makes it worth getting up in the morning. I've got something that makes it worth going on for another day. Because I found a hope. I found a hope. I found a hope, and people can tell when you've got hope. They don't always know what it is. They may think just think you're a little off, and there's something strange about you. We had a teenage girl come to church many, many years ago. And we were talking to her, either before or after the service. And we're just having some informal conversation. And she looks at us and she says, "There's something really strange about you people." She says, "You know, I can see it in your eyes." And we just kind of looked at each other and smiled, because we knew she could see it. We knew she could see it. And she didn't have it. And it intrigued her. She knew there was something there. What is it? She wanted to know: What is it? Well, that puts an obligation on us.

First Peter, chapter three, he said, "*Sanctify the Lord God in your hearts, and be ready always to give an answer to every man that asketh you a reason of the hope that is within you, with meekness and fear."* Be ready to tell them, because they're going to notice if you've got the hope. If it's really there, and you got hold of that hope, they're going to see I; they're going to know that something's different, they're going to want to know what is it. What is it? I can still remember my old pastor saying that people would come up to him and they'd say, "Lee, you've got something! What is it?" And he'd tell them what it is.

If you've got the hope, share it! Hope Broker! I've got something for you! I've got what you're looking for! I've got a hope. I've got a reason to go on. It's not just for this life. It's not just for the material things that people look for. It's none of that. It's totally beyond that. It's totally beyond that. But it's a hope. And it's a powerful hope. And it's a hope that I'm never going to let die. How do I keep it from dying? By sharing it. Because the more I share it, the stronger it grows. The more I hear myself say it, the more I believe it. The more I know it's the truth, the more I feel that hope inside of me, the more I want to give a reason for the hope. So that if somebody doesn't ask, I'll drop the hint until they do. Because I've got something to share. I've got good news to tell. That's what the gospel is supposed to be. The word gospel from Old English *god spell*. Good news, good news. Catch *that* Christianity: Too many out there preaching bad news. Too many people out there preaching judgment. Too many people out there preaching hellfire and damnation, and nobody spreading any hope. Nobody given any hope. I want to be a Hope Broker.

I wonder what the IRS would do if I put that on my tax return next year, occupation: *Hope Broker, you want some?* You want it? That's what my old pastor used to say when they'd say, "You've got something. What is it?" He'd tell them what it was, and then the last thing he'd say is "Do you want it?" *Do you want it? You can see it! Do you want it?*

I've got hope. I've got hope. You know what? It's contagious. Its contagious! It's better than any life insurance policy we're going to buy. It's more like an *eternal* life insurance policy. You can buy any life insurance you want, but they can't promise that you're going to keep on living. Sooner or later, you're going to die. But I can sell you a life insurance policy that has hope: You'll never die. *You'll never die!*

I love to read the account of when Jesus went to the home of Mary and Martha after Lazarus died. Oh, I love to read that! They both said the same thing to him: "Lord, if You'd only been here, our brother wouldn't have died." He said, "You know if you believe, you'll see the power of God. Your brother will rise again." *Oh, I know at the last day at the resurrection.* Yeah, she knew. It was just a fairy tale to her. She knew the right words. She knew that at the last day he'll rise again at the resurrection. And Jesus answered her with words that probably could have knocked her right off her feet: "I **am** the resurrection!" Don't be looking for some future thing. This is the hope! This is it. I'm the resurrection. "The one who believes in Me will never die." And less than 15 minutes later, he was at the tomb and saying, "Lazarus come out of there!" Come out! Because He **is** the resurrection. And Lazarus came out. There's a hope there!

When He left that house that day, do you think Mary and Martha had hope? You'd better believe they had hope! All of Bethany had hope that day, because they saw what happened. They saw a man who said the most unbelievable thing to Lazarus sister: "I am the resurrection and the life." Nonsense words... Until the minute He said, "Lazarus, come out!" He put His money where His mouth was. He put His words into action.

That's what we have to do: Put our words into action. It's not enough to talk Christianity. It's not enough to say *"Oh, yes, I've got the hope. Praise the Lord. Praise the Lord, Praise the Lord, I'm a Christian."* It better be in what we're doing! That hope better be real! It better be shining out of our eyes! And it better be in everything we do.

I knew a lady one time, years ago. We had called her up on a Saturday and asked her if she wanted to go someplace with us. She says, "Oh, no, I can't." We said, "Why not?" And she said, "I have to clean the attic today." Why do you have to do that? *Now?* Couldn't you leave that? Why do you have to clean the attic at all? Who's going to see your attic? She said, "Jesus is coming back. You think I'm gonna let people find a dirty attic?" This was a woman whom I believe had the hope to the point where she was cleaning her attic, so that people wouldn't find a dirty attic after she was gone. I've never understood that, you know, move out of the house and clean it so that the people come in don't find a dirty house. What do you care what they think? She cared. But she proved her hope. She proved that that it was not just a fairy tale to her, that she fully expects Jesus to come back. She fully expects it. That's the kind of hope we got to have.

If you're going to be a Hope broker, you'd better have it. Don't be advertising something you don't have. I preached a sermon here some time ago. Sister Thomas, you probably remember it, where I dressed up like a used car salesmen with that hideous red jacket. Were you here for that service? I had a sign that says *"I have got just what you're looking for."* And I offered them a bridge in Brooklyn. I offered them swampland in Florida, and of course they're all laughing. I said "What's so funny?" They said, "You don't have those things." So what? Can't I offer them for sale? Can I offer to sell you something I don't have? Well, no, I can't. I can't deliver the Brooklyn Bridge to you. I can't give you any swampland in Florida. I don't have it.

But then I showed them the fruit of the Spirit. Love, joy, peace, all those good little things. I said I've got just what you're looking for. There they are. But the problem is, if I don't have them, I can offer them. If I don't have the hope, I better not be offering it to anybody. If I don't believe in it, I better not be offering it to anybody. There's no point in me praying for people to be healed, if I don't believe in healing. There's no point in me praying for people to receive the Holy Ghost, if I don't believe they're going to receive the Holy Ghost. I'd better believe it! I better have that hope. I better know! It better be real if I'm going to be a Hope Broker. Because otherwise I'd just be a Nope Broker! Just be selling one great big Nope! You got it? No. You go to the country store and look for things on the shelf. I don't see any faith here. You got any? Nope. How about hope? Nope. Got any love? Nope. You're in the wrong store. And that storekeeper better get out of business: He ain't got anything for sale! If you're going to be a Hope Broker, you better have the hope. And not the Nope. Or you're gonna look like a dope!

We need hope, real hope, everlasting hope. Not just hope in this life only, because Paul said that would make us more miserable than anybody out there! We were doing all this, and it was all going to end when we died? We'd be more miserable than anybody. Look at all the things we *could* have done! But we've got a hope that goes far beyond that. The eternal life insurance policy! Be ready to give a reason of that hope. Make sure you've got that hope. Keep that hope burning inside of you. Don't ever let it go away. Don't ever let it burn out.

You know, we have to have from time to time revivals, where somebody will come and preach and stir the church up. We're not supposed to need those, you know that? We're not supposed to need those. Paul told Timothy, **you** stir up the gift in you.! You do it yourself. We shouldn't need anybody to come and stir us up. We shouldn't need to have somebody rekindle the fire of hope inside. We're supposed to do that ourselves. Scripture tells us to stir up the gift that's within you. **You** keep that fire burning! One good way is to share the hope: it'll keep on burning. The more you give away, the more you're going to have.

Remember the story in the Old Testament about the woman with a little jar of oil? The woman was poor; she had almost nothing in the house. She and her son were going to starve, and she asked the prophet, "What do we do?" She had to know. She had nothing but a little tiny bit of oil. Just a little tiny bit. There's not enough to do anything with. He told her "Go to your neighbors and borrow vessels. Borrow anything that will hold oil. Not a few; borrow as many as you can. Bring them all into your house." And so she did what she was told. Then he told her take that little bottle of oil, and start to fill up all those others. And she did... and kept filling them and kept filling them, and when every one of them was full, that little bottle of oil still had oil in it, and they sold all the oil and she and her son had money to live on. It's that way with hope: you've got a little bit of hope inside, start pouring it out into other vessels. The more you pour out, the more you're going to have. It won't run dry if you keep pouring it out!

But I'll tell you the truth: If that woman had not obeyed the prophet, if she had not gone out and borrowed those vessels, and had now poured out that little bit of oil, that little bit of oil would have run out, and she wouldn't have had it anymore, because she hadn't shared it. And so it is with hope.

You want to be a Hope Broker? You want that hope to continue to burn inside of you, and be able to give it to other people. You'd better give it to other people, because that's how you'll keep it. Give it away. *Be ready always to give an answer to every man that asks you a reason for the hope that's within you. Having a good conscience that whereas they may speak evil of you, as if you were evil doers, they may be ashamed, who falsely accused your good conversation in Christ.* They may say all kinds of things about us. It doesn't really matter, as long as we know we're doing it right. As long as we're speaking in that hope, living in that hope, walking in that hope. Let them say hopeless. Let them say there is no hope. I'll go out there and show them there **is** a hope. I've got a hope. Do you want it? Do you want it? Amen.

The Second and Third Epistles of John

1996 Northeastern District Conference
  Schenectady, New York

We're going to have a teaching on two overly neglected books in the New Testament, 2 and 3 John. If you would turn to those, we're going to start with Second John. These epistles are believed to have been written between AD 85 and AD 95.

I don't ever remember hearing teaching on either of these books. I have no recollection of ever having heard anyone teach on them, or having heard anybody take a scripture from them and preach on it. It's like they've been there all these years, but we haven't used them very much. And people say, "Well, they're just little books; maybe there's nothing in there we need." But *all* scripture is given by inspiration of God and is profitable, etc. It would not be in there if there was not something in there for us. One of the tests for canonicity, that is whether something belonged in the Bible or not, was that a writing had to be for all ages. If it applied only to the people it was originally written to, and didn't have anything for anyone else, it wouldn't have been included in the Bible. And there are things that were not included, either they were lost, and we don't have them because God felt we didn't need them, or they were left out deliberately because they couldn't meet all the canonicity tests. For example, we have two letters from Paul to the Corinthian church that we call 1 & 2 Corinthians. In truth, those are technically 2 and 3 Corinthians. We don't have the actual 1 Corinthians. We know he wrote an earlier letter to them, because in the book we call 1 Corinthians, he referred to his earlier letter. He apparently wasn't direct enough in it, since it didn't solve the problems. 2 and 3 John *are* here, so it seems to me, we must need them. From the Bible dictionary, I learned that there is no doubt in any scholar's mind as to the authenticity of these two books, that John definitely wrote them. There's no question they're written in the same writing style as 1 John and the Gospel of John. And that's good to know. Not that I was going to doubt in any way, but it's nice to know that other people agree. It just makes it easier.

There has been some controversy over the years, as to whom 2 John was addressed. 2 and 3 John are not general epistles, that is, they're not addressed to the church in general. Rather, they are addressed to specific people, or so it appears. 2 John, verse one:

The elder unto the elect lady and her children.

Now the word translated here as *elder* is the word *presbyter*. In fact, the word in Greek is πρεσβύτερος (pres-VEE-ter-os):

The presbyter to the elect lady, the chosen lady, *and to her children, whom I love in the truth; and not only I, but also all they that have known the truth.*

Now, I'm going to come back later to who this lady might be, some of the theories on who she might be, and who I think she is. But I want to talk about some of the things that were said to this woman and her children.

In verse 2, John spoke about his reason for writing the letter. In the old days, they started off a letter not only with who it was to, but who it was from. More accurately, with who it was from, and then who it was to. So if I were writing a letter, I would say, *Brother Carey to Brother Roberts, I'm writing because...* And this is what John did, he followed this format in this letter. It's interesting: The length of this letter is the exact number of words that would comfortably fit on a single sheet of parchment, like a single sheet of paper. He wasn't going to write a long-winded letter. He wanted it to fit on one sheet, and it did fit... exactly.

So, the Elder, the presbyter, to the chosen lady and her children, whom I love, and everyone who knows the truth loves, for the truth's sake. That's why he's writing: for the sake of the truth. Now, I'm not going to generally write a letter to somebody with the topic being "for the truth's sake," unless there's something that might be jeopardizing the truth. I have occasionally had to write letters to ministers that I thought were straying from the path of Apostolic truth. And, in fact, anybody in our fellowship would do that. If we see another minister who looks like they're straying off the path, and we see it, we're going to try to do something. That's our responsibility, all of us, to each other, if you see a brother or sister start to stray off the path.

I know in some places, they'll brush you off and say, *"ha-ha!"* But our job is to help you back onto it, to point out the path. *"This is the way: Walk ye in it."* So John is writing to the elect lady and her children for the truth's sake, for the purpose of the truth, the truth that dwells in us and will be with us forever. Truth is not something that alters or changes. Truth is truth. I've had discussions with people, theological discussions, on whether truth is unchangeable, about whether there is an absolute truth. Everything I see in Scripture suggests the truth is absolute. It doesn't say by *a* truth, it says by *the* truth. Jesus didn't say I am *a* truth. He's *the* truth. There is an absolute truth that will be with us forever. And we will be with Him forever.

Following the introduction, the purpose of the letter, comes, a greeting, a blessing kind of thing: *Grace be with you, mercy and peace, from God the Father and from the Lord Jesus Christ, the Son of the Father and truth and love.* Be careful with punctuation. Sometimes in these blessings, a lot of times, they are punctuated in a way to look like it's talking about more than one person. Sometimes if you play around with the commas, you'll get a better picture on how things are supposed to be. Don't be afraid to play with punctuation in Scripture. It's not part of the original scripture; there was no punctuation used. They didn't even put spaces between words back then. Verse 4:

I rejoiced greatly that I found of thy children walking in truth, as we have received a commandment from the Father.

It's a wonderful thing: When you find out that people that you don't know how they're doing, when you haven't seen or heard from them in years, you suddenly find out they're still walking with God, they're still living for God. I was talking with sister Karen this week. We had been talking about a lot of the folks we used to go to church with years ago. Not too much in detail. But she mentioned that Sister So-and-so and Sister Such-and-such had all gotten together with Sister Thus-and-so who we used to go to church with years ago. Sister Thus-and-so I remember as a little girl, because I taught her in Sunday School. But she just had a baby shower. She's married and living in Maryland. And all these sisters from the church, from the old church, had gotten together and gone to this baby shower. And I said, "You know, it does my heart good to hear that the folks from the old church are keeping in touch with each other, which suggests to me that they still have something in common." Now, these particular people I know, and the only thing they ever had in common was that we have the same Father. And it's good to know that at least some of those folks that I used to go to church with are still living for God. It's a good feeling to know that. And yes, I can rejoice in that. Because I'm saddened when I find that other people who I used to go to church with aren't living for God anymore. So it's a source of uplifting and joy when we find somebody who is still walking with God.

Anyway, John went on to give a very interesting commandment to the lady. He wrote in verse 5:

And now I beseech thee, lady, not as though I wrote a new commandment unto thee, But that which we had from the beginning, that we love one another. And this is love, that we walk after His commandments. This is the commandment, That, as ye have heard from the beginning, ye should walk in it.

It's an interesting thing that he had to say this to this woman. He had mentioned that she was elect, chosen. *Many are called, few are chosen.* He's trying to make sure she's not only called and chosen, but faithful. And he loves her. And yes, everybody who knows the truth loves her. So she was well known in the church. And he's telling her the most basic of all Christian commandments!

Now, we know that this was something that was very close to the heart of John. If you read 1 John, what was the main topic of it? It was always very important to him, that we love each other, and that we understand that God loves us and that we love Him, and that we act and move and share in that love. It's interesting, though, that John would have to bring this up in writing to someone who, from the sound of his opening introduction, was a pillar in the church; not just a local church, but the entire church community. I'm going to come back to the reasons why I believe he had to say this when I talk about who I think she was.

He went on to say that many deceivers were entered into the world who confess not that Jesus Christ has come in the flesh. This is a deceiver and an antichrist. This was in the late first century. We know from reading the Epistle of Jude, which was written 66 years after the church began, that at that point, the church was already beginning to backslide, and it was a frightening thing. There is something about second and third generation Pentecost that takes things for granted and doesn't have the same zeal and fervor the first generation Pentecost had. We saw it happen in the first century, we have seen it happen in this (20th) century. We have seen the children of the preachers, who have grown up from the time that they were born in Pentecost, who take it for granted, who don't understand in their hearts what it's like to be saved from sin because they've never been in the world. And so the church experienced this in the late first century, and had begun to backslide. Whereas earlier in the century, if anyone had come into the church and had begun to teach false doctrine, or anyone had begun to create any kind of division, or had moved in any spirit other than the Holy Ghost, not only would it not have been tolerated, but the church would have been aware of it. And immediately, somebody would have said something, whether it was one of the apostles coming in and saying stop, or writing a letter and saying this can't be, somebody would pick up on it. Jude's main warning was not only were these things happening, but the church couldn't tell anymore. They didn't recognize the problem, that they had lost their ability to discern between what was the Spirit of God and what was not. And there were false teachers in the first century who had come into the church.

John is also warning about false teachers. The main controversy, in the first four centuries of church history, was the nature of the Godhead, who is God. And this is exactly what he dealt with here: They do not confess that Jesus Christ has come in the flesh. That refers to two different heresies that had become manifest in the church. First, the one that was influenced by Greek thought. This was the one that was actually the first of the heresies. This was the one that was strongest at the point when this epistle was written, although it later died out for several centuries. And that was the idea that there was one Mighty God, but he was not the only god. There were many, many, many lesser gods, millions of them, in fact, demi-gods, or *æons* they called them, and that Jesus was one of those, and that He was not the Mighty God in flesh, but one of the lesser gods. We find the resurrection of that kind of heresy in the mid 16th century: The original Unitarian doctrine which denied the deity of Jesus, and in the 19th century, the Jehovah's Witness view of the Godhead. These are resurrections of that early heresy that make a division between Jesus and God, and deem Jesus a lesser being than the Mighty God.

And also, this is a little early for it, but it wasn't long before the Trinitarian heresy would begin, when Montanus took the Babylonian doctrines and modified them, twisted them, so that they would look Christian, and began to teach them in the church. Although Second John was written a few decades before that, it comes down to the same thing. Any doctrine that denies that the one Mighty God took on flesh and came down to live among us was deceit. It was a lie. And it was antichrist. In speaking of antichrist, we would almost always think of the one who is coming during the time when, God willing, we'll be out of here. But antichrist is not simply a person. The Scripture tells us the spirit of antichrist is **already** working in the world. Antichrist is anything, any spirit or any teaching, that comes against the teachings that Jesus taught, anything that works against what He taught. In fact, in a sense, it's a form of witchcraft. Witchcraft is not, you know, what we usually think of, like the Wicked Witch of the West, or even the New Age kind of witches. Witchcraft was anything that went against the established order of the way God had created things, that challenged the way God had set it up. When Jewish Christians came to the church in Ephesus, they began to tell them, as Bro. Roberts taught us before, "You've got to be circumcised; you've got to keep the Law." Paul, when he wrote to them, asked "Who bewitched you?" He was not using that word lightly. When these people came in, it was a form of witchcraft because they were subverting the order that God had set up there, and they were teaching another way. That was witchcraft; it was antichrist.

Many deceivers, John told the lady, had entered into the world, and they will not acknowledge that He came in the flesh. Personally, he tells her to do something very unusual. **Look to yourselves.** It's so easy to turn your focus outward. Just stop doing that. *"Did you hear about Sister So-and-so? She's doing such-and-such!"* Look to yourself. Look to yourselves. Because that's the only person, that's the only one you have permission to judge: Yourself. If we judge ourselves, the scripture told us, then we would not need to be judged by Him. See, some people's sins go ahead of them, others' follow them to the judgment. So we judge ourselves now, then our sins don't follow us to the judgment, because we've repented of them and they're gone. Look to ourselves, that we not lose those things which we have worked for, or those things that we have gained, but that we receive a full reward. Something here was in jeopardy: The things that were gained, or the work they had done. Everything they had accomplished was in jeopardy. And the solution, John told her, was to look to herself... because she was in danger.

What could possibly jeopardize the work? Think in terms of modern day Apostolic works: Something is jeopardizing them, that we could lose them all. And the solution is looking to yourself. The answer is obvious: It's judgment. The church is destroying the work by judging. But if they would look at themselves, being only in charge of themselves, then they would not lose what they had gained.

Whosoever transgresseth, and abideth, not in the doctrine of Christ, hath not God. He that abideth within the doctrine of Christ, he hath both the Father and the Son.

He's drawing it back again to the knowledge that there was One. They were trying to draw that split again between the Mighty God and Jesus. And they weren't understanding. Whoever sins, transgresseth, whoever sins, and does not remain in the teaching of the Messiah, in the teaching of Christ, does not have God. If you don't have Jesus, you don't have God. It was that simple. He was saying that, by not staying with that teaching, they were sinning. Whoever stays in the doctrine of Christ, in the teaching of the Messiah, has both the Father and Son. You don't need to look for anyone else if you've got Jesus.

And if any come to you and bring not this doctrine, receive him not into your house, neither bid him Godspeed, for he that biddeth him Godspeed is partaker of his evil deeds.

We need to keep this in mind in the context of the first century. Remember, they did not have church buildings. The church met in the house of a pastor. There would be one Bishop, Presbyter, over a city. And then there would be smaller groups in the city and each would meet in the house of the person who was the pastor of that small group, all under one Bishop of the city. So what John was saying was, don't invite them into your house, that is, don't let them come and preach in your church. When somebody comes to you and proclaims to be a believer and a minister, an evangelist, whatever, but they're not teaching the Apostolic doctrine, they don't have the doctrine of Christ, don't put them up in the pulpit! Don't invite them in there, if they're going to come in and teach some kind of heresy.

We're not saying don't give hospitality. The Scripture tells us, you know, don't worry, don't hesitate, or don't be careful, about entertaining strangers: many have entertained angels unawares. We are supposed to show hospitality, but that does not extend to allowing them into the pulpit to teach, because all they're offering is poison. It's not good hospitality to allow someone to poison your household. That goes a little beyond hospitality, I think. And don't bid him Godspeed, don't wish him success in his efforts, if what he's doing is evil and wrong. Because if you do that, then you're partaker of it.

You've given your stamp of approval to it.

Having many things to write unto you, I would not write with paper and ink. But I trust to come unto you and speak face to face, that our joy may be full.

Now I've never, from what I've seen in the scripture, never known any of the apostles to hesitate to take the time to write something down if it really needed to be said. I think that John had managed to say everything that it was essential for the lady to hear at that moment.

He closed with *The children of thy elect sister greet thee.* Another lady and her children. Now, I've heard, especially in Catholic circles, where they would teach that the elect lady that this epistle is written to is the virgin Mary.

And honestly, in the first century, if it were written to an individual female, that's probably the only choice, if it was someone that the entire church knew, or knew and loved. However, I hardly think, from what we know of the personality of Mary, that she would need to be exhorted to love. Or to stay in the doctrine of Christ. And to beware false doctrine. I don't think she was prone to those kinds of things. That go doesn't go along with her personality, which puts us back, again, to the question of who is the lady?

And I had a thought on this. And after some research, I found that I was not the only person with this thought; that many others have had it, too. The idea is that the *lady* is not a single individual, but represents the church. This is especially significant for our time period. And I wonder sometimes, if there's a reason why we haven't looked at things to a certain time. More than 100 years ago, almost nobody ever opened up the book of Revelation. It was kind of almost as if it was locked up so tight they could not look into it... because few understood anything in it. The entire book was a mystery, and many were afraid of it. And so they would not open it. However, as we drew closer to the end times, preachers began to open up the book of Revelation, and things began to make sense. Not all of it. There are still things in there that we can't make heads or tails out of. And yet as we get closer and closer, more and more things begin to make sense. There is a reason for that. The prophet Daniel was told to seal up his book. Well, it wasn't done physically, because it's there. It's open, you can read it. But the prophecies that refer to the end times in the book of Daniel were sealed up in the sense that nobody understood what it was talking about. And now as we get closer, it begins to make sense as it's opened.

As I mentioned at the beginning, I can't remember anybody ever teaching on 2 and 3 John. They've been ignored, it seems for the past 2000 years, that nobody's done anything with them. It may be that the message that was contained in these two books was specifically for our time, and maybe now we need to look at them and see what it is. The reference to the two ladies, the lady and her sister, strongly suggests something to me that I want to pass along to you: And that is the end time Apostolic Church, which is divided in two parts. Both Apostolic doctrinally, but not both Apostolic spiritually. One bound in judgment, and the other motivated by love. We call these Philadelphia and Laodicea. The things that were written to the elect lady in this epistle suggest that there was some of Laodicea in her and in her household, being told the simplest of all Christian commandments, one that should be so basic that it shouldn't even need to be repeated, that she needs to love. Being told not to look at others, but to look at herself, so that she didn't lose the work that had been accomplished. Those are not things you say to somebody who's walking in full truth, spiritually. Those are things you say to somebody who is in spiritual danger from being bound by judgment.

She also has a sister, and yet nothing needed to be said to her. If you would switch over with me to the book of Revelation, chapter three, verse fourteen: "*And to the angel of the church of the Laodiceans, write...*" For many years in Apostolic churches, they loved to preach that Laodicea refers to everybody but them. *That's everybody else!* Because God didn't have a good thing to say about them. They have nothing going for them. It's very easy to be able to do that. And so they say the rest of Christianity is Laodicea. But if we look into it, honestly, we have to acknowledge that all seven of those churches mentioned in Revelation were doctrinally Apostolic at one point. Laodicea was an Apostolic church, doctrinally. The scripture mentions that those that erred in spirit shall come to understand, they shall come to know the doctrine. But their error was in spirit and not in doctrine. Laodicea translates as *the people of judgment* or *the people who judge.* Such was the nature of the church of the Laodiceans: They are the ones who judge other people.

These things say the faithful and true witness, the beginning of the creation of God: I know thy works, that thou art neither cold or hot. I would that thou wert cold or hot. So then, because thou art lukewarm, and neither cold nor hot, I will spew thee out of my mouth. A better translation would be *vomit you.*

Think about these next few verses in the context of the Apostolic churches of our world today that are so proud of having the Apostolic truth. You'll hear them say we have all the truth, full truth, and no one else does.

Because thou sayest, I am rich, and increased with goods and have need of nothing, and knowest not thou art wretched and miserable, and poor, and blind and naked, I counsel thee to buy of me gold tried in the fire, that thou mayest be rich, and white raiment, that thou mayest be clothed and that the shame of thy nakedness do not appear. Anoint thine eyes with eyesalve, that thou mayest see. As many as I love, I rebuke and chasten. Be zealous, therefore, and repent. Behold, I stand at the door, and knock. If any man hear my voice and open the door, I will come in to him and we'll sup with him and he with me. To him that overcometh will I grant to sit with me in my throne, even as I also overcame and am set down with my father in his throne. He that hath an ear, let him hear what the Spirit saith unto the churches.

This sounds a lot like the situation the lady in Second John was getting into, that she couldn't seem to see herself, but was looking at everybody else, and was failing to love them, which falls right into judging them. And so John wrote to steer her back, and then just closed with a greeting from the children of her sister. Who's the sister? Let's go up to verse seven in the same chapter of Revelation:

To the angel of the church in Philadelphia, right? Now, of course we have a Philadelphia in this country, and we've been taught to translate it as the City of Brotherly Love. A better translation of Philadelphia is *"love between brothers and sisters,"* because the Greek word for *brother* and the Greek word for *sister* are identical, except for the ending you put on to signify gender. And if you wish to say brothers and sisters, you would use the masculine plural. So *brothers* also means *brothers and sisters.* Philadelphia is the love of brothers and sisters.

These things saith he that is holy, he that is true, he that hath the key of David, he that openeth, and no man shutteth; and shutteth, and no man openeth; I know thy works: behold, I have set before thee an open door, and no man can shut it: for thou hast a little strength, and hast kept my word, and hast not denied my name. Behold, I will make them of the synagogue of Satan, which say they are Jews, and are not, but do lie; behold, I will make them to come and worship before thy feet, and to know that I have loved thee.

Who's he talking about when he says "the synagogue of Satan?" No, not real Jews, not the physical Jews. This is speaking in spiritual terms, so not the physical children of Abraham, but the ones who *say* they are spiritual children of Abraham. That is, people who say they're Christian, but are really the synagogue of Satan, the assembling of Satan. They name the name of Jesus, but they don't look like their Father, they don't act like their Father. Why? He said, *I will make them to come and worship before thy feet.* We need to be clear on this: They're not worshiping the Philadelphia church; that's just the place where they're being made to worship God, in the presence, at the feet of, the Philadelphia church. *...to worship God, and to know that I have loved thee.* Now, why would He need to do that? ...unless those particular people had denied that God loved the Philadelphia church? Does that sound familiar to anybody? *Jesus doesn't love you?* Sounds very familiar. *I'm going to make them know that I **have** loved you. Because thou hast kept the word of my patience, I also will keep thee from the hour of temptation which shall come upon all the world to try them that dwell upon the earth.* Now that word *from* is translated from the Greek word ἐκ (ek), which means *out of.* People tell you "We're going to go through the tribulation period." It says to me here I will keep you **out of** the hour of temptation which I'll come upon all the world. We will not go through that.

Behold, I come quickly. Hold that fast which thou hast, that no man take thy crown. Him that overcometh will I make a pillar in the temple of my God, and He shall go no more out. And I will write upon him the name of my God and the name of the city of my God, which is New Jerusalem, which cometh down out of heaven from my God. And I will wrote upon him my new name. He that has an ear, let him hear what the Spirit says to the churches.

To me, the two women in 2 John seem to be these two end-time Apostolic churches that are sisters. Now, it's interesting that John would have to convey greetings to this woman from her sister. Why didn't the sister's household write? Why weren't the sisters in communication? Something had happened that made a break in communication between the two sisters, that John is sending the greetings instead. Surely, if the relationship was close enough that they could write to each other, John would not have needed to have said anything. There was no communication between the two sisters. And one of the sisters was falling into judgment. It very much to me suggests the end-time Apostolic church. It suggests the warning against judgment. It suggests the urgent exhortation to love. And it's not a new commandment.

It's not a complicated commandment. He said it's the same one you've had since the beginning, that apparently, this elect lady had not followed... wasn't following. And from what I can see, there's no indication in this epistle that she ever followed that commandment. Her entire Christianity built up with all the Apostolic truth, this elect lady, and the very foundation of love was missing from it. Something was very wrong. And I wouldn't be surprised if that lack of love was the reason there was no communication between the two sisters.

What happens to the two sisters? Jesus never says He is coming to take two brides away. I love the suggestion in the two letters we read in Revelation of a connection between Laodicea and Philadelphia: In no other letters were doors mentioned, only in those two. He mentioned doors. The Philadelphia Church has a door that is open and nobody can shut it. He never said anything about what was on the other side of it. He never told them what they should do about it, but it was implied they should go through it. It was there. And it was open. Laodicea, on the other hand, also has a door, but it's closed. And He's knocking on it. And only *they* can open it. Have you ever seen the picture that shows Jesus knocking on the door? Generally, you'll notice there's no doorknob on that door. He can't open it from His side. They've got to open it from within. He said if anybody opens the door, I will come in. What would happen to the Laodicean church if Jesus walked in? Could it be that the judgment would be thrown out, and from His example of love, they would learn to love each other? What would happen if the Philadelphia church walked in with Him, since they have an open door, that they are to go through?

Now we wouldn't have two end-time Apostolic churches anymore. We'd have one, a united Apostolic church, a single, powerful united lady, which takes us back to Song of Solomon, where Solomon told the love story between Jesus and the church. And I know you've all heard me teach this before, so I'm gonna make this brief. Where Solomon had been telling the story of the church and Jesus, and suddenly didn't recognize the church anymore. Halfway through the book, he said, *"Who is this?"* Solomon, you're getting senile; you're forgetting the characters in the story! She's the one you talked about from the very first chapter, the first couple of verses. You mentioned her, you quoted her. How come you don't recognize her? *Who is this coming up out of the wilderness?*

You know, sometimes those wilderness experiences are where God refines us and purges out those who aren't going to make it, so that those who come into the promised land are the ones who belong there. She's coming up out of the wilderness, she's coming up out of the trial and tribulation, out of the fire. Terrible as an army with banners. A better way of translating *terrible* might be *awe-inspiring.* That implies strength, and it implies unity. And she's leaning on whom? On her Beloved. And that's **not** who she was leaning on when she went down into the wilderness, and then she wasn't strong and united. Then she was trying to lean on her own devices, in her own denominations, and everything she built for herself. Now she's coming up out of the wilderness, leaning on her Beloved, terrible as an army with banners. And Solomon was so taken with the change, he didn't know who she was anymore. I think it's the two women, the two ladies, the two sisters united into one powerful church. And I think that's what we're going to see happen.

Third John starts off:

"The elder [or the presbyter] to the well-beloved Gaius, whom I love in the truth." Alternate translation, *"whom I truly love."*

I tried to find out who Gaius was, if he represented anything. I didn't find anything. The Bible dictionary wasn't a lot of help. They could not connect conclusively him with anyone else in the New Testament who had that name. There was no clue as to who he was, but the dictionary recognized him not as a leader of a church, not as the pastor in a particular church, but as someone of prominence in a particular church. That was the best they could do at identifying him.

Beloved I wish (another translation: *I pray*) *above all things that thou mayest prosper and be in health, even as thy soul prospereth.*

I think that's important. It reminds me of the "Sister Sicker-than-thous" in the church, who dwell on their illnesses and their shortcomings, and think that it's God's will that they suffer these things. You know, *"We all have our cross to bear, and mine is sickness!"*John's wish for Gaius was that he would prosper and be healthy even as his soul prospered. Apparently, Gaius was doing OK spiritually, and that's good, but apparently he was having some physical problems, and John wanted his physical health to match his spiritual health. Certainly makes it a lot easier to do the work of God if you have the freedom from your body to do so, and it's not got you bound.

For I rejoiced greatly when the brethren came and testified of the truth that is in thee, even as thou walkest in the truth. I have no greater joy than to hear that my children walk in truth.

This suggests to us that Gaius was someone that John had converted, someone John had witnessed to, who had heard the word, and perhaps he had not heard from him in a long time. And sometimes you lose track of people, and you wonder, *Is this one that I haven't seen in years still living for God? Is that one still living for God? This one who I witnessed to, I haven't heard from them.* John got word: *Remember that guy Gaius you preached to? He's living for God! He's preaching the truth! He's living in it!* John had no greater joy than hearing that. I can sympathize with that. I can understand that. I can empathize with that. I think that's the most wonderful thing I could hear, that somebody I reached out to years ago is living for God. I think that's a wonderful thing!

Beloved, thou doest faithfully whatsoever thou doest to the brethren, and to strangers; which have borne witness of thy charity before the church: whom if thou bring forward on their journey after a godly sort, thou shalt do well:

Another translation of *"after a godly sort"* is *"worthy of God."* Charity is an area where Gaius was not lacking. Too often the church is lacking. It's kind of ironic that of all the denominations that call themselves Christian, and I know the Schenectady folks have heard me say this, the one that does best when it comes to taking care of the poor and needy is the one that has the least Apostolic truth. That's a frightening thing; it shouldn't be that way. It very much brings back the story of the Good Samaritan. Of the three people who passed that man, bruised and beaten, on the road, the one who had the least chance of knowing about compassion and loving his neighbor was the one who stopped and helped him. The priest and the Levite, who should have known about those things, crossed over to the other side of the road and acted like they didn't see him. But the Samaritan, the Samaritan who shouldn't have known any of this stuff, did. When you say to people today, charity, taking care of the poor, taking care of the hungry, name a person, most are going to come up with someone like Mother Teresa. And yeah, she puts the Apostolic church to shame. And the Catholic church in general, when it comes to charity. One of the letters in the book of Revelation is directed toward Catholicism, and their charity, their works, the good works that they do, is mentioned TWICE because they are so good at it. Now, he didn't hesitate to point out the spiritual idolatry that is going on in the church, and that doctrinally, they were a mess, that they were an abomination in a sense. But when it came down to taking care of the little ones, they knew how to do it. That's OUR responsibility! That's something for us!

Jesus said that not everyone who calls Him "Lord, Lord..." gets in. Many, He said, Many will come to Me in that day, saying "Lord, we cast out devils in Your Name, we did miracles, we prophesied..." All these things they said they did IN HIS NAME, which means we're talking Apostolic folks here, and He says, "I... NEVER... NEVER... NEVER... NEVER KNEW YOU!" How?! They're filled with the Holy Ghost and baptized in Jesus' Name! Well, He can't recall having met them, because He was hungry, and they didn't come and feed Him. He was naked, and they didn't bring Him clothes. *"I never met you before! Where were you when I was in prison? Where were you when I was sick?"* That's for us! That's part of OUR responsibility. And unfortunately, for a large measure, the Apostolic church as a whole, both halves of it together, have tended to neglect our responsibility. We're afraid of being accused of preaching a social gospel. We want to make sure we stick to teaching the Apostolic truth, so we tend to overlook the fact that there are people who are hungry. There are people we can help. Yeah, that's real nice to hand them a tract, but if their stomach is empty, that tract isn't going to take care of them. It's not going to meet the need. Feed them first, THEN give them the tract! You're going to have to take care of the needs of the body. It doesn't do any good to tell them to be warm and filled if you haven't given them the things they need.

Gaius knew how to do it. He faithfully took care, not just of the brethren in the church, but strangers, too. And John had even heard the stories of the faithfulness of Gaius, of his charity before the church. And he went on to mention that these people, if you bring them on their journey in a godly fashion, you're really doing good. Not only taking care of the poor, but helping them find their way in. You know, some have tried to use that as a form of coercion. There are actually charities in this world that will not give food to people unless they convert. I had signed up for one of those things one time, where you send a monthly amount to sponsor a child. But before I did it, I said to them, "I want to ask you a question. Is this help given to any child, or do you insist they be Christian children?" And they said, "No, of any faith." "I said, "All right, then I'll do it." I'm not going to have anybody forced to convert in order to eat. There's a particular food pantry in this city that is run by a Pentecostal church. They will give food to anybody... the first time. But after that, if you are not a Christian, they are not going to give you food. There is something very wrong with that attitude. It kind of brings us back to something that I think Bro. Roberts will touch on later, if you love only those who love you, what have you accomplished? If you greet only those who greet you back... The heathen can do those things! We're called upon to love those who do not love us... and to feed those who may not feed us in return. Yes, we need to meet all the needs of the people, as best we can, and try to bring them along. But don't make it conditional: *You get the food if you're willing to convert.* You're not going to win anybody that way. Jesus never used blackmail or extortion to convert anybody.

Because that for his name's sake they went forth, taking nothing of the Gentiles. We therefore ought to receive such, that we might be fellow-helpers to the truth.

In a sense, he's talking about a continuation here: You've helped these people, you've brought them along in this way, now they can go forward doing the same thing. These things are, in a sense, contagious: We show charity. They learn charity. They'll show charity. When you show people the path, they'll show people the path. Who among us, if we see a good movie, won't tell our friends: *Oh, you've got to see this; it was wonderful.* Or if we find a new restaurant: *You've got to try their food. It's great.* Or *You've got to read this book I just got!* It's a natural thing to do. How about *I just found a brand new way to live. I found a path that leads to glory!* Wouldn't you want to share that, too?

I found people who helped me when I was down. I see you're having some trouble. Here, take this. Let me help you. Let me show you what I've found.

We've got a little subject change coming up here.

I wrote unto the church: but Diotrephes, who loveth to have the preeminence among them, receiveth us not.

He didn't mention which church here, so I'm going to assume that he's referring to the church Gaius belonged to. And apparently, Diotrephes must have been the bishop, because he was the one who had refused to be receptive to John's letter to the church. And yet, Diotrephes loved to have the preeminence, he liked to be in charge, he liked being the boss. He wants the big chair up front. He wants to sit in that one, so everybody could see him. *He would not receive us.* That, to me, is mind-boggling, that in the first century there would be a church that called itself Christian that would not receive one of the apostles who had walked with Jesus. That is, to me, the epitome of... I can't think of the word I'm looking for. That they would think they that knew... *Arrogance,* yes! To think that they could know more than the apostles, or be better than the apostles, and not need the apostles. Hey, you can choose the most boring among them: *I'll* listen to him preach! I don't care! I want to hear what he's got to say!

Wherefore, if I come, ... that's going to be difficult: There's an "if" there, John said. He's not even sure he's going to be able to visit. And he's going to go on to say why he may not be able to come there...

I will remember his deeds which he doeth, prating against us with malicious words: and not content therewith, neither doth he himself receive the brethren, and forbiddeth them that would, and casteth them out of the church.

Not only would Diotrephes not welcome John and his party, but if any of you folks bring him into your house, you can't come to church here anymore. Unbelievable! At this point, if I were John, I would have interjected something to my beloved Gaius, my dear son in the Lord: *Get yourself out of that scene, and find another church to go to!* There's something really wrong with Diotrephes: Throwing people out of the church for receiving the apostles! The scripture gives us permission to throw someone out of the church for one reason only: Heresy. And they get warnings... even they get warnings! We have whole steps to follow if people fall into sin, and if, after the second warning, they don't repent, you take it to the church, it does tell us to treat them as an unbeliever, treat them as a heathen. What does that mean? Well, some churches think it means you throw them out and you never speak to them again. There are still folks in this city who, when they see me, will not speak to me, as if they never knew me. That is NOT what that means. Good Lord, we're supposed to be *reaching* the unbelievers. You don't win them by turning your back on them! You don't win them back by giving them the cold shoulder. You win them back with love! Isn't that how we treat the unbeliever, when the visitor comes to church? You know, everybody wants to fawn over the visitor, and love them, and win them. That's how you win them. That's how you win the brother who's backslidden, too, who's fallen into sin. They may not be considered Brother or Sister anymore, but you want to get them back to their original place as best you can. The scripture says, "If a brother be overtaken in a fault, you who are spiritual, **restore** such a one." That's our responsibility. The horror stories I've heard! One particular horror story I heard from one of the other Apostolic churches: A few of the ministers got wind that one of the other ministers was having a problem with a particular sin that he kept falling into. The Christian thing to do would have been to go to him and say, *"We know you're having a problem. How can we help?"* Instead, they set him up, and videotaped it so they could throw him out of the church! I wanted to cry when I heard that story.

Beloved, follow not that which is evil, but that which is good.

Remember what I said, that if I were John, I would have inserted there "Get yourself a new church?" I think that's kind of what he's saying here. Don't follow that which is evil. He had just finished talking about the evil deeds of the leader there, Diotrephes, and then said, don't follow that which is evil. That's an example NOT to follow. But follow that which is good.

He that doeth good is of God: but he that doeth evil hath not seen God.

No matter how much they call themselves "Christian," or pretend to be Christian, if they're doing evil, if that's what you're receiving from them...

In one of the other epistles, John asked the question *"How can you say you love God, whom you have not seen, if you hate your brother who you have seen?"* It's not possible. If you can't love the people you see, how can you love the One you haven't seen?

He went on to talk about someone named Demetrius, and I think it's connected, because not only did he say don't follow that which is evil, referring to Diotrephes, he also said follow that which is good, and now he's going to bring up somebody else:

Demetrius hath good report of all men, and of the truth itself: yea, and we also bear record; and ye know that our record is true.

How about if I paraphrase verses 11 & 12: *You've got to get yourself out of that church. Here's a good pastor; go follow his example.* Yeah, he did put it in there. A lot of times I've had to tell people, you're going to have to get out of the church you're going to. Many years ago, I got a call from a dear Sister in Tennessee, Sis. Wanda. She used to live here; she was our youth group leader. She did more for the UPC [United Pentecostal Church] in Schenectady than anybody other than Bro. Hanby himself, and received only evil from people in the church as a result of it. She moved to Tennessee, and she was attending a little church there, and she called me one day and she said, "I am so torn; I don't know what to do." I said, "What's the matter?" She said, "I know I'm called to ministry." Well, that came as no surprise to me; I'd known for years that she was called, but it wasn't my place to tell her, because I'm not the One calling her. But she said, "My pastor doesn't believe in women in the ministry. He won't let me pursue it." She said, "I don't know what to do. The scripture tells me to obey my pastor." I said, "If you have a pastor who tells you to do one thing when God is telling you to do another, it's time to find a new pastor. It is time to find a new pastor!" Don't follow the pastor if the pastor doesn't do what's right. But Demetrius had a good report of everybody. There's no one in the church who could find a bad thing to say about Bro. Demetrius. I tell you, he was all right! And of the truth itself... he wasn't going to swerve from it. He was going to teach it exactly the way it was. We also bear record... John could say, "I know Demetrius is a good man; you can follow him. ...and ye know that our record is true. That is, you know

I wouldn't steer you wrong. You know I wouldn't lie to you, and that if I tell you he's a good pastor, he's a good pastor. You can trust him.

I had many things to write, but I will not with ink and pen write unto thee:

The same thing he wrote to the elect lady: I'm not gonna write all these things now. But he had said the things that I think needed to be said. The main purpose of that letter was *You're in a bad church; you'd better get out of there!* You know, he went in to great detail about how well Gaius was doing, how good an influence he had been spiritually, and how he'd been taking care of people. I think he was concerned that 'if you stay in that church much longer, you're going to be poisoned with what's happening there. You're going to have to get out.' I think that was the reason he wrote this, just a short little letter. That was what needed to be said. Anything else, when we speak face to face:

But I trust I shall shortly see thee, and we shall speak face to face. Peace be to thee. Our friends salute thee. Greet the friends by name.

It's interesting, in most places, the people in the church aren't referred to as friends. Usually, it's "Greet the brethren," "Greet the brothers and sisters." And especially in the Apostolic and Pentecostal churches, where we call each other Brother and Sister, it's good that we have that knowledge of family, and we keep that, and I like that, and I think that's important for us. But we're friends, too. We *are* friends. It's important to be friends to each other, and we want to be His friends. He said we were His friends if we obey His commandments, not the least of which was "Love one another." And if you love somebody, I think you can call them your friend.

So the friends who were with John sent greetings to Gaius, and he asked him to greet the friends by name. Maybe there's another reason there, because the people in the church who were not always doing what they should, maybe still Brother and Sister, but maybe they weren't friends. So I think Gaius knew which ones he should be greeting for John. I don't think Diotrephes wanted to hear *"John says hello!"* I don't think he wanted to know that. In fact, Gaius could have found himself put out of the church just for receiving this letter from John!

I think there is some good stuff in both of these epistles. There's some good meat there for digestion. There's some good steering on how we should be living, how we should be treating each other, what things we should beware of. I preached a sermon one time, if you want to look back at the very end of 1 John, the very last verse:

Little children, keep yourselves from idols.

It's interesting that he put it in there, because, in the sense that we usually think of idols, the statues of Diana, and all the others, the only church that we know of that had a real problem with it was Ephesus. And yet, 1 John was a general epistle that went to all the churches. They weren't all having problems with idols. Most of them were only too glad to give up their gods and goddesses that had eyes, and couldn't see, and ears, and couldn't hear, and mouths, and couldn't speak, and hands, and couldn't help, for a God whom they couldn't see, but who could do anything. They were only too happy to get rid of those statues. So I don't think that's the kind of idols he was warning against, if he's writing to everybody.

Sometimes there are things that we think are more important, things that we put before God. You know, you'll have churches competing with each other for attendance, competing with each other for the nicest building, competing with each other for the best program. Even evangelistic programs: *Ours is better than yours. Our outreach works better than yours. Our music ministry... You should hear **our** choir!* There are things that they make so important that are of no consequence at all to the Kingdom. We're supposed to have a common goal. We're supposed to be working with each other, not competing with each other. And sometimes competition becomes an idol itself. We need to always remember to keep our priorities correct. Anytime we have trouble remembering the priorities, go back to Matthew chapter 6, verse 33. He set our priorities for us. And as many times as we have to reset them, we need to reset them:

Seek ye first the Kingdom of God, and His righteousness, and then all these other things will be added unto you.

Never mind about the biggest Sunday School attendance, or anything like that. You know, sometimes the little stunts are funny. I was invited by some friends of mine in high school... I hung around with a group... I was the only

Pentecostal in Galway [New York] at the time, so the friends that I hung around with were the product of a Baptist revival that had happened, and I have to give them credit: It was good of them to be my friends, because most went to Baptist churches that taught that Pentecostals were devil-possessed! And yet, my friends knew better. One of them was the brother of one of those Baptist pastors, someone who was really nervous about his younger brother hanging around with me. But I went to visit one of the churches with them one time. They were having a drive to reach a certain number in Sunday morning service, and the pastor had promised that if he got that many in Sunday morning service, he would go preach on the rooftop. And of course, they all wanted to see the pastor on the roof. Well, that's a nice, fun little game, but it really accomplishes nothing for the Kingdom. The people who were brought in as visitors to that church were not given the kind of attention that a new visitor to the church should have. There was no one there to take them by the hand and show them the way to salvation, which, of course, that church didn't know anyway. They were simply cattle, numbers, crowded in so the pastor would go preach on the roof. They didn't get anything out of that spiritually. I don't think anybody did. They were playing a game. It was like having a party, to see who could have the biggest party. Their priority was wrong. It wasn't the Kingdom of God at all. It was something that *they* were making.

We need to watch our priorities. We need to look and see what is most important. Nothing is more important than the Kingdom of God. Nothing matters more than His Kingdom, His righteousness, to do the work that He sent us here to do, that He put here: *Go into all the world and preach the Gospel: Judea, Samaria, the uttermost parts of the world.* Witnesses. What does a witness do? Testify. What does that mean? What I saw, what I heard, what I experienced. That is what a testimony is. "Well, I don't know how to witness." Have you had an experience with God? *Yes.* Can you tell me about it? *Yes.* That's witnessing. What happened to you. Not what happened to somebody else, but what happened to you.

We used to do witnessing with the youth group that Sis. Wanda founded here. We'd go door to door, two by two, and people would be scared, thinking,

'*Here come the Mormons, or the Jehovah's Witnesses.*' And it was completely different, because they were used to opening up the door to '*Have you ever thought about God's kingdom?*' Some memorized speech! Instead, you've got a thirteen or fourteen year old kid who'd say, "*Can I take just a minute to tell you what the Lord did in my life?*" And they'd offer a personal testimony about a change that had taken place in them. And there is nothing in the world more powerful than that. Nothing that will change people's minds and their lives like hearing what God has done in your life. If you do it that way, they've got something to build on, and it won't be long before they can say to somebody else, '*Let me tell you what God just did for me. Let me tell you what God has done in my life.*

Labor to Bring Forth, O Daughter of Zion

I'm going to be reading a few passages of scripture, starting in Isaiah chapter 37. This was one of those days when I didn't have a clue what I was preaching about until about a half an hour before service. I was doing so many things at once that I kept thinking *What's going to happen?* I finally took a moment to sit down with the Bible.

I have just three passages of scripture. I'll have to trust on the Lord to supply the rest of it. I like reading Isaiah, because he said some pretty profound things. I always liked reading some of the things he said. If you ever need to prove who God is, Isaiah is the book to turn to. And he didn't pull any punches when he quoted the Lord.

I enjoy reading how Isaiah got his call to Ministry, when he found himself standing in the throne room of God, knowing full well he had no business being there, probably hiding behind a pillar. And the Lord said, "Who am I going to send? Who's going to go?" And Isaiah just stepped out and said, "Here am I; send me!" Now, that's dedication! I like that.

Isaiah chapter 37 and verse 3:

And they said unto him, Thus saith Hezekiah, This day is a day of trouble, and of rebuke, and of blasphemy: for the children are come to the birth, and there is not strength to bring forth.

Turn to chapter 66, in the same book. Beginning at verse 7:

Before she travailed, she brought forth; before her pain came, she was delivered of a man child. Who hath heard such a thing? who hath seen such things? Shall the earth be made to bring forth in one day? or shall a nation be born at once? for as soon as Zion travailed, she brought forth her children. Shall I bring to the birth, and not cause to bring forth? saith the Lord: shall I cause to bring forth, and shut the womb? saith thy God.

And finally, the book of Micah. Micah is another prophet I enjoy reading. He was the one who predicted where the Messiah would be born. Chapter 4 and verse 10:

Be in pain, and labor to bring forth, O daughter of Zion, like a woman in travail: for now shalt thou go forth out of the city, and thou shalt dwell in the field, and thou shalt go even to Babylon; there shalt thou be delivered; there the Lord shall redeem thee from the hand of thine enemies.

All of these verses that I've read spoke about bringing forth children. Hezekiah had mourned the fact that it was a day of trouble, because it was time for birth and there was no strength to bring forth the children. Obviously, I can't speak from experience, but from what I understand, giving birth is quite a traumatic experience, that it does take quite a bit of strength. I've seen videos of women giving birth, and how sometimes they feel like they just don't have the strength to continue. And this is where a coach comes in handy to encourage them: *You've got to continue! You can't give up halfway through. You've got to deliver the child!*

It speaks of travail, which is an old English word for being in labor. And Hezekiah, again, complaining that there was trouble, because the children came to the birth and there was no strength to deliver. And then later on in the same book, it talks about the fact that before the travail even came, before the labor pains even came, she was delivered, that the earth was made to bring forth in one day, a nation born at once. And God asking the question: Would He bring to the birth, and then not cause to bring forth? Or would He cause to bring forth, and then shut the womb at the last moment?

And finally, Micah encouraging the daughter of Zion, which is symbolic of the church, like a woman in labor, to go out. Now that doesn't make sense from a natural standpoint. If somebody is in labor you don't tell them to go for a walk! You don't tell them to go to work. Generally, if somebody's in labor, the place to bring them is the hospital, or if they're going to give birth at home, at least go to bed. Don't go out! And yet, here's the daughter of Zion, a woman in travail, in pain and laboring to bring forth: Go out of the city and go live in the field. Even go to Babylon, which is symbolic of sin, and there you will be delivered. To have children in a place where it doesn't seem to be natural to give birth, in a place that's unusual.

The whole thing speaks of the mission of the church, what our responsibility is. For so long now, the church has had a day of trouble, a day of rebuke, and a day of blasphemy, because there were children waiting to be born and the church had no strength to deliver; because there was a harvest waiting to be reaped, and there wasn't enough labor, there wasn't enough power to go out and reap the harvest.

What I want to tell you today is that things have begun to change, that we have begun to see a change in the church. The church is still in labor, the church is still ready to bring forth, but we've finally found strength. We finally found the strength to bring forth! Just in the past few months, with the changes that we've seen across the country, as new churches have opened up, we've seen strength come forth. We've seen the power to reap a harvest where before there wasn't any. And the end result is a nation being born in a day, is the church bringing forth many children at once, to the point where we'll be bringing forth before the pains even come, before there is even labor, bringing forth children. bringing forth people. And not just in the place where we thought we would do it.

For too long, the church has tried to shut itself in, lock itself in its buildings to protect itself. Too much of the church world has made the mistake of trying to do things backwards. They try to keep the world out of the church. We had a woman in a play one time announcing that they only let holy people in her church. Well then, what's the purpose of the church? Jesus said those who are well do not need a physician. It's the ones who are sick who need the doctor. Those are the ones you're supposed to be inviting in, the ones who need to know. But for too long the church's shut itself up, playing holier-than-thou and not letting those in who were different. Not letting those in who needed to hear the message of truth. And they've alienated people over the years. And the result was that no children were brought forth, because the children need to be born outside of the church and then brought in. The harvest needs to be reaped in the field, not in the house. The farmer can't reap his harvest if he stays in his house. It won't happen. It's not going to reap itself. You've got to have laborers out there working. You have to have the church in labor, not in the church, but out of the church, out in the field, and even into Babylon, the midst of the evil religions that are not teaching the truth of God. Even out there, where they're relying on things that are not of God to save them, to go out right there in the midst of that, and to bring forth children, to go out there with a message of hope and a message of truth, to go out into the darkness with a light and say there's a better way.

The doors of the church need to be opened up. The windows of the church need to be opened up. And the people who for too long have sat around the table feasting need to go out and labor in the field. They need to go out and travail in the world, outside of their safe and secure city. because it is indeed a day of trouble. It is indeed a day of rebuke and of blasphemy, because for too long children have come to the birth, and there was no strength to bring them forth. We've lost too many over the years because we did not have the strength to give birth.

We've got to have that strength. We've got to have the spiritual strength to bring forth children, the courage to step outside of our walls, the courage to step outside of our safe haven, and to go out into the world.

Jesus was in trouble more often than not with the Pharisees, because of the company that He kept. Because, instead of hanging out in the synagogues and hanging out in the temple, He spent precious little time in those places. Oh, He'd go to the synagogue on the Sabbath. And if He was in Jerusalem, He'd go to the temple. But He didn't spend most of his time there. You could find him at the seashore, preaching to a crowd, or on the mountaintop, preaching to a crowd, or in the red light district, meeting with the people that the church didn't want anything to do with, meeting with the people that the religious leaders of His day said were not worth the time.

When He talked to the tax collectors, he talked to Zacchaeus, and the people wanted to know, Why is He talking to him? Why is He spending time with him and then, to fly absolutely in the face of the Jewish tradition, he told Zacchaeus, *I'm going to your house today!* Unheard-of! You don't go to the house of a sinner! But he did. And when it was all over, Jesus was able to say to the world that salvation has come to this house today; one who was lost has been found.

But if Jesus had waited for Zacchaeus to come to the synagogue or the temple, He would have been out of luck, because Zacchaeus wasn't welcome in those places: He was a sinner. The only way to reach him was for Jesus to go to where he was, to go to his house.

Last winter, I got an invitation which was kind of unusual and it was a first for me. I was invited to go and and teach a gathering of people, most of whom were pagans and witches. And what they told me on the phone was, *We can't get a Christian who will come and teach us. Will you come and teach us?* And I said, yes.

And people would ask me, *But why are you going there?* And I said, "What would have happened in ancient Greece if Paul had refused to go to Athens because the people were idol worshipers?" They had so many different gods and goddesses, and even the altar to the unknown god. Paul could have said, *I'm not going there.: They're heathens! and* refused to preach the gospel. He never would have come to Greece. The Gospel never would have reached there. In fact, it never would have reached anybody. It's our responsibility to go!

If a door opens, go through it. One of our new ministers called me the other day and asked me if could he go preach in another church. He'd been invited to go preach in a church of another denomination. He said, "I don't know, should I do this?" I said, "Is the door open?" He said, "Yes." I said, "Go. They need to hear it." They won't come to you, you go to them. You go to them. If the sick people can't go to the physician, the physician's got to go to the people. We still make house calls!

We still make house calls; it's our responsibility. They're not going to be born in the church. They're not going to be born in here. You know, the church I used to attend in Southern California: I've had to use this as an example so many times of what the church should not be, and it's a sad thing, because they were a nice group of people. But they didn't have a clue what the mission of the church was. There was not one whit of evangelism in that church. Nobody reached out to anyone else. Nobody invited anybody.

Nobody told the good news to anybody there. The baptismal tank had been empty for 20 years because there was nobody to baptize.

Well they weren't going to have anybody born there. Nobody was going to come into the kingdom there, because everybody in the church was already in, and they had no interest in anybody outside their doors. And I asked them, but they had no good reason why they weren't. But it's not going to happen within the walls of the church. It's for the same reason that we don't look for our salvation doctrine in the epistles. It's because they were written to people already saved, and we don't look to see people saved in the church because they're already saved. If we want to see people brought into the kingdom, we've got to go out into the world, out of the city, out of the the enclave of our church, out of our protective hedge, and go out there where it's not safe. Where it's not comfortable. Where there are hardships to face.

Paul was on his way to Jerusalem. And prophets came from Jerusalem to him to warn him that he was going to be arrested and that he was going to face terrible hardship. And they were hoping he wouldn't go, because they didn't want to see him go through that. But Paul was not the least bit hesitant to continue on to Jerusalem, because he was willing not only to face imprisonment, but even death, if there was a chance to reach a few more people. And in every situation that Paul found himself in, no matter how incredibly difficult it was, he preached the gospel.

When he was on trial, being accused by the Jews of being all kinds of terrible things, rather than really making a defense for himself, he used the opportunity to preach the Gospel to the rulers. He preached before kings, he preached before governors. And he didn't pull any punches. It didn't matter who he was preaching to. He spoke to the king just the same as he would have to a prostitute, or to a tax collector, or to the governor. No respecter of persons. It didn't matter to whom he was speaking: His message was the same.

He preached the good news. He preached the good news every place and it didn't matter what hardship. Even when he'd been shipwrecked on the island of Malta, he preached there too. He brought Christianity to that little island. He was a prisoner, but it didn't matter. It didn't matter! He considered himself not a prisoner of men, but a prisoner of the Lord. And in a sense, so are we.

He said, "Woe unto me if I preach not the gospel!" He said, "A generation of the Gospel is committed to me."

And now a generation of the Gospel is committed unto us. How will we answer for ourselves if we try to keep it within the walls of the church, and we don't go out to where the people really need to hear it?

You know, if I tell you good news, and then I tell you the good news again and again and again, eventually that good news is going to lose some of its emphasis, because you heard it before. And eventually, the good news becomes boring news because you already know it. What's the point of me standing up here and preaching good news to people who've already heard it? My responsibility is to others who have not heard; those who still think the Gospel is bad news; those have been burned by the churches, who have been told there's no place for them; and those who have never found their way into the churches. They need to know.

They need to know the good news: The news of unconditional love. The news of salvation. The news of Hope in a world that doesn't know any. Only then will the church bring forth children. Only then will we reap a harvest, when we're willing to go out and do the work.

Back in the 70s, Gospel singer Lanny Wolfe wrote a song, and I know I preached this here before, that was based on a prophecy that was given in a church service where he was in attendance. And they had been having a wonderful service. People were being blessed, and the Spirit of God was moving, and people were shouting, and singing, and probably dancing and running in the aisles. And then the Lord spoke and said, "My house is full, but My field is empty. All My children want to sit around the table, but nobody wants to work in My field."

But this is the responsibility of the church! I heard a message taught one time that I had to disagree with, and it was taught by a friend of mine who's a minister, who said that the main purpose of the church is worship. And I thought, no, the lifeblood of the church, our very reason for existence, is evangelism: The good new,s to reach out to others. Not to keep ourselves locked in here so we can worship all the time and enjoy the blessings, but to go out there, sometimes all alone, and to preach the gospel.

We have wonderful examples. The first century church: Persecution came to Jerusalem, and the Jerusalem church was dispersed and scattered. If that had happened in one of our cities today, the church would cease to exist. But the Jerusalem church wasn't like that. These people who were scattered and dispersed, who lost everything, lost their homes, lost their Church and the ones they loved, every one of them went out and preached the Gospel every place they went! So the persecution of the church backfired. Instead of destroying the church, it spread everywhere like wildfire. And so it should be today, that even when there isn't persecution, or there's only a little bit of persecution, that we go out with it, and take it every place we go. Every opportunity, when a door opens, tell the news. If somebody asks a question, give them the answer. If they don't ask, drop enough hints until they do. Find an opening. And if there's a door open, go through it. Whether it's preaching to pagans and witches, whether it's preaching to someone on the street, whether it's sharing the news with the family, or with a friend, or with someone who's been told that God doesn't love them. It's our responsibility. It's our responsibility.

For too long now, the church has been pregnant. You know what happens if a woman stays pregnant too long? After about nine, nine and a half months, the placenta starts to break down and can't nourish the baby anymore. You going to wind up with problems. If we don't deliver the children, we'll lose the children. We've got to deliver them, and we can't do it in the church. We can't do it here. It's got to be done out there. We've got to go out, even into Babylon, even into the places of sin, and preach the good news, every place we go.

And the promise is that there, out there, where we think we don't belong, is where we'll be delivered, and there the Lord will redeem us from the hand of our enemies. That's where our salvation is, not hiding in here. This is just a filling station. A car is of no use if you park it at the gas station and keep it running there next to the pump and just fill it up when it gets low. it won't take you anywhere and the church is the same way. This is our filling station.

We can get full here, but if you just stay here, you're not going anywhere. You're not reaching any destination. You've got a responsibility to go.

The very first word of the Great Commission Jesus gave to his disciples was GO. Go and teach All Nations. Go. It implies motion. It implies action, it implies responsibility.

And just as it was in Micah, Go forth out of the city, dwell in the field, live out there in the mission field, out where there's work to be done, out where there's a harvest to be reaped. The whole Northeast part of the country, we have one red pin up there [on the map], we've got one church in the whole Northeastern District. We've got work to do. We've got a harvest to reach. We've got children to bring forth. We can no longer let it be a day of trouble. We can no longer let it be a day of rebuke and of blasphemy. We've got children that are come to the birth, and we must have the strength to bring them forth. We must go out and deliver. We must!

In our district, in our state, in our city, and in the whole country and in the whole world. Yes, we've only got one church up in the northeastern District. But there are districts where we have no churches. There are districts with nothing!

There's work to be done. There's a district here that has church property and no pastor. No congregation, just a building sitting empty. That should never be. It shouldn't be.

If we were out there bringing forth the children, there would be people, and out of those people, God would choose laborers, workers, men and women with a call, and tell them go here and preach, go there and preach, just the way it was in the first century church, the Apostolic church. If we're going to follow the pattern of being Apostolic, we have to be open to the voice of the Spirit of God when He says go here and preach, go there and teach, go here and meet this person, go there and meet that person. It's got to be that way!

When Philip found himself at the place just where the Ethiopian eunuch was, he preached to him. And then Philip was found later on at Azotus, because he was needed there. He was open enough to the Spirit of God that God was actually able to move him one from one place to another. He didn't even need to travel there! He was just *found* there! And so it needs to be in this century, that when we're needed some place, we're able to go.

For too long, God's been getting a busy signal. He's been calling the church and calling the church with the message: Go here, go there, go teach, go preach, and He's getting a busy signal, because we're too busy! We're too busy with our own agenda. We just don't have time to preach the Gospel, and if we don't have time to preach the Gospel, we don't have time to be the church!

And if we don't do it, He'll give it to somebody else. It's always been the pattern in history when the church got tired of doing things God's way and began to do with their own way, they ceased to be the church, and He gave it to somebody else. Somebody else had to carry the ball. Someone else would get more truth. Someone else would get the burden, and we'd lose it.

We've carried children for a long time. It's been 14 years this week that we've been working in this country. We don't have enough to show for it. I'm thrilled to death about the things that are happening. I'm excited especially at the growth in the Southeastern District, in the South Central District. I'm excited, but it's not enough, I'm not satisfied. I'm not satisfied till we have fulfilled the Great Commission, until we have preached the gospel to every nation, until we have evangelized the whole world, until every person on the face of the earth has been told.

Not only the *name* of Jesus. Some churches think the whole world has been evangelized, because everybody in the world has heard the name of Jesus. Well, that's fine. How many of those people know He loves them unconditionally? How many people know the sacrifice He made? How many people know that they're welcome in His kingdom? And until they know that, our job is not done... until we have re-enfranchised the disenfranchised. Our work isn't done until we have gathered in those that were driven away. Our work is not done!

Ezekiel talked about the pastors who had fed themselves instead of the sheep and had driven the flock away. There's too much of that going on in the churches, where the sheep are actually being driven out. And we've got to go gather them in. Somebody's got to bring them back to the fold. Someone has to go out and look for the one that was lost. Somebody's got to do the job, and if we don't do it, someone else will. But we'll lose our place as the church. Because that's our responsibility. That is the church's job. That is the mainstream. That is the lifeblood of the church. Not just worship, but evangelism: Good news, bringing the good news.

And it **is** good news, and it needs to be told like it's good news. It needs to be preached like it's good news.

That same play I mentioned before had Sister Hatemore, and she had the news, but to her it was bad news, and she preached it in hate. She didn't know anything about love; she only knew judgment. And so she preached the truth in hate. But the scripture tells us to preach the truth in love: Agape love, which is an unconditional love, a *no matter what* love.

That's our responsibility, because that's the way God loves us. And it's the way we must love others, no matter who they are. Even those who have set themselves up as our enemies. Those who, in the name of Christianity, have chosen to hate us. We gotta love them. We've **GOT** to love them.

It's tough: Pat Robertson makes it awfully difficult to love him. He really does. Jerry Falwell makes it difficult to love him. But if I don't love them, then I failed in my job as a Christian, and then I'm no better. If I'm going to be a Christian, I've got to love them unconditionally. The same love for the president, for the tax collector, the IRS, the prostitute, the drug addict, the saint in another church. The same unconditional love, the same *no matter what* love, because it's the love that God has for us.

The church is in labor. We've been in labor too long. It's time to deliver.

Lieutenants in God's Army

I'm turning to Isaiah chapter 35, beginning at verse 4:

Say to them that are of a fearful heart, Be strong, fear not: behold, your God will come with vengeance, even God with a recompense; he will come and save you. Then the eyes of the blind shall be opened, and the ears of the deaf shall be unstopped. Then shall the lame man leap as an hart, and the tongue of the dumb sing: for in the wilderness shall waters break out, and streams in the desert.

Turning now to Acts chapter 3, and I'm beginning at the beginning of the chapter now:

Now Peter and John went up together into the temple at the hour of prayer, being the ninth hour. And a certain man, lame from his mother's womb, was carried, whom they laid daily at the gate of the temple which is called Beautiful, to ask alms of them that entered into the temple; who seeing Peter and John about to go into the temple asked an alms. And Peter, fastening his eyes upon him with John, said, Look on us. And he gave heed unto them, expecting to receive something of them. Then Peter said, Silver and gold have I none; but such as I have give I thee: In the name of Jesus Christ of Nazareth rise up and walk. And he took him by the right hand, and lifted him up: and immediately his feet and ankle bones received strength. And he leaping up stood, and walked, and entered with them into the temple, walking, and leaping, and praising God. And all the people saw him walking and praising God.

And finally, Acts chapter 14, beginning at verse 8:

And there sat a certain man at Lystra, impotent in his feet, being a cripple from his mother's womb, who never had walked: The same heard Paul speak: who steadfastly beholding him, and perceiving that he had faith to be healed, Said with a loud voice, Stand upright on thy feet. And he leaped and walked.

Hallelujah!

When I was a very little boy, I saw a movie on TV. I was very young and I remember very little of the movie. I don't know the name of it, I don't know anyone who was in it, and since I was that young, I'm not even sure I understood the whole plot of what was going on. But I remember in this movie there was a man who was a lieutenant. I don't know a lieutenant in what: I have no idea what branch of what service he was in, but I remember he was a lieutenant and the lieutenant had a machine.

I don't know how to describe it, except that it looked like a submarine, but it wasn't in water. It was just inside of a room. It was kind of a chamber, that was shaped like a submarine. And the lieutenant took children who were crippled, unable to walk, and he brought them into this chamber. And in there, they were able to walk. I was so impressed by what he was able to do, and not just that he was able to do it, but that he wanted to do it. These children weren't related to him. They weren't anything to him. And yet he had made this for them so that they could walk. And I remember being so impressed that I sat down and I wrote a paper about how, when I grew up, I wanted to be a lieutenant so I could help crippled children walk. I was very young and didn't understand what lieutenant meant, but to me, lieutenant meant someone who was going to help the crippled children to walk again.

I had forgotten very much about that movie. Every few years, it pops back into my head again, and sometimes I associate it with my work at O.D. Heck.[1] I can't make any of my clients walk, but I do help them as best I can. But I think, well, in a sense I did grow up and do something similar.

This popped into my head again the other day and I was thinking again about the lieutenant and how he helped the crippled children to walk. And I tried again comparing it to my job at O.D. Heck and there's just wasn't a comparison anymore, because I just don't feel that same feeling of accomplishment that I used to.

And I began to think, what about my dream of being the lieutenant? How is that going to happen? Now, if it's not being fulfilled through my work, is there some way that I can still be that lieutenant to help the crippled children to walk? And that's when I remembered that one or two services ago, we had read those scriptures in Isaiah and it talked about the lame walking. Yeah! We *can* help the children to walk, the crippled children! And I remembered the man at Lystra, who had never walked, who had been lame from the time he was born. And I remembered the man at the Temple gate, how he jumped up, and he went into the temple with them, jumping and leaping and praising God. He must have look like quite a spectacle, I thought, yes, there is a way to make the crippled children walk,

What does it take to be able to do it? Being a lieutenant in God's Army.

I began to look at the word lieutenant. We sometimes just, you know, name off the different ranks in the service, and we don't stop to think that some of them have meanings. Lieutenant comes from French, and it means *taking the place*. Lieutenant is one who takes the place of another, takes the place of a higher-ranking officer. And that's exactly what we've been called to do: We've been called to take the place of the Higher Officer: Our General, who is Jesus, who is not here on the battlefield with us right now physically. So therefore, we take His place. And what do we do as we take his place? Exactly what he would have done! Isaiah told us that when the Messiah came, the lame were going to walk, and the blind were going to see, and the ears of the deaf would be unstopped, the tongue of the dumb would sing. All these things would happen when the Messiah came.

Well, if we are His lieutenants, His place takers, then it's our responsibility to carry on that work. Yes, I *can* make the crippled children walk again, and no, I don't have to build a chamber that looks like a submarine. I don't need that. I've got the authority to tell the crippled children to stand up and walk!

That man that Paul healed at Lystra didn't ask for anything. He didn't ask, "Would you heal me? Would you let me walk again? I've never walked. I'd like to be able to walk." Paul looked at him and saw that the man had faith to be healed, and without even asking permission, told him to stand up, and he did.

Peter and John at the temple didn't ask that man, "Do you want to be healed?" They didn't ask the High Priest's permission. They didn't check with the man's doctor to see what his prognosis was. They didn't ask anybody.

The man had asked them only for money. They didn't happen to have any. They happen to be flat broke. "I don't have any silver or gold," Peter told him, "but I'll give you what I do have." I can give you something else!

The Jewish people have what's called the Ladder of Tzedakah. Tzedakah means *righteousness*. But it's also a word that's used to mean *charity*. And there are different levels of charity, the lowest being where you've given something to somebody, and everybody knows about it. But one of the highest things you can do, rather than giving somebody something, giving them charity, is enabling them to provide for themselves, so that they won't have to take charity anymore. In other words, which is it better to do: Give a man a fish, or teach him how to fish? It makes a difference!

No, Peter and John didn't give the man at the temple a dime, but they gave him the ability to stand up on his own feet so he could go out and earn a living, something he'd never been able to do because he couldn't walk. But they didn't ask anybody's permission. They were the lieutenant's of Jesus Christ, taking His place, and that's what Jesus would have done. Any time He saw someone in need, He met that need.

There was a woman who had been ill, had an infirmity for many, many years, and she came and even though it was the Sabbath, Jesus healed her. It didn't matter to Him that it was the wrong day to do healing. He did the healing; she needed Him. Even the Syro-Phoenician woman, who had no legitimate claim to His abilities, to His power: Eventually, she got what she wanted because of her faith and persistence. She had tremendous faith, and she had the persistence, and Jesus met her needs.

His place-takers, His lieutenants, have to do the same thing. We have a responsibility. It's not just "nice" that we can help the crippled children to walk. We have a responsibility to help the crippled children walk! We're supposed to be the place-takers of the Messiah, and when Messiah comes, Isaiah promised us, the lame would walk, the blind will see, the deaf would hear, the tongue of the dumb would speak or sing. He promised those things would happen.

Well, yes, the Messiah was here and gone. That was nice. That was 2,000 years ago. We're His place-takers. Messiah is still walking this earth in the body of every Christian: Every person filled with the Holy Ghost is just one more little Messiah walking around. They call us Christians, which means *like Christ.* Christ means Messiah, anointed one, we are messiahs. We are little messiah's walking around through this Earth, taking the place of our general, who's gone to prepare a place for us.

That means we have to do what He would do. We can't live any other way, but to live the way He would have lived. We can't treat people in any other way other than the way than He would have treated them, and when we come across those who are sick, those who are crippled, those who have some form of deformity or illness, we have a responsibility to them to set them free from it. That's our job as the lieutenants.

You know, Jesus said these signs would follow them that believe. He talked about some of the miracles that would happen, and He told us the miracles that He did, we would do, too. Well, that wasn't just because it would be nice if we could, or because we want to get excited and jump up and down. It's because He did them. So we're supposed to, too. He wasn't giving us a marvelous little gift; He was giving us work to do. *This is what you do, while I'm gone!* The same things He did while He was here: Preach the good news, set the captives free, tell the blind man to see, tell the deaf man to hear, tell the lame man to get up. Set the crippled children free! The Lieutenant's in God's Army!

I always was rather fascinated by the Salvation Army. Doctrinally, they may not have much on the ball, but they know how to take care of people, and I always admired their military structure. It was nice to see a military structure that wasn't devised solely for the purpose of killing people. That's rather unique. There aren't too many armies that are that way, but this is such an army. Yes, it is a Salvation Army.

Now, they have all different ranks in the Salvation Army. We really just have two. We're all lieutenants. We're all taking the place of the one General. That's all this army needs: two ranks, the General and His lieutenants to take His place. That's all He needs. But if we're going to be His lieutenants than we have got to take that place; we've got to fill that place. We have to fulfill that role of being messiahs in this earth.

There's a song that I dearly love that is called *Lucifer's Illusion*. It talks about how Satan deluded himself into thinking "Now, Jesus is dead. Everything's going to be just fine!" And three days later, Jesus rose from the dead. But then, after that, when Jesus ascended into heaven, things got worse for Satan. Because now, instead of one Jesus, there were hundreds in His place!

You know, Jesus told us that repentance and remission of sins would be preached in His name. In the Old Testament, Second Chronicles, it says, "My people which are called by My name..." A better translation would be "upon whom My name is called." That's the name that was called on us when we were baptized: Jesus. That's *our* name! Now, the whole family in Heaven and Earth is named Jesus. That's the name where there's power. We are not just lieutenants in title, we are lieutenants in name. That's the name we do everything in. Whatsoever you do in word or deed, you do in the name of Jesus. We go against the enemy in the name of Jesus. But we also go to those who are in bondage in their own bodies, crippled, in the name of Jesus. That's the name we use. It's the name we come in. We are actually taking His place by using His name.

We've got to live up to that name. We've got to live up to being Lieutenant Jesus under the command of General Jesus. Yes, I'm Lieutenant Jesus. Yes, you are Lieutenant Jesus. We are little messiahs in this earth and doing the same things that our General did when He walked the earth. And if we're not doing the same things, I don't know whose army we belong to, and we better get our act together and find out what our orders are.

We **do** have orders. Yes, we have the order to come against the enemy, to come against the gates of hell, and He promised that [the gates of hell] weren't going to win; we were! But we also have other responsibilities. One is to set the captives free. He said, "The Spirit of the Lord is upon me because He has anointed me." And he talked about some of the things that He'd been sent to do: to set the captives free, to preach the good news, to proclaim the acceptable year of the Lord. Well, all those things are now **our** responsibility: To set the captives free, to preach salvation, to preach the opening of the eyes of the blind, and the unstopping of the ears of the deaf. That's now our job to do that, because it's been passed on to us. The first time in history that it happened was when Jesus stood up in Nazareth and said, "Today the scripture is fulfilled in your ears!" But it didn't end there; it just began there. It's still going on, and that scripture will continue to be fulfilled through us, if we will take our positions as lieutenants in God's army.

Till the day that trumpet sounds and he calls us calls us Home, tells us that the battle is over, and we've won, and we can go home now... Until then we're lieutenants. Until then, we're on the front lines of the battle. And every time we find somebody that the devil's kept in bondage, somebody that the devil's had in captivity, we set them free. We've got to set them free! It's the church's responsibility!

Too many churches are killing them when they find them. They find people in bondage, and instead of setting them free, they kill them! What good are they doing? They're just causing more harm. Micah himself talked about the Lord, talking to the church and saying, "My people have risen up as an enemy..." But that wasn't what they were supposed to do. They weren't supposed to be the enemy; they were supposed to be the deliverers: To deliver those who are in bondage, to set them free. That's something the devil never has done with his captives. One of the scriptures that talks about Satan says it: "[he] opens not the house of his prisoners." He never lets them out of prison! Someone else has got to go do it.

One of the scriptures I think I read on Sunday talked about how Jesus went and preached to those who were in prison in captivity after He died. He was talking to those who died in captivity. He'd gone to set them free, too. But He set **us** free. And now we're the ones setting free. Now, we're the ones bringing redemption. Now, we're the ones bringing salvation. We're the ones bringing healing. We're the ones bringing wholeness. We're the ones helping the crippled children, setting them free.

I always wondered why I was so impressed by what the lieutenant [in the movie] did with the crippled children. Maybe I saw beyond the physical crippling, the fact that these children couldn't walk. And maybe I saw some of my own spiritual condition, some of my own emotional condition. There is hardly a person in this world who isn't severely in bondage, and severely crippled. Even if they can walk, they're crippled emotionally, or they're crippled mentally because of the things that they've gone through. The battle scars of this life, they've crippled us. They've crippled us!

But we're lieutenants of a General, and that General can heal the cripples. Not just the crippled in body, but crippled in spirit and crippled in mind, crippled in heart: All the things that we were, when we came to Him. He can set us free, and the others, too.

We've got a message of Good News. We have some hope to bring out there into the darkness. We can let the light shine from the lighthouse, because we **do** have something to tell them. We **do** have a new message. We **do** have something they haven't heard before.

It's sad that so many people won't go to church because the message they'd hear is one they've heard before, and it isn't a good one. I was reading Ann Landers' column today: A man was upset because his daughter was marrying out of the faith, but he acknowledged he hadn't been to church in 10 years! What's his problem? Why hasn't he been to church in 10 years? Maybe it's because he didn't like what he was hearing there. Maybe it's because the church wasn't preaching him any Good News; it was preaching bad news: That they don't have any deliverance, that they don't have any hope, that they don't have any freedom for the people.

My Bible says, "If the son therefore shall make you free, you shall be free indeed." And "where the Spirit of the Lord is, there is liberty." We're talking about freedom: No more chains! No more braces on our legs! No more dark glasses to cover blind eyes! No more hearing aids!

We're talking about setting people free. We're talking about real freedom, brought to this earth by the lieutenant's in God's Army. It's our job. It's our calling. Those are the orders we've been given.

We're going to be good soldiers, and we have to obey orders. Good soldiers don't question orders. They don't disobey orders. They obey orders. They don't disobey, they obey. The only response to an order should be *Yes, Sir*. I want to be a good lieutenant. I want to live up to the name of lieutenant, taking the place. I want these hands to be the hands of Jesus on earth. I want these feet to be the feet of Jesus. I want this mouth to be the mouth of Jesus, to do and say and the things He would do and say, to go to the places He would go, to be a real lieutenant, taking the place of the General.

[I need to be] a legitimate lieutenant, so that when I use the General's name, I have the authority to do it. I don't ever want to hear a devil say to me "Well, I know who your General is, but who are you?" I want to be a legitimate lieutenant. I want to be a lieutenant in God's Army, using the name of my General to set the crippled children free.

It wasn't just a movie, or a dream. In a sense, it was a prophecy of where we were going to be someday, setting the crippled children free. I want to see lieutenants all over the world, bringing the word of the General, and setting the captives free. That's the kind of battle, that's the kind of warfare I want to be involved in. That's the kind of army I want to belong to. I know my General, and I want to follow him.

Thank the Lord!

Lord Jesus, help us to be faithful lieutenants in Your army. Help us to serve You faithfully, to do the things that You would do, to take Your place here on this earth. Wherever we go, whatever we do, and whatever we say, to follow Your example: To take away the chains from those who are bound, and to let the crippled children walk, to set them free. Doing it all in the name of our General, the name that sets everyone free, the name of Jesus. Amen!

[1] O.D. Heck Developmental Center was a NYS facility that housed developmentally disabled and autistic individuals.

Monsters Under the Bed

We're turning to three different sections of scripture, possibly four. I haven't decided if I'm going to use the fourth or not. I guess we'll have to wait and see what God says. The first one is the Book of Micah, chapter 2, verse 8:

Even of late, my people is risen up as an enemy: ye pull off the robe with the garment from them that pass by securely as men averse from war.

Over to the book of Ephesians, chapter 6 and verse 12:

For we wrestle not against flesh and blood, but against principalities, against powers, against the rulers of the darkness of this world, against spiritual wickedness in high places.

Finally, turn to 2 Corinthians, chapter 10, beginning at verse 3:

For though we walk in the flesh, we do not war after the flesh: (For the weapons of our warfare are not carnal, but mighty through God to the pulling down of strong holds;)

Hallelujah! We are right now between Halloween and election day. And I'm not so sure anymore that it's just a coincidence that those two days are so close together. We expect that once October 31st is past, that we won't see any more monsters.

I looked out my front window on Halloween evening. And the street was just crowded with Frankensteins and ghosts and witches and Mighty Morphin Power Rangers, and even probably a few Ninja Turtles, and I thought, *Oh Lord, here we go again!*

Norma downstairs and I have a Halloween custom that we do every year: We turn off all the lights, including the porch light. We disconnect the doorbells and we pretend we're not home. My theory is if there's any chocolate candy in this house, it's for me! But I saw all the kids, all the monsters on the streets. And of course, all the TV sitcoms had their Halloween episodes where people were dressed up as monsters. But once Halloween is over, we pretty much expect that that's the end of it; no more monsters.

And yet I find that, especially as election day draws closer, there seem to be more and more monsters hiding under the bed. I read that on a particular Sunday, the Christian Coalition was going to be sending booklets to all the churches. Thankfully, we did not receive one here. These booklets contained the survey results of all the different candidates who responded to them. And I thought about some of the questions that they were asking the candidates. I thought about the concept of enemies.

You know, it seems that Christianity doesn't function well without enemies. When things go too smoothly, the church becomes complacent and starts taking God for granted, and the church doesn't grow. But persecution has always allowed the church to grow. Satan learned that in the first century when the Jerusalem Church was dispersed and the saints of the church were just scattered in every direction. Satan thought, *Well, that's the end of that!*

You know, he might've gotten rid of the Jerusalem Church, but he didn't realize that it was kind of like shooting water at the base of certain types fires: Rather than putting them out, it spreads them. And that's what happened with the Jerusalem Church: As the people were scattered around the known world, they took the Gospel with them. and the church spread. The persecution actually help the church to grow!

The first century church, for the most part, understood who their enemies were, and who their enemies were not. And lest at any time they should forget, Paul reminded them of who their enemies were and who their enemies were not. He told the Ephesians that they were not wrestling, or fighting, with flesh and blood, but against spiritual powers, the rulers of the darkness of this world.

Now, some people want to take that to mean the government, the rulers of the darkness of this world, like President Clinton or this one or that one. But Paul just finished saying we're **not** wrestling against flesh and blood. The last time we checked, and I'm sure that the Secret Service will back me up on this, President Clinton is flesh and blood. Hillary Clinton is flesh and blood. The whole cabinet is flesh and blood. The Congress and the Senate, they're all flesh and blood. We aren't supposed to wrestle against them.

So then, the rulers of the darkness of this world are not flesh and blood. He told the Corinthians, we are walking in the flesh, but we don't fight after the flesh. The weapons that we're fighting with are not physical. They are not carnal, but they are mighty and they pull down strongholds. They understood that their enemy was not the Roman government, the Roman Empire. Their enemy was not Caesar. It took them a while to catch on to that, because while Jesus was still on earth, the apostles still considered the enemy to be Caesar. They still thought that Jesus was going to restore Israel as a world power and overthrow Rome.

It was after the Holy Ghost came that they understood that the kingdom of God had nothing to do with the kingdoms of this world, that there was no connection and there was no conflict.

During the time of Jesus' ministry, people kept trying to create, the Pharisees especially, kept trying to create a conflict between the message of Jesus and the Roman government. They kept trying to find some way to show a discrepancy between the two, some conflict where they couldn't coexist.

Tell us, Jesus, is it lawful for us to pay taxes to Caesar?

His answer was good and it would work today, to. Show me a one dollar bill... Whose picture is that? Washington? Then give it to Washington. Whose image are you created in? God's? Give yourself to God.

There's still no conflict between the kingdom of God and the government, regardless of what the Christian Coalition says, regardless of what the religious right thinks. There is no conflict between human government and the kingdom of God. It's comparing apples to oranges, because the kingdom of God is not flesh and blood. It's not those things. It's things that you can't hold in your hand. It's things you can't measure.

But the church needs enemies. Somewhere after the first century, the church lost sight of who their enemies were. They lost sight of the spiritual powers, and they began to focus on the physical powers. They lost sight of the devil and his angels. They lost sight of the fact that those things are behind the things that go on in the world.

And they began to set their sights on the things of earth. And any power that they couldn't overcome physically, they merged with! If you can't beat 'em, join 'em! You can't overthrow the Roman Empire, then join with it.

And sure enough, in the early fourth century Christianity became the official religion of the Roman Empire, neatly combined with the Babylonian religion. And all the while from then on, Christianity looked for enemies.

We have the horror stories of the Spanish Inquisition, where countless numbers of Jews and Muslims, or people of any other religion you can think of, were tortured until they would either convert or die. And then, finally, it attacked the Protestants. After the Protestant Reformation, the Inquisition turned against them. Many were burned at the stake. Some were thrown overboard from ships with rocks tied to them. Killed in many different ways, because the church felt it needed enemies. It had to be fighting against somebody in order to be strong, and so it fought against the people.

As Micah said, *My people, the church, risen up as an enemy...* An enemy of everybody, an enemy of everything. But not fighting against the principalities. Not fighting against the powers. Not fighting against the rulers of the darkness. Instead, fighting against the people. Fighting the wrong battle. Fighting the wrong war.

The Christian church today has monsters hiding under the bed. There's a paranoia that throughout [the 20th] century has raced through Christianity. And yet, as we read the history books, we can see it's been there for centuries. It just changes its focus every few years.

During the time of the Protestant Reformation, The Catholic Church's monsters under the bed where Protestants. The Protestant churches' monsters under the bed where Catholics and Jews. In Spain and Portugal, the monsters under the bed were Muslims. There's always a monster under the bed.

In the twentieth century, up until the late 1980s, there were Communists under the bed. Monsters! And don't look now, but there are homosexuals under the bed! Don't look now, but they're running an abortion clinic under the bed! There's pornography under the bed!

Some of these things may be good. Some of these things are bad. But the point is, the church has missed the point. The point is, there are no monsters under the bed! Those aren't the enemies; those are people.

Whether we like what they're doing or not, they're people, and according to Ephesians 6:12, they can't be the enemy, because we don't wrestle against flesh and blood. We're not wrestling against Bill Clinton. We're not wrestling against Cuomo or Pataki. We're not wrestling against them, and yet, every one of them is a monster under someone's bed, and nobody's got more monsters under the bed than the *religious right.* Nobody has more monsters than the Christian Coalition. I wonder how Pat Robertson sleeps at night. He's got so many monsters under the bed, so many people tormenting him! He projects so much paranoia, thinking that somehow he's got to protect the kingdom of God from all these people.

Well, my Bible said that the gates of hell would not prevail against the church. If the gates of hell cannot prevail against it, how does he think people are going to? If the devil doesn't have the power to overthrow the church, why are they worried about what people can do?

But what really scares me about all these Christians with monsters under their beds, what really scares me, is that, although they claim to be Christian and to believe the word of God firmly, they are spending all their time, all their effort, and all their money, to make sure that the things the Bible predicts do not come to pass! They're trying desperately to create a dictatorship in this country where their ideas of morality, their ideas of right and wrong, are the law of the land, and that nothing else is allowed to exist.

What they're trying to create is called Utopia or Heaven. Now, that would be all well and good if the scripture told us to do that, but it didn't. That would be all well and good, if the scripture said that the church could do that. But it didn't.

In spite of the best efforts of the church, my Bible tells me the world is going to get worse and worse, but rather than trying to reform the world, rather than trying to patch up a sinking ship, we're supposed to be launching the lifeboat and getting as many people into it as we can. We cannot stop the ship from sinking. The word of God is forever settled in heaven. It's not going to change. No matter what the Christian Coalition does, this ship is going to sink. It's going to founder. Call it *unsinkable* if you want; it's going down.

They've got monsters under the bed. They got to get them out of there. But it's sad, because every time they manage to eliminate a monster, another one pops up.

You know what, little kids are afraid at night because there's a monster in the closet, or there's a monster under the bed. You know what makes that monster go away? You turn on the light. You turn on the light, and the children can see there's no monster, and they're not afraid anymore. They can go to sleep. Maybe if the Christian Coalition had a light in their life they wouldn't be afraid anymore. Maybe if the Light of the World was the light of the church, they wouldn't be afraid. Maybe they could see there are no monsters under their bed, only people.

The real monsters are above us, the devil and his angels, who have free rein to do anything they want in this country because the very people who are supposed to be fighting them are fighting each other.

You talk about getting a wrong message! The church has got a wrong message. They totally ignored the commandments from our Commander, the orders that He gave before He left. They've ignored those completely. They've rewritten their orders, and they're doing any old thing they please.

Politics: A nasty, dirty game that the church shouldn't have anything to do with anyway. I read about the interactions of the first century church with the Roman government. I can't find any place where the Christians in Rome tried to get into the Senate. I can't find any of them running for any kind of political office.

There were Christians who lived in Caesars household, but I can't see where they made any effort to overthrow Caesar. In fact, I can't see where they really involve themselves with the government at all. They acknowledged its authority in civil matters. And when convenient, they used it. When Paul was about to be beaten, he pointed out the fact that he was a Roman citizen, and they had no legal right to do that. It doesn't hurt to point out your rights now and then. But that was about as far as their interaction with the government went. When Paul was arrested and brought before governors, before kings, and eventually, before Caesar, he didn't stand there arguing over the evil of the government.

Now, you know, we have people in this country who think our government is so evil. But it's nothing compared to ancient Rome. That was an evil government. It was no question about it that the people in the government were evil, because they were idol worshipers to begin with. They were worshiping many different gods and goddesses.

They had very little sense of morality for the most part. If it moved, they slept with it. They would eat... Talk about gluttony: They would eat till they couldn't hold anymore, then they'd go throw up and come back and eat some more.

It was an evil government. There was no question about it, and yet I can't find the apostles involving themselves with it, or preaching against it, or worrying about it, or ever acknowledging it, other than acknowledging, yes, it's there. It's the government. We pay our taxes. We obey them in civil matters although the word of God has final authority. If necessary, we invoke our rights, if we need to. And other than that, we ignore it.

Why can't the Christians today do what the Christians in the first century did? Why can't we learn to ignore the government, to just realize that it's a temporary thing, that the only government that we're forever bound to is the kingdom of God. That's where our Allegiance is.

There's no monster hiding under the bed. There's no requirement for the church to infiltrate the government. But they're pushing candidates for all these different positions from school board all the way up to president. The Christian Coalition has someone they want in every spot. God help the people of this country if they ever get their way, because they'll make Nazi Germany look like a picnic in the park.

They don't know how to read the history books any better than they know how to read their Bible. Because if they did, they would see that every time the church gained political control, innocent people died by the thousands or the hundreds of thousands, and sometimes by the millions. The church has no business seeking political control. It was never meant to be a political entity. It was never meant to have political power. It only ever does harm when it has political power.

But they've been blinded by their enemy. Their **real** enemy, not the monsters under the bed. They have been blinded by the devil who has sent them a spirit of judgment and a spirit of blindness so that they can't see. The spirit of Laodicea is alive and well in Christianity today.

Halloween may be over, but the monsters are running rampant through the streets. The monsters are running rampant through the government. There are no monsters under the beds. The Christian Coalition have become the monsters. They have risen up as the enemy, made themselves the enemies of the people, the enemies of the word of God, by trying to change what it says is going to happen.

The enemies of the people. It's sad when they make themselves the enemy. It's sad when they set themselves up as the opponent. In the long run, we get hurt because we can't fight them back, because we can't ignore the scripture. And it tells us not to wrestle against flesh and blood. It tells us that the weapons we fight with aren't physical weapons. We cannot fight the Christian Coalition. We cannot fight the religious right, at least not the way they're fighting. But there is one weapon we're allowed to use and that's unconditional love.

They don't know how to fight unconditional love because they've never felt it. They've never seen it. They've never experienced it. They don't know what it is. It'll be as much of a mystery to them as the atomic bomb was to Japan, and will take them as much by surprise. They know how to fight against hatred. They know how to fight against words and rhetoric. They know how to fight against everything except unconditional love. They don't know what to do with it. There are only two possible responses to unconditional love:

One is to try to stop it, either by running from it, or killing the source of it. You got to make it stop one way or another... or else surrender to it. And the surrender to unconditional love is an unconditional surrender.

It is possible to win them. It is possible to conquer them with love. It's not easy, because they've been blinded, but I speak as one who was once blinded by that very same spirit. It is possible to be set free from it. It is possible to have the scales taken away from one's eyes, to have the log removed from one's eye, to be able to see again. It is possible.

All it took was somebody loving me unconditionally. All it took were the words *I love you just the way You are.* And the scales began to fall away.

All they need is someone to love them. And then maybe they'll learn to love themselves and someone else.

What do you do when the monster under your bed loves you? They think we're monsters under the bed, but we're going to love them. We're going to love them when they hate us. We're going to love them when they hurt us. We're going to love them when they legislate against us. When they rant and rave and tell lies about us, we're going to love them anyway. They get on TV and say the most atrocious things... And we're going to love them.

Being Christian demands no less of us. All people are sinners. And yet, God loves us unconditionally. If He can love me, I can manage to love anybody. Thank the Lord!

Multitudes in the Valley of Decision

I'm turning to Joel, chapter 3. Joel is one of the shorter books in the Bible, but for such a short book, he had an incredible amount of things to say. There are only three chapters in the book of Joel, and yet, he foresaw the outpouring of the Holy Ghost, he foresaw the church, and the falling away of the church and the restoration of the church. He saw many exciting things!

I enjoy reading the Book of Joel because of the the alarm that he spread in the church. He would say things like *"Blow the trumpet in Zion and sound an alarm in My holy mountain!"* Things that are exciting, that are meant to get the attention of the people. Joel chapter 3 and verse 14:

Multitudes, multitudes in the valley of decision; for the day of the LORD is near in the valley of decision.

This has been a verse that I've been fascinated with, oh, for many years. Since I was back in Bible school, this verse has fascinated me. There's something about the concept of the valley of decision. In the past, I've preached about other valleys. Now too many weeks ago, I preached on the valley of the shadow of death, and the fascinating concept of the shadow of death and how it's it's such a unique concept. Hebrew actually has a single word that means the shadow of death, and I was just impressed by that. But this is a different valley. This isn't the valley of the shadow of death, but it's the valley of decision. And there are multitudes.

Multitudes! Now, that's a lot! I try to avoid giving Hebrew lessons when I preach or teach, but I sometimes wind up doing just that. One of the ways in Hebrew that you can emphasize something, rather than using a lot of adjectives or putting numbers in front of it, you can put the word twice, and this is what Joel has done here. The word *multitudes*, which already means a lot of people: He put it twice, which in Hebrew intensifies. He has multitudes multitudes.

An incredible number of people, probably without number, unable to count, more people than we can possibly imagine. Multitudes, and all of them in the same place. All of them crowded into the valley of decision. Why? Because the day of the Lord is near in the valley of decision. I was reading some scripture about the day of the Lord, and some of the prophets, and people had a misconception about the day of the Lord in the Old Testament.

Well, they kept thinking of the day of the Lord as a day of glory and a day of light. The Jewish people, of course, had been waiting for thousands of years for their Messiah to come. But when they read the scriptures, they only saw the second coming of the Messiah. They didn't see His first coming, which was two thousand years ago. So, they were waiting for His glorious second coming, thinking it's His first, and they're expecting this wonderful day of light and deliverance and freedom. And this is what they were thinking of when they spoke of the day of the Lord.

But the prophets said no, and you should not be looking for the day of the Lord, because, they said, it's not a day of light, but a day of darkness. And it's not a day of joy, but it's a day of trouble. It's a day of sorrow, it's a day of everything being shaken, the world being shaken right to its foundations. The day of the Lord: It's a time of terror. It's a time of trouble. It's a time of fear. It's a time of decision.

The day of the Lord is near in the valley of decision. What does that mean, that it's near? Does it mean that chronologically it's closer? No, the time doesn't change. The times of everything are fixed in scripture. We don't always know what they are. Jesus told us, No man knows the hour of the day of the things are going to happen. We know only the times and the seasons, but the times are appointed ahead of time. We're just not given to know them. The day of the Lord doesn't grow any closer chronologically in the valley of decision, but it grows closer in another way. It grows closer because people suddenly realize it's coming. *It's coming! I've got to make a choice!*

People who've spent their entire life sitting on the fence, suddenly think

I've got to make a choice! I have to make a decision! I have to decide what I'm going to do, and I've got to decide soon, because the day of the Lord is coming. When you're in the valley of decision, the day of the Lord seems very near, very near. And it pushes us to make a decision to make a choice. Life is full of choices and decisions. Abraham Lincoln once said that most people are about as happy as they make up their minds to be. In other words, it was a choice. Some people choose to go through life with a negative aspect, complaining and whining; Everything is wrong, and nothing could possibly be any worse than it is. And poor me, poor me!

We did a wonderful church play years ago. It was the only play I was ever in where the director gave the cast permission to laugh all the way through, because it was so funny we couldn't help it. But it had a powerful message. It took place in a Pentecostal church. But these people were not living for God. There was one woman whose name was Sister Tell-it-all, whose idea of a testimony was to gossip about the other people in the church. But one of the worst was Sister Sicker-than-thou, whose idea of a testimony was to stand up and tell everything she had been through that day, and *nobody's ever been through what I've been through,* and *the devil's just chased me around all day!* But there are too many Sister Sicker-than-thous out there. Too many people who choose to have a negative attitude about everything, and everything is just terrible.

I saw a poster in the 70s that said, *If life gives you lemons, make lemonade.* Somewhere in the 80s, I decided lemonade wasn't good enough for me. If life gives me lemons, they're **MY** lemons: I'm making lemon chiffon pie! I can be as happy as I want to be. It's a choice for me. It's a choice. It's a decision, that I can choose to look at the positive instead of the negative. It's just one of many choices in my life. Sometimes we think we live in a world where we don't have any choices. The government makes too many choices for us, our parents make choices for us. Families make choices for us. All these choices! And we think, well, I really don't have any choices left to make. My life is planned out for me, and I don't have any choice of what to do. And yet, there are still dozens of decisions. We can make dozens of choices, dozens of choices. We can do anything we want to do. We can be anything we want to be. The only limitations are really the ones we set on ourselves. We have an incredible amount of potential, if we just believe that.

Unfortunately, we're brought up in a world that teaches us to think so little of ourselves that our motto, everybody's motto, and middle name is **I can't.** I can't! And so we don't. And so people don't get anywhere, and they don't do anything, and they never make the decisions they have to make. Someone once told me *Not to decide is to decide.* In a way that's true. If I refuse to make a decision, in a sense, the decision's been made for me. I want a hand in this! I want to choose some things. I want to choose, and if I'm in the valley of decision, I want to know the facts, and I want to make a choice and decide what I'm going to do.

When the Jewish people entered the promised land, Joshua called them all together. Joshua had been watching them. He was one of only two people who came out of Egypt who lived to reach the promised land. Everybody else died in the wilderness. Even Moses was only allowed to see it from far off, and couldn't enter into it because of his sin. But Joshua and Caleb were allowed to enter in. So Joshua had seen the Jewish people from the moment they left Egypt until the moment they entered the promised land. He'd watched them in everything they'd done. And everything they'd done wrong! He watched them worship the golden calf. He'd watched them murmur against Moses in the wilderness. He'd watched them complain at every opportunity. He thought, we can't go any further until some decisions are made. He couldn't take them all the way into the promised land, because they had to make some choices. They had to make some decisions. You would think, Well, their decisions made: They left Egypt. They wandered in the wilderness. Now they're here. They might as well go in. Joshua thought it wasn't that simple, because he wouldn't let them go in until he had cornered them. And he said to them, "Choose today whom you will serve. You can choose to serve the gods that your fathers served over on the other side of the Red Sea; you can go back and serve the gods of Egypt. They're still there, all those statues. Or, you can serve the Lord." You've got to make a decision! And Joshua said his own decision was made. He said, "...but as for me and my house, we're going to serve the Lord!"

That was his decision; he'd made the choice. The people of Israel didn't understand the seriousness of what he was doing to them. This was just, you know, multiple choice: Check the right answer and let's get in there and let's get this over with. And they said, *Oh, of course, we're going to serve the Lord!* But they hadn't even thought about their answer. They weren't making a decision. This was just something they'd been taught to say. This was repetition, like parrots.

And so Joshua said no. *No, you can't serve Him. He's a holy God, and He's not going to forgive you.* Does that mean that God's not forgiving? No, it means that they weren't going to repent. They thought they could continue with life as usual. They thought they could go on the way they'd always gone on, still worshiping whatever they wanted to. And if things got boring, build a golden calf! Break whatever commandments you choose! They thought they could do anything they wanted, and still say that they were followers of the Lord. They did not understand the seriousness of the decision.

So Joshua was pointing this out to them by saying that the Lord was a holy God and wouldn't forgive them. He was pointing out to them that the day of the Lord is near in the valley of decision. You can't put off this decision. You've got to decide *before* you go into the promised land. What are you going to do? What are you going to do? And he demanded a serious response from them. He would not let them go further until they came up with the answer he wanted to hear: either that they were going to go back and serve the old gods of Egypt, or that they were going to dedicate themselves to the Lord.

And they finally came around and said, "God forbid that we should serve anyone but the Lord, because He brought us out of Egypt!" That was the answer Joshua needed. That was the decision he wanted to hear. At least for that time, in that generation, the decision was made. Subsequent generations didn't always stick to it. It's a decision each person has to make. Too many people think, *Well, I'm a Christian because my parents went to church.* That doesn't do it. That was a decision for *their* day. It's up to each one of us to make a decision. We're in the valley of decision and we've got to decide. But it's not simply a one-time thing either. It's not simply, *Okay, I've decided this now and I don't ever have to worry about it again.* Well, no, because tomorrow,

I may change my mind and I've got to rededicate myself again tomorrow. Each day, I have the same choice again. Today I can live for God, or today. I can live for myself, Today I can live for God, or today, I can live for the world. Today I can do whatever I want to. A day has been given to me. The scripture says, *this is the day that the Lord has made.* I've got it on a sign in the window: This is the day... It's a gift given to me. What I do with it is my gift back to God. And I have a choice, the same choice every day. And every day, I find myself in the valley of decision with multitudes of decisions to make, and multitudes of people not making any decisions.

I've got to make a choice. *I've got to make a choice!* I can't live in limbo anymore. I can't live wishy-washy. I can't live on the fence. I've got to decide something. I can't keep just going on the way I've been going on. Too many times, Pentecostal churches fall into this rut that I call "Pentecost as usual." They've been doing the same thing for the past 90 for years, and nothing's any different. I was attending a small church in Southern California for a few months when I was in my teens. I thought it was wonderful because that was the first time, the first real Pentecostal church I'd ever really gotten to go to. But I went back to visit that church in my 20s, when I knew something a little more about the way things were supposed to be. And I realized those people had been stuck in a rut for the past 20 years. They didn't even have any water in there baptismal tank! Nobody had come to that church and been saved in 20 years, because those people were too busy playing *Pentecost as usual.* They had wonderful services. Those people had music that was incredible. I remember sitting in their service with the music, oh and the pastor's son was playing the trumpet, the pastor had a bass guitar and his wife played the organ. There's a piano, and all the music's going, and I looked out of the window to the neighbor's house, and the neighbor's boogieing past his window... to our music!

There was good music, and the people knew how to shout, and they knew how to wave their hands in the air, and they knew how to speak in tongues. They knew how to do everything except live for God. They knew how to go through the motions, how to play *Pentecost as usual,* how to play church. And it looks great, but it doesn't accomplish anything. They'd never made any decision. They'd never really made the decision. It was just like the Jewish people: *Of course, we're going to serve the Lord... and anything else we want to do along the way.*

But it's not that simple. There are responsibilities with this decision. There's a Great Commission that Jesus gave before he ascended back into heaven. He said, "You are My witnesses. Go out and be witnesses to all the world." What does a witness do? Well, if you go up to a courtroom and there's a witness on the witness stand, the witness tells what he saw, the witness tells what he heard, what he experienced: This is what happened. And that's OUR job as witnesses to go out into the world and witness. Be witnesses: Tell them what you've seen, tell them what you've heard, tell them what you've experienced. Tell them about it! Why? So they can know it too, and then they can go and tell somebody else. We've got a responsibility to evangelize the world. A job to do. That's our decision that we've got to make. Am I going to do this job, or am I going to fence-sit? Am I going to do this job or am I going to be just another person in just another pew and play *Pentecost as usual?* I can't live that way anymore. There are too many people doing it, and the world's not finding the answers it needs. The world sits in darkness while people play games in church. It can't go on that way. It can't go on that way!

Times before, when I preached this verse about multitudes in the valley of decision, I spoke mostly of the world: They hadn't decided whether or not they were ever going to live for God. But this verse applies just as much to the church, that we have a responsibility each day to make that decision. What we're going to do with this day? Who am I going to live for today? Who am I going to give all of myself to today? What am I going to do? Yesterday's decision doesn't matter today, because today's a new day. I've got to decide today what I'm going to do.

You know, if I decided yesterday, *Okay, I'm going to live for God.* And I lived for God yesterday, but today I go out and live like the devil, I've messed it up. Yesterday's decision has been canceled because I made a new one today. And I don't believe in the doctrine of eternal security that some churches teach, that once you're saved, you're always saved, no matter what you do after that. There's something wrong with that kind of thinking, that I could be saved today and murder someone tomorrow and still be saved. Not unless I'm willing to repent for that! That's still a pretty serious crime. It tells me that I'm not demonstrating the fruit of the Spirit, not living as a Christian, because Bible says they'll know us by our love.

If I've gone out and killed somebody, then I am not acting like a Christian. There's something wrong with the decision I made. There's something wrong with my faith, and I'd better get back down at the altar and pray until I find out what the problem is, and get right with God, because the day of the Lord is near. I don't know when it is, but I feel like it's close. I feel like there's not a lot of time that I have to make this decision now. Just as I felt yesterday that I had to make it then. I can't put the decision off for tomorrow, because I don't know what tomorrow brings. I don't have tomorrow promised to me. None of us do. Nobody ever gave us a written guarantee that we're going to wake up tomorrow morning. No promises. No promises. But I've got now. I've got now, and it's an opportunity. It's an opportunity.

The Chinese use pictures for writing. Their writing is very difficult for people to learn, because it's all these elaborate pictures. Their character that means *crisis* is made by putting two other characters together: the character for danger and the character for opportunity. The valley of decision is a crisis place; there's danger if you make the wrong decision, or refuse to make a decision. But there's opportunity, there's a chance. There's a chance for all the things that we read about in [the Bible], all the promises. All the things that God promised to His people. There's a chance in the valley of decision. But the choice is ours. God has never forced the choice on anybody. Right from the Garden of Eden, when Adam and Eve were given a choice, they made the wrong one. But we've had a choice ever since.

He'll never force us. He'll never force us to make the choice. He's never forced anybody to live for Him. That's useless. If He wanted that, He would have built robots instead of people. It's meaningless to have someone serve you if they have no choice.

But I serve Him because I want to serve Him. I made the choice, because when I was alone, He came and stayed with me. Because when I was hurt, He made me feel better. Because when my family rejected me out and said they didn't want me anymore, He said, "You come to Me and I'll never throw you out!" My choice, my decision.

And I have a responsibility to the multitudes in the valley with me, to say "This is the choice I made, and this is why. This is what He's promised if you'll make this choice. We can't just stay here and not make a choice." You've got to make a choice, and the church has a responsibility to make that choice too. Today I'm going to walk with the Lord, and today I'm going to do something for His kingdom. Today I'm going to tell somebody else. Today I'm going to make a difference for somebody else.

I'm a witness. I'm going to take the stand. I promise to tell the whole truth and nothing but the truth: This is what he's done for me! This is what he's done!

We used to have a youth group here in Schenectady years ago, mostly teenagers and a few early 20s. We would get together on a Saturday morning and pray for an hour. And then the youth group leader would drive us out to remote parts of the county where there was no church, like Duanesburg and Esperance. All these places I couldn't find if my life depended on it! She'd divide us up into groups of two. Then we would go door-to-door.

This really knocked people for a loop! Now, they were used to opening the door and seeing a Jehovah's Witness there, or something like that, or a Mormon. But those were adults, and these were teenagers. One would pray silently, while the other one would just say, "Can I take just a minute?" Not to give you literature, not to preach hellfire and damnation or to tell you what you got to do. But I want to tell you what Jesus did for me, and I'll tell you, the people out in those rural areas were absolutely floored to see boys and girls between the ages of 12 and 19 standing there and saying, "I want to tell you what Jesus did for me." Let me just take a minute. I just want a minute of your time. I don't want to preach anything to you. I just have to tell you what He did for me. And they'd share their own testimony, and it makes a difference. That's the most powerful sermon! I mean, I can stand up here and holler and shout and pound the pulpit if I want to, but there's nothing as powerful as saying *This is what Jesus did for me:*

That I was lost, now I'm found; that I was homeless and He took me home;

that I was without a family and He adopted me; that He cared enough about me when no one else did. That's what He's done for me.

There aren't too many people in this world who haven't felt rejection, who haven't felt that they just don't fit or just don't belong. That's something we've all experienced at one time or another. And I could say I felt that way, but I don't anymore, because now I found where I belong. And that powerful testimony, just of what He's done for me, that's all He asks: To be a witness. To be a witness.

There are multitudes in the valley of decision; the day of the Lord is near in the valley of decision. We've got choices that we've got to make. As for me and my house, we will serve the Lord. Amen!

No More Poison

Scripture tells us that your young men shall see visions and your old men shall dream dreams. I know when I was in my teens and my twenties, the Lord often let me see things that were fantastic. I haven't seen any of those since then, but the Lord does talk to me in dreams. I don't want to think about what that means as far as me no longer being young!

What I'm going to share is one that I had this week. Sometimes I don't even realize that a dream has come from God for several days. Then I'll be sitting in church, and all of a sudden I understand what the dream was about. I had a very strange dream where I walked out the back door of the house I was living in. I walked out into the backyard, and there was a white alley cat off to the side, lying on her side. As I watched, it seemed as if her stomach was open, and other alley cats began to come out of her. I thought that was very strange: Three, four, five cats, just stepped out from inside of her. And when I went over to take a closer look, there was nothing inside of her. She was completely empty inside, but she was alive, and she was talking to me, explaining that this is how she keeps the other cats safe.

I thought it was very strange, but there wasn't too much more to the dream than that. But it came to me today about how this cat very much symbolizes the Lord. In the same sense as that cat, He emptied himself out of all of His glory, and became just like us: We're the other alley cats.

Alley cats aren't exactly known for all their endearing qualities, but in a sense, neither were we. We were lost in sin. We had no protection from the devil. We had no protection of any kind from the world.

But He emptied himself out of His glory, and came to protect us from those things, and now we hide ourselves in Him. When we put on Christ, we're safe inside.

After Jesus died on the cross and they buried Him, it didn't seem possible that He could live again. But we know He did, and just like that cat with nothing inside who shouldn't have been alive but was, a miracle took place.

And I just sum up the dream by saying *Because He lives, we live also!* Hallelujah! Hallelujah! And that dream has absolutely nothing to do with my sermon today!

If you would turn with me to the book of Hebrews, chapter 12, we have two portions of scripture to read.

Hebrews chapter 12, starting at the 12th verse:

Wherefore lift up the hands which hang down, and the feeble knees; and make straight paths for your feet, lest that which is lame be turned out of the way; but let it rather be healed. Follow peace with all men, and holiness, without which no man shall see the Lord: Looking diligently lest any man fail of the grace of God; lest any root of bitterness springing up trouble you, and thereby many be defiled;

Turn with me now to Matthew chapter 5. The Sermon on the Mount, beginning at verse 7:

Blessed are the merciful: for they shall obtain mercy.

Verse 9:

Blessed are the pure in heart: for they shall see God.

Same chapter, verse 43:

Ye have heard that it hath been said, Thou shalt love thy neighbor, and hate thine enemy. But I say unto you, Love your enemies, bless them that curse you, do good to them that hate you, and pray for them which despitefully use you, and persecute you; That ye may be the children of your Father which is in heaven: for he maketh his sun to rise on the evil and on the good, and sendeth rain on the just and on the unjust. For if ye love them which love you, what reward have ye? do not even the publicans the same? And if ye salute your brethren only, what do ye more than others? do not even the publicans so? Be ye therefore perfect, even as your Father which is in heaven is perfect.

If I offered you a choice between a bowl of ice cream and a bottle of castor oil, which would you take? Ice cream, definitely. if I give you a choice between a candy bar and liquid erythromycin, which is the nastiest tasting stuff I've ever had, what are you going to choose? I want the candy bar. If I give you a choice between a slice of your favorite pie and boiled spinach, which do you want? You can keep your spinach; I want the pie!

We would always rather have the things that taste good rather than the things that we sometimes need. But how would we have grown up, and I'm speaking physically and possibly mentally, if our parents fed us only ice cream and candy and pie, and never gave us good nourishing food? And if we came down with an infection, like an ear infection or strep throat, they treated it with chocolate, there's a good chance we might not have lived to adulthood. But even if we did, we would not be as strong and as healthy as we turned out.

This is true spiritually as well. I don't think that there's a preacher in the world who wouldn't love to stand up in the pulpit and dish out spiritual ice cream every week. It makes you popular. You can get people running, shouting and jumping and feeling good. Unfortunately, a lot of times when the preacher says *Lord, what do you want me to give the people?*, the Lord hands down boiled spinach or a bottle of medicine.

And it's not going to be popular, but there's a reason for it. I promise you, your parents didn't give you penicillin or spinach because they were mean and nasty and hated you. They gave you those things because you needed them. And when the Lord gives us those things, it's not because He wants to be mean to us or is mad at us. It's because we have to have those things, and if we don't get them, if we live our entire spiritual lives on sermons of ice cream that get us shouting every week, we'll never grow. We'll stay children. And growth is necessary.

We know the story of the Prodigal Son. I didn't read it today, but I'm going to tell the story. There was a man of some financial means who had two sons. And the day came when the younger son said to his father, "Give me my share." The father took one half of everything and gave it to his younger son. And we know that the younger son left town and squandered everything his father gave him.

At that point, the scripture continues on following the younger son. It doesn't tell us anything at all about what was going on back home until the prodigal returned. So if you will permit me a little bit of license here, I'm going to fill in between the lines and tell the rest of the story:

When the oldest son came home that day, he noticed half the furniture is gone. Half of the land had **SOLD** signs on it. And when the bank statement came, half the money was gone.

Now, Dad, I realize this stuff is yours. But what's going on? Where's the furniture? Where's the money? Where did half of the estate go? Why is my brother's room empty?

Son, your brother wanted his inheritance, and so I gave it to him.

You gave him half of everything? Where is he?

He's gone.

Where did he go?

I'm not entirely sure.

I'm sure that the older brother had to find out what's going on. Half of this estate was his; he does have an interest in this. Where is everything? He did the best he could to find out where his little brother was, but none of the reports he got back were good. It wasn't hard to find out, because his brother was making quite a splash in the country he went to: Spending money like it was water, and going through everything, and wasting it all.

It didn't make the older brother very happy. He didn't like the way his little brother was wasting the things their father had worked so hard for, the way he had treated his family by taking everything and running off. And he didn't keep his feelings inside either, because every time he got together with his friends, his favorite topic of conversation is what his little brother has done now. *Let me tell you what he did this time!*

One of the things I kid my little brother about is something he used to do when we were kids: John seemed to, in his mind, have this running conversation going with my mother, because he would walk up to her out of the blue, and say something to her that sounded like it was part of an ongoing conversation: *You know what else Billy did?* as if he had been all along giving her this whole list of things I had done wrong.

Well, the prodigal son's older brother was doing kind of like that with his friends: *Most of the money is gone now, and I can't believe he treated our father this way.* He didn't have a good thing to say about his little brother, and granted his little brother wasn't doing anything good, but big brother made sure that he poured out the venom to his friends.

Did they knew how rotten the kid was, how he had disrespected their father and had treated callously everything their father had ever done for him, and how worthless he was, and how useless he was? And I hope he stays gone. I hope he never comes back.

And we go back to the scripture, when the youngest son had run out of everything, and found himself reduced to feeding pigs for a living. The ultimate disgrace for a good Jewish boy! And then reduced to eating whatever he could fight away from the pigs. After pigs eat, there isn't much left. Yes, and pigs are not noted for eating very neatly. They're also not noted for knowing the difference between the food trough and the bathroom. And this poor kid had to dig through that to try to find something to eat!

And we know the story, that he finally came to his senses and wondered if he could go back home. Maybe if I ask my father for his forgiveness... I'm not worthy to be called his son, but even the servants there eat better than I do. And so he went home.

And we know that his father ran out to meet him, and put a ring on his finger and threw a fine robe around him and brought him into the house. They killed the fatted calf, they had a party and everything was great... until the older brother came home.

What is going on in there? Your brother's come home! Your father's killed the fatted calf. He's having a celebration.

There was such a great difference between the way the father handled this and the way the older brother did. The father wasn't happy about what the younger son had done. He had worked all his life for those things. He had worked hard, he had saved, he'd used wisdom, so that he could provide a good living for his family. And his youngest son had thrown it all away. He wasn't happy about that. But something the father understood that perhaps the oldest son didn't, was that that young son was worth more than all of that money, all of that land, all of those possessions. All of those things could be replaced, but his son could not. To him, his son was worth everything, and he'd have done it all again, if it just meant getting his son back.

The older brother didn't understand. From the moment his brother left home, he took a daily dose of emotional poison, a dose of bitterness. Everyday taking more. It wasn't enough though, the light stuff. He had to go on to the hard stuff, and started taking a dose of hatred. Poisoning himself day by day. And that wasn't enough for him either, because he began to poison his friends with it, too. To poison them, so that even when his brother did come home, his friends couldn't rejoice over this either, because all they could think of were all the terrible things the younger brother had done.

There was joy that day for the father. There was joy for the youngest son. But there was no joy for the oldest brother.

Poison is a terrible thing. We like to talk about Miss Mary. Most of us knew Miss Mary, who passed away recently. Miss Mary was famous for her chicken soup that she made for her husband. She was angry at her husband, perhaps with good reason. So she made him chicken soup, with an extra special ingredient: Drano! "Not enough to kill him," she said. "Just enough to make him sick!" But sometimes that's all it takes. Now, thankfully, the Drano soup didn't hurt her husband at all. He didn't even get sick from it. But a little bit of poison, taken over a period of time, builds up. It builds up.

We don't use lead-based paint anymore, because kids were eating little chips over a period of time that caused sickness, that caused brain damage. We have to be careful with mercury, because mercury can build up in your system, and in time, it can kill you.

But we seem to be oblivious to spiritual poisons, and we ingest them regularly and share them.

I'm going to tell another story. And I need you to understand right at the beginning that this story is only an example. It is not a real story; it's a parable.

Now I'm going to tell the story about Sister Wester. I'm picking on her because Sister Wester has gone to be with the Lord. I can say what I want; it's not going to hurt her. But I need you to understand me: Sister Wester never did any of the things I'm going to say she did in this story. I don't want you someday over in Glory, saying, *Oh, you're Sister Wester! I heard you did this, this, this, and this!* I don't want that coming back. Sister Wester did not actually do any of these things. This is an example only.

Sister Wester was having a little bit of financial trouble. She went to her pastors and asked, "Can I borrow $500?" "Well, what's it for, Sister?" And so she explained, and they agreed: Her need was legitimate.

The need was not the result of anything she had done as far as mismanaging. She had a legitimate, unexpected need, and so they lent her $500.

She borrowed a few other things from people in the church over time. But then something happened, and I can't tell you why. God knows. Sister Wester knows. Sister Wester backslid, and it didn't take long before she left the church... Taking with her the $500 she had borrowed, the various other items she borrowed from the congregation, and all the choir song books... And a few other little items in the church building that we're not nailed down. She took them all with her. She was backslidden. She stole. It happens. We'll leave Sister Wester for a moment. We'll stay with the church that she left.

Once it became apparent, what happened? A sister told a brother, "Boy, I heard she borrowed money from the pastors and didn't return it!" And he told someone else, "You know, she stood right next to me in the choir, and now she's taken all the songbooks! Do you know how much it's going to cost to replace all those books?" Another person said "That's nothing! Do you know what she took from me?"

And the favorite topic of conversation in that church among most of the saints was what Sister Wester had done before she left. All the things she had taken and never returned.

No one really knew for sure why she backslid, but she had. You couldn't dispute the fact that she was backslidden. She was gone, and she had really taken all those things. We can't just ignore that; those are facts. She did do it. It's truth. The facts were never in question. The reaction to them was the question.

So the poison began to spread from one to another. It started with just plain shock. Okay. Okay, somebody does something unexpected like that. There's going to be shock, like the older brother coming home, finding out half the furniture's gone, half the money's gone. My little brother's gone. Yes, they're shocked at first. *How could Sister Wester do that?* She's been in the church so many years! She was a pillar in the church! What was it that she had said when she was first saved? Oh, yes, she said, I am determined! Someday, I'm going to be a pillar in this church! And Sister Wester **was** a pillar in the church. She was so spiritually strong. How did this happen? The shock.

And then the anger, that she hadn't returned any of the things that she borrowed. And then the other things that she didn't actually borrow: she just walked out with them. Shock turned to anger.

It was no longer Sister A saying to Brother B, "I can't believe she did that!" It was the rehashing of the fact over and over. "Yeah, she took all the choir books we had, too? You know how much it will cost to replace those things? Now we've got to get new ones."

Anger. But it didn't stop with anger, because then it became bitterness. Anytime her name was mentioned, there were people there willing to rehearse everything she had done when she backslid.

Odd, how nobody remembered the things she'd done for the church while she was there, before she backslid. Nobody seemed to remember the help she'd been the years she'd lived for God, the things she'd done for the Sunday School, the things she done to help out people in need. All that was forgotten. All they remembered now is Sister Wester backslid. She took all the Sunday School money, she took all the choir books, she took money from the pastors. The anger had turned to bitterness.

Now, let me ask you something: Sister Wester is gone. She had no contact with the folks in the church anymore. Is any of the anger in the church hurting Sister Wester? She doesn't even know it's happening. Is any of the bitterness hurting her? She doesn't know it's going on. She's separated from all of that, because she's out of the church right now.

So, who is the anger hurting? Who is the bitterness hurting? It's hurting the church! It's hurting the very people who are passing the spoon full of poison from member to member! It's not hurting Sister Wester now, but it's going to.

Now let's switch back to Sister Wester who's backslidden. I'm not sure how long she's been out. Weeks, months, years? It doesn't matter. But all the while she's backslidden, the Spirit of God is trying to draw her back. There are one or two old saints in the church still praying for her. We'll pick on somebody else. Let's say Sister Lily Kowal. I'm saying nice things about her, so I think I can use her name. She remembers that Sister Wester was the first witness to her, the one who brought her into the truth. She's not happy about any of the things that Sister Wester had done. But more than anything in the world, she wants Sister Wester to be saved. She wants her back in her position in the church. She wants her restored, and so she's praying *God, please bring her back. Please!* And day after day, she's praying and she's fasting, because she wants Sister Wester back.

And of course, God doesn't ignore things like that. He wants Sister Wester back, too, even more than anybody in the church possibly could. And so the Spirit of God is wooing her. You talk about having dreams that seem to come from God! Sister Wester can't get any sleep, because every night, she's dreaming about the things of God. Her mind keeps wandering back to the things of God, and she can't escape from it. And the day comes when Sister Wester realizes what she traded away, that, in a sense, she's finding herself fighting with pigs just to get a bite to eat. And she's asking herself, *What was I thinking? How can I undo this?*

She gets down on her knees and she repents and she says, I have to go back. I have to make it right in whatever way I can. I've got to go back.

And so, the very next service day, Sister Wester went back to the church. But she was in for a surprise. Most of the congregation was dead. They died of poisoning. Oh, they were still there, but they were dead. They poisoned themselves. Those who weren't dead were dying. Only a few lonely souls were still trying to hang on.

We're so careful about some things, and rightfully so. We're careful about false doctrine. We would never let a preacher up in the pulpit was going to preach something that we knew was not true. You'll never hear from the pulpit of this church somebody preach that if you sign your name after this little prayer, you're saved, that you never have to do anything else to get to heaven. We're really careful about that. When it comes to doctrinal poison, we're on the alert; we guard our doctrine carefully. There's nothing wrong with that: We should! There's nothing wrong with that. The scripture tells us *Buy the truth and sell it not.* It tells us the first century church continued steadfastly in the apostles' teaching, in their doctrine. We do exactly the same thing, and that's good. I'm thankful for that. I won't go to a church where they don't guard the doctrine carefully, but I'm telling you, it's not enough.

There is so much more to this Christianity thing than just having the right doctrine. Because I will promise you as a man of God, that there are churches preaching the absolute gospel truth, and they're on their way to hell, because there's something more to it than just being doctrinally correct.

The Pharisees in the day of Jesus were doctrinally correct. Their problem was never their doctrine. There were two basic schools of doctrine in Judaism at the time: Pharisaism and Sadduceeism. One was right, and one was wrong. The Pharisees were right, the Sadducees were wrong. Doctrinally, Jesus was a Pharisee. Paul was a Pharisee, something he freely admitted.

The Pharisee's doctrine was never their problem. When Jesus rebuked the Pharisees and called them a generation of vipers, it wasn't because of their doctrine.

Jesus met the woman at the well in Samaria, and they began to have a conversation about religion. And He said that God is a Spirit, and they that worship Him must worship Him in spirit and in truth. Not one or the other, but both.

You will find people who have one and not the other. When I was in my teens, my mid-teens, my parents would not allow me to attend an Apostolic church. So I had to settle for "second-best." When I describe to you, where I was worshiping, It may not sound like second-best. They had a congregation that ranged between 800 and 1000, and nearly all of them had the Holy Ghost. They knew how to worship in ways that sometimes would put a Pentecostal to shame. They loved each other.

I think in all the years that I attended that group, I never once... I take that back... *only* once did I ever hear anybody in that group say anything bad about anybody else. In fact, that was such an uncommon thing, the one time I did hear it, I was so shocked. No one in that group had ever done anything like that before. But they really did love each other. There was a powerful spirit of worship, a powerful spirit of love. It sounds like a great place.

Their doctrine was wrong, though. They worshiped in spirit, and it was beautiful and it was powerful, and I loved it. They had not just the Holy Ghost, as we talk about worshiping in spirit, but they had the right spirit from brother to sister, from sister to brother. They had the right way of treating each other. They were living their Christian lives in the correct way, but short on truth. They were missing the truth.

I also known other people, and this is where the Pharisees fit in, that worshiped God in truth, but with the wrong spirit. Now, when I'm talking about Apostolic churches that worship in truth but with the wrong spirit, I'm not saying they don't have the Holy Ghost. Doctrinally, they know they can't be saved unless they've received the Holy Ghost with the initial evidence of speaking in tongues. They've got that part. When I say that they have the wrong spirit, I'm talking about their basic Christian attitude.

I know I've told this story before. I had a young man who had been a Pentecostal minister for years, with absolutely no success to show for it. Every time he'd try to start a work, it would cave in on him. He'd worked for years with not a single convert, and he didn't know what the problem was. And finally, he said to me, if I come there and enroll in the Bible school, will you teach me how to be a minister? He said, "I must be doing something wrong." And so of course, I agreed. My goal, basically, in all of my ministry, is to help equip other people to do it to it. If someone has a call, he or she needs to be equipped to do it.

But after about a month or two, he noticed something very odd. I wasn't teaching him anything about how to be a minister, and he asked me why. And I said, "Because when you arrived here, I found out you didn't know how to be a Christian. You're going to have to learn that first."

When you see someone on the phone, angry about something and cussing out the person at the other end, and then slamming down the phone on them, something is wrong. I can't see Jesus doing that. This man didn't even know how to treat people! You don't win people treating them like that; it won't happen.

There are churches where Apostolic truth is taught. Nothing else. Some of us, probably most of us, have read the letters to the seven churches in the Book of Revelation. The last two letters are such opposites, such extremes. With the Philadelphia Church, even though it was small and didn't have a lot of strength, the Lord didn't have one bad thing to say about it. It seemed, in every respect, they were perfect, and in a sense, it's what we aspire to be. Every church who reads that says we want to be just like that. We want to be like the Philadelphia church.

But then the opposite end of the extreme was the church of Laodicea. Because they didn't seem to be doing anything right. They were a mess. And it's very easy to accuse everybody else who's not just like us of being the Laodicean church. When I was back in Bible school, they tried to make us think like the Assemblies of God was Laodicea. Or other non-Apostolic Pentecostal churches will be Laodicea. They miss something really important in there: Laodicea's problem was never its doctrine. It's doctrine was exactly the same as Philadelphia. They're both Apostolic churches doctrinally. The difference was the spirit.

To make it very simple to find out what was wrong with the one and what was right with the other, translate the names of the two churches into English: Philadelphia means the love between brothers and sisters. That was the basis of that church; that was the foundation of the church. Yes, they had the right doctrine, but they had something else: They knew how to love each other. Nobody could divide them. Nobody could destroy them, because they were found together by a cord of love that could not be broken.

The Laodicean church: Laodicea translates as judging people, or people of judgment, and that is what they were founded on. That was what they were based on, judging everybody else but themselves. *You're not as good as us, because you don't believe like we do!* But it wasn't enough to judge the people outside of themselves: They began to eat away at each other, to tear each other apart. No church can grow spiritually while its members are consuming each other. It isn't possible.

Before Jesus was crucified, He took time to pray for the church to pray for us. The one part of the prayer that almost seems impossible is when He prayed that we be one the way He was one. That's difficult. As an Apostolic church, we understand very clearly that God is one. If you divide one it's not one anymore, but only a part of one. There's no such thing as a part of God. He's either all of God, or he's not God. We understand that, that the Holy One of Israel is not divisible. He cannot be divided up into pieces or parts. There is one God, and that won't change. But Jesus prayed that we would be one in that same way. How is that possible?

How many cells in the human body? I'm sure that at one time or another I must have studied that information in school. A general idea, the number of cells that make up the human being. And yet it's only one person made up of those tiny little parts. But if you take them all apart from each other, you don't have a person anymore. They have to be held together, intact, to be one person.

We're cells in the body of Christ. Paul talked about it as being different members of the body, but that was really the best he could do because there was no such thing as a microscope in those days. They couldn't look at the body down on the cellular level and see that it's tiny little cells. Each cell holding on to the cell next to it, because the only way it can stay alive is to hold tightly to the cell next to it.

Now, I don't know all about cellular biology. In my mind, I think that probably each individual cell doesn't have much as far as consciousness goes, but let's assign consciousness to each one for a moment. And let's decide that this little cell gets mad at the cell next to it, because of something it thinks that cell did or maybe something that cell didn't do. *I won't hold onto him anymore!* Then it turns to the cell on the other side, and says, "That cell did this! Don't hold on to him!" Before long, the cells in the body are not holding on to each other anymore. You've got little groups, they can get along together, but they want nothing to do with other groups. And before you know it, the body is falling apart and dies.

The body of Christ does not have some magical power that enables the parts of it to hold together if they refuse to do so, if they don't want to do so. God has never forced people to be part of His body. It is a privilege and a blessing to be a part, but it's up to us. If we cannot learn to get along with each other within this little group, how could it be any wonder that the other Apostolic organizations cannot get along with each other? Is it any wonder that His body is fragmented when within a small group like this we have trouble getting along with each other. And if a prodigal son does walk away, we're willing to say, "Oh yeah, he can always come back." Except when he comes back and find so much poison that there's no way he could stay. We poisoned each other, and made it impossible for us to hold together.

There are many different kinds of glue in the world. There are different glues that work for different things. If you're going to stick two things together, you need to make sure you're using the right kind of glue that isn't going to damage what you're working on. When I made the posters for the foreign missions dinner, I had to be careful what kind of glue I bought, because I'm gluing paper on top of poster board. Some glues wrinkle when they dry, and that would have wrinkled up the papers I was gluing.

People can be held together by many different things, for example, a common cause. You will find that sometimes people who absolutely can't stand each other will work together if they have a common goal, a reason to work together.

You will also find that, if the circumstances are right, people who one minute ago were enemies are now the best of friends. It all depends on what's between them, holding them.

What holds us to each other? I won't even answer that one right now. Let's look at some other folks. Let's look at the folks over at Affirmations [LGBTQ community center]. There are many different kinds of groups that meet there. But what holds it all together is something that they have in common: it's a place for sexual minorities. That's what holds them together. That's what they have in common. They may have absolutely nothing else in common.

But you'll find even over there that politics sometimes gets working, and people can't work together anymore, and people will split off. And then from time on, they don't have anything good to say about Affirmations after that. So politics can do it, it can destroy. What it really means is that the glue that was holding them together in the first place was not strong enough to weather a storm.

Some of the glues that the body of Christ has been trying to use to hold ourselves to each other are not strong enough to survive persecution, because they don't even survive the small storms we go through now. We're using the wrong glue.

You buy a glue, check the label. See what it can be used on. See what its strength is: Is it strong enough for the job you're doing? Is it the right one for the job you want to do? We've been promised persecution: *All who live Godly in Christ Jesus will suffer persecution.* That tells me that we need the absolute strongest super-glue that we can find to hold us together no matter what happens, a glue that will prevent us from becoming offended.

Look at Brother So-and-so: He doesn't do what I think he should. Or he does it a different way than I would have done it. I need a glue that prevents me from dosing myself with poison if a brother or sister backslides. There is only one glue in the whole world can do all of that. There is only one brand on the shelf that will get you through all that, and still keep you holding on to the brother or sister next to you. I'm talking about *agape* love.

This is the right spirit. This is the spirit that we need to worship in. It's not a matter of the Holy Ghost here, because the Holy Ghost is part of our doctrine, having it. And yet, it does have to do with the Holy Ghost. But is the Holy Ghost, is that glue? The Holy Ghost is love.

We need a dose of medicine because the body is sick. We don't want the dose of medicine because it doesn't taste good, and it means we have to change. But the sickness is serious enough that, without it, without the medicine, the body is going to die.

Some of you are thinking that I'm overreacting. How many churches do we have to see die before it happens? I've watched churches die. I'm not just talking our organization. because I've watched United Pentecostal Churches die. I've watched them die because they wouldn't take the medicine the spirit of God offered. They preferred to use an inferior brand of glue, and there wasn't anything to hold them together. There was no reason to be one anymore.

Day after day, we ask God to do this for us, to give us that, to provide the other thing. And yet, for all of that, we somehow ignore the request that He made of us. And that is that we would be one as He is one, that we would be one body.

We're stuck in... It's not really a rut... in a groove. We're all old enough to remember records. When you play a record that has a scratch or something, it gets stuck in a place of the same groove, over and over and over, and it never moves on to the next one until something gives it a push. We're stuck in the same groove, going around and around and around, doing the same thing over and over and over, and looking for different results. I was once told that was the definition of insanity, when you keep doing the same thing over and over again, but you expect the result to be different next time. But it's not going to.

Do we want the church to grow? Yeah, I do. I assume everybody wants to see it grow. And yet, it doesn't. We don't see the seats filled up with people. We see the same approximate number, week after week after week. Are we doing something different to change that situation? Or are we doing the same thing? The very beginning of service, we pray for those missing, and mention the names of people, some of whom I've even forgotten. They've been gone a long, long time. But why are they gone?

I'm not here to tell you that we can prevent every person from leaving who wants to leave. We can't do that. We don't have control over what other people do. But there is something we can do. If a change happens in the way we treat each other rand a change happens with the way we treat people when they come in and if a change happens in the way we treat people after they've gone out, then there's hope. Then there's a possibility.

I've got to be careful here, I try very hard when I'm preaching just to preach what God says, and not to put in some of my own emotions, but sometimes I can't help it. I get so frustrated. And the next time somebody comes to me and tells me what Brother So-and-so did or what Sister So-and-so did, I might have the urge to slap somebody! I'm tired of being poisoned! I don't want to hear it anymore!

My grandmother used to say, *if you can't say something good about somebody that don't say anything at all.* If you can't tell me something good about somebody, don't bring their name up in conversation. I don't want to hear it anymore! I'm sick! And I'm sick because I've been taking poison. But we've all been taking poison. It's time to stop and look for an antidote.

The antidote is love. Where would we be if God kept throwing in our faces the sins that have already been forgiven? Or even those that haven't been forgiven? If every time I delay repenting for something I did wrong, the Spirit of God went around to everyone in the church and kept reminding them that I hadn't repented, where would I be? Where would we all be?

It's time for us as a church to grow up. And if we can't do that, it's time for us as the church to shut up. We're destroying ourselves. The scripture tells us that with the very same tongue we bless God and curse man. It's a shameful thing when that applies to the church, and not just the world. With the very same tongue, I can say I love God and badmouth my brother.

How long can it go on? I'm sick of it. How long before God is sick of it? Sick enough that he puts a stop to it Himself? *Why won't the church grow?* Maybe it's sick. Maybe it needs medicine. Maybe it needs help. Maybe it doesn't need a revival but a renewal.

Earlier in the service when we were asking for testimonies, we wanted to talk about the things that have changed in us. But I can't help but see the things that haven't. I don't have to tell anybody in here what the devil is like, but he doesn't make us do these things.

Oh, because we know what he's like. We know he's looking for our weakness. For any area where we're prone to do something we shouldn't, that's what he's going to work on us. The devil will never waste time working on an area where you're strong.

If you know the word of God, I doubt the devil's going to bother you doctrinally. He's not going to challenge your doctrine, or plant false doctrine in your head. But if we have an attitude that we can judge others, where we can be ruled by anger, that is where he's going to work. He doesn't make us do it. All he has to do is plant the seed, and we do it on our own.

We can pray all we want for God to stop it, but until we're willing to stop it, it's not going to stop. It's not going to change until we heal the sickness that's in here, until we heal our own spiritual sickness, until the only glue that is used in this church is the Holy Ghost and *agape* love.

Until then, it's not going to change. We can sit here and go on year after year with six or seven people in attendance, and we'll fit the definition of insanity for trying the same thing over and over. Physician, heal thyself... Before you try to heal the world.

Look in *your* eye before you tell me that Brother's got something in his, because I think every one of us can find something in our own eye that needs to be fixed, that needs to be taken out, that needs to be changed.

I don't like preaching like this. Frankly, I hate it. I'd rather preach what people want to hear. But I don't have that luxury, because I promise you, if I ignore what God says to preach, and I start to preach what I'd rather hear, I won't be preaching much longer. If I'm unwilling, there's someone else who's willing to preach what God says to preach.

But if we'll make a difference in ourselves, if we'll change what we're doing, we won't ever have to hear this message again, and I can go along with that, because I don't ever want to hear it again. I hate boiled spinach. I hate liquid erythromycin. But if I'm spiritually sick, I know I'm not going to get better unless I take my medicine. Unless I eat the right spiritual food, I'm not going to get spiritually strong. If I take daily doses of poison, I'll die. It's that simple.

Prepare to Meet Thy God

Before I read my text, there's something that was kind of on my mind last night. I was thinking about it and I thought I'd like to share it. A lot of times, we're hesitant to talk to people about the Gospel, to tell them about the things the Lord has done, or to invite them to church. We have all kinds of excuses that are kind of built in, that we don't want to bother them, we don't want to frighten them, we don't want them to think that we're strange or weird or, God forbid, that we're Jehovah's Witnesses! And we tend to think that if we somehow, by some miracle, get somebody to come to church, they're doing us a tremendous favor!

I think we've sold our Gospel short. The Gospel is Good News, and when we go out to the world and we tell it to someone else, they're not doing us a favor if they come to church. We are doing *them* a favor by telling them! We're demonstrating the highest form of love by sharing good news with them, and sharing good news is only natural. It's just a normal part of who we are. If I go to the movies and I see something that's just fantastic, I want to tell my friends, *I just saw the greatest movie! You've got to go see this!* If I find a new restaurant, and I eat there in the food is good, and the service is good, I'm going to tell my friends, *I had dinner at such-and-such a place; You've got to try it! It's great!* Any time I try something new and it's good, I'm going to share with my friends because that's what friends are for.

I've found the greatest news of all. It beats any movie or restaurant. I found eternal life, and it's only natural that I'd want to share it with other people. I've got good news! There's a song that we sang, oh, 15-20 years ago: *Come on and shout it from the mountaintops! Proclaim it in the city streets! Sing it everywhere you go! Tell everybody you meet! Shout it: Jesus is coming!* That's news to be shouting from the housetops!

No man lights a light and then hides it under a bushel. You put it up on a lamp-stand, where everybody can see it. What good is our light if we hide it from the world? We are the salt of the earth, but if we don't have any flavor left, what good is our salt? Or as Godspell said, *If that salt has lost its flavor, it ain't got much in its favor! You can't have that fault and be the salt of the earth...* and *You've got to stay bright to be the light of the world.* Hallelujah!

You've got to let your light so shine before men. Shine brightly, because there's an awful lot of darkness out there. But you know, it doesn't matter how thick the darkness is; even the smallest flame will give some light. Even a spark can be seen in the darkness, and it only takes a spark to get a fire going.

When we studied Pentecostal history, we studied, I think his name was Brother William J. Seymour, who was a Baptist Minister. As I recall, he traveled to Houston where there was a tremendous Holy Ghost revival going on in the early early years of [the 20th] century, and he got so excited by what was happening there, that he took the message with him to Los Angeles to a church where he was expected to preach. But they didn't want the message. Now this is fantastic, because he had not even received it himself! He didn't even get the Holy Ghost in Houston, but he carried a spark to Los Angeles, and even though the church he went to in Los Angeles didn't want to hear it, and they locked the doors to him, he went and preached in an old livery stable. Los Angeles was dry wood and he had a spark! Hallelujah! And that flame just spread around the world. They weren't doing *him* a favor. He was doing *them* a favor when he brought that spark there.

There's a lot of dry wood in Schenectady and Albany and Troy. And the whole area is a lot of dry wood. I've got a spark, and I see what I can set on fire. We're going to have a little Holy Ghost arson! Hallelujah!

I'm turning to the Book of Amos. This is one of those times when I have some scripture, but I have no idea where God's going with it. He gave it to me at work last night.

Amos chapter 4, beginning at verse 4:

Come to Bethel, and transgress; at Gilgal multiply transgression; and bring your
sacrifices every morning, and your tithes after three years:

And offer a sacrifice of thanksgiving with leaven, and proclaim and publish the
free offerings: for this liketh you, O ye children of Israel, saith the Lord God.

And I also have given you cleanness of teeth in all your cities, and want of bread
in all your places: yet have ye not returned unto me, saith the Lord. And also I have
withholden the rain from you, when there were yet three months to the harvest:
and I caused it to rain upon one city, and caused it not to rain upon another city:
one piece was rained upon, and the piece whereupon it rained not withered. So
two or three cities wandered unto one city, to drink water; but they were not
satisfied: yet have ye not returned unto me, saith the Lord. I have smitten you
with blasting and mildew: when your gardens and your vineyards and your fig
trees and your olive trees increased, the palmerworm devoured them: yet have
ye not returned unto me, saith the Lord. I have sent among you the pestilence
after the manner of Egypt: your young men have I slain with the sword, and have
taken away your horses; and I have made the stink of your camps to come up unto
your nostrils: yet have ye not returned unto me, saith the Lord. I have overthrown
some of you, as God overthrew Sodom and Gomorrah, and ye were as a firebrand
plucked out of the burning: yet have ye not returned unto me, saith the Lord.
Therefore thus will I do unto thee, O Israel: and because I will do this unto thee,
prepare to meet thy God, O Israel. For, lo, he that formeth the mountains, and
createth the wind, and declareth unto man what is his thought, that maketh the
morning darkness, and treadeth upon the high places of the earth, The Lord, The
God of hosts, is his name.

This chapter has always fascinated me because it shows us an aspect of
God's personality that we don't see often. We don't often see God being
sarcastic. And yet, in Amos chapter 4, this is the epitome of sarcasm. He
started off by telling them to go to Bethel, which means *house of God.*

And God told them to come to Bethel and to sin, and then go to Gilgal and
multiply their sins. They could bring their sacrifices every morning, but if
they wanted to wait three years to pay their tithes fine, no problem. Offer
a sacrifice of thanksgiving with leaven, that is with sin. And proclaim and
publish the free offerings. Like, take out a full-page ad in the newspaper and

let everybody know what you sacrificed! *No one's ever given as much as I have!* For this is like you: This is exactly what you're like, you children of Israel.

It's not that He *wanted* them to do those things, but He told them to do them because they were going to do them anyway. *Go ahead, do what you want to do!* He tried everything to get them to repent, everything he could think of. He started off by saying he gave them cleanness of teeth in all their cities. Well, we may think that's a wonderful idea: The dentist will be thrilled by cleanness of teeth. He actually meant there was nothing for them to eat: Their teeth were clean because they had no food and had no bread, and yet they didn't repent. The hunger wasn't enough to drive them to their knees, to make them pray, and so He kept the rain from them, so that the crops withered, there was thirst, but they still wouldn't repent.

He gave them blasting and mildew and withered all their trees and the palmerworms came and ate them: all their figs, and their olives, and their grapes, and yet, they wouldn't repent. The pestilence of Egypt, the plagues, came. The young men were killed, the horses were taken away. They wouldn't repent. God even overthrew some of them like Sodom and Gomorrah, sending fire to destroy them. And still they wouldn't repent.

Well, He's done everything short of killing the whole nation. What more could He do? What more could He do? *Go ahead and sin. It doesn't matter anymore, because I've made up My mind now. This is what I'm going to do to you, Israel: Prepare to meet your God.*

Through the ages, God sent messengers. Prophets we call them. It's like Western Union. God sent Western Union to the northern Kingdom of Israel to tell them that what they were doing was wrong, and to tell them to repent. Unfortunately, Israel was not interested in hearing what the prophets had to say. They weren't interested, and so they killed the prophets. Jezebel was real good at that, killing the prophets. She didn't care much for the prophets of the Lord. She liked her own prophets because they'd say exactly what she wanted to hear. And as a thorn in her side, it seemed every time she turned around, there was a man of God telling her the truth. Good old Elijah, there to tell her *Thus saith the Lord...*

But instead of listening to the messengers, Israel killed the messengers.

They killed them, they starved them, they burned them, they cut them in half, they stoned them, anything but listen to them.

Jesus told a parable about a man who owned a vineyard. When it came time to collect from the people who were working in the vineyard, he sent a servant. And they beat the servant and threw him out.

And so he sent another servant, and they treated him worse than the first one.

And finally, the owner of the vineyard said, "I will send my son because him they will respect."

They saw the son coming and they said, "Here is the heir to the vineyard. Let's kill him, and then his heritage will be ours!" And so they killed him.

And Jesus said, "Now what do you think the owner of the vineyard is going to do to those people? He will go to the vineyard himself and he will destroy them!"

Israel was the vineyard, and God sent messengers. He sent His servants. One after another, they threw them out. They wanted no part of them. They would not hear the words.

His messengers weren't just prophets. His messengers were also plagues, things to remind the people that they needed to repent, the curses that He'd promised in Deuteronomy if they would not obey the Law.

And they came upon the people, but the people would not repent. It seemed that nothing in the world was as important to them as continuing to walk in the way that they wanted to walk. They were willing to go without food. They were willing to go without water. They were willing to give up their figs and their olives and even their grapes, so they had no wine. They were willing to let the young men die. They were willing to let fire fall out of the sky. Anything other than repent! Anything other than surrender to God!

He did everything He possibly could for the northern Kingdom of Israel, to get their attention, to turn them around, to make them come back to Him, "And yet," He said, "you would not come back to Me." *So go ahead to Bethel and sin. Go to Gilgal and multiply your sins. Go ahead and bring me a sacrifice with sin. Go ahead and wait three years to pay your tithes, so the priests have to go out and work in the fields just to make a living. Who cares anymore? Israel prepare to meet thy God!*

I can't deal with you in any other way. You won't hear My messengers. You won't heed the plagues. There's nothing more to do but have a face-to-face meeting. We're going to sit down and we're going to discuss this together, Israel. Prepare to meet your God!

Of course, in the Old Testament, there was only one way to do that. They had to die. That was the only way to meet your God in the Old Testament, to die. And that's what He told them: "Prepare to meet your God!" *Your time is up. I've run out of options. The only way to get your attention is to bring you here and stand you before My throne. So prepare, get ready. You're about to die.*

And the northern Kingdom of Israel was destroyed because of their sin, because God couldn't get their attention in any other way.

A lot of times, Christian people will moan and complain about the terrible time they're going through. Good old Sister Sicker-than-thou: *No one's ever been through what she's been through today!*

And all the problems and all the trials of being a Christian! It seems to me from reading the Bible that being a Christian was supposed to be a joyful experience, that we were supposed to go from victory to victory, and that any time the devil threw a monkey wrench at us, it was supposed to be turned around into a victory.

Look at some of the things [the devil] threw at the apostles: Peter wound up in jail. John wound up in jail. Paul wound up in jail. James wound up in jail. Everybody wound up in jail at one point or another. Persecution, and yet, it always turned around to victory, because God kept releasing these people.

Well, we went to the prison, and it was securely locked, but there is nobody inside. And the men that you threw in there? Well, they're out in the Temple teaching again! We don't know how they got out there! It was a joyful thing, because there was victory. They knew the message, they knew the good news, they knew Who was in charge, and they went out and did what they had to do, and there was victory and every time trouble came. They turned it around so that it was a victory.

And yet, too many times today Christians aren't living a victorious life. They're living from trial to trial instead of victory to victory. They're living from valley to valley instead of mountaintop to mountaintop.

Something's wrong with the way we're living the Christian life if we're down in the dumps all the time, if we're Sister Sicker-than-thou. Or if we've, you know, got more problems than the people in the world. Something's wrong.

Sometimes Christians get a persecution complex, too. They feel like if they're not being persecuted, they must be doing something wrong, and so therefore they go around trying to stir up persecution.

But it's supposed to be a joyful experience, and maybe if the Christian is having trouble in his or her life, maybe if there's problems, maybe if there's trials, maybe if it seems like the hand of God is against us, maybe we're doing something wrong. *Oh no, no, no! It's just the persecution. It's just the devil attacking me.* Well, why is God allowing the devil to attack you? Maybe He's trying to get your attention. But Israel didn't want to hear that either. There was famine, there was thirst, there was drought, pestilence, plagues, death, fire.

No, God's not trying to get our attention. Don't be silly! Those are just... that's... that's life. That's just the chances of the way it is. That's just luck, you know? We're just having a run of bad luck, right? Couldn't possibly be the God's trying to get your attention now, Israel, could it? Couldn't possibly be that maybe you're not living right, and you need to turn around and repent. Oh, no.

I fear for the Christians who are in the same position that Israel was in, enduring all these trials, but not getting anywhere with them, not realizing what the purpose of some of these things are. When the hand of God is against the church, it means the church is doing something wrong! And if He can't get our attention any other way, there is always the last resort. There's always the last resort if they ignore the messengers.

I listen to a wonderful sermon years ago, back in the 70s. It was preached in a United Pentecostal Church. Shortly afterward, the church became independent. The preacher was talking about all the messengers that God had sent to the United Pentecostal Church over the years, with a vision from God, or a message from God about the way things should be done, and he said, we didn't want to hear them. And so we threw them out, He said. Any man or woman that ever came to this [organization] with a message from God about what we're supposed to be doing, if it didn't line up with what we were already doing, we threw them out. That's a scary thing! But they didn't want to hear the messengers. This still don't want to hear the messengers.

God sends us messengers. He's given us the Gifts of the Spirit so that we can hear His voice, so we can have the messages, so we can know what *Thus saith the Lord.* Whether it's through prophecy, whether it's through tongues and interpretation, whether it's through a word of knowledge, or a word of wisdom... So that we can know how we're supposed to be doing things.

Far too often, were stuck in what we want, to do it our way: *Well, this way works fine. We've always done it this way.*

Then why don't we see what we're supposed to see? If this way works so fine, why haven't we evangelized the world? if this way works so good, why has it been two thousand years, and we still haven't reached the world? The world's not getting smaller for us; its getting bigger. We're getting more people, not less. The job is getting harder every single day, and we're not getting any closer to our goal of evangelizing the world, while we sit on padded pews and wait for Jesus to come.

He's not coming till we do the work! Two thousand years and we haven't figured out. He's not coming till we do the work. Yes, we're preparing to meet our God, but we may not be meeting Him the way we think we're going to. Not if we don't get out and do what He told us to do. Not if we don't start listening to the voice of God, and stop blaming all our troubles on the devil, when it may very well be God trying to get our attention.

Just say do it His way. Do it his way. We have a dear Sister in the ministry who's got a wonderful sense of humor. And she likes to tell how God will let her mess up a situation beyond belief. And when she's totally fouled up everything, He'll just sort of tap her on the shoulder and say, "Excuse Me! *This* is what I told you to do. Would you mind doing it now?" I told her I could definitely empathize with that. I've been in that position before too many times, because it's all too easy to listen to myself and all too difficult for me to listen to God.

I'll tell you the body of Christ has a very bad case of cerebral palsy, because the brain, the head, who is Jesus, gives the command, and somehow, it never reaches the body of Christ somehow. We've got our own mind, and we're doing our own thing, and doing whatever we want to do, and the thoughts of God elude us completely.

And so He tries to get our attention: A little slap on the hand, and we blame the devil. Grab by the wrist, and we blame the devil. We blame the world. Or certain branches of Christianity, they check under the table because there are *whatever their current enemy is*, whether it's the Communists or homosexuals. There's someone under the table, and it's all *their* fault. It's Republicans... I mean, it's liberal Democrats.... That's what it is! There must be liberal Democrats under the table!

Always ready to blame anybody but ourselves, always ready to look for someone else, instead of thinking, maybe I'm not doing it right. Maybe I need to listen.

King Saul was one who thought he knew the ways of God, and he didn't. He thought he knew how everything should be done, and that he was just so important in the eyes of God, and that he just had it all sewn up. There was an appointed time when the prophet Samuel was supposed to offer a sacrifice. Saul got there early with his men, and they decided they didn't want to wait for Samuel. Saul figured he could offer the sacrifice just as well as Samuel could. And so he did, but it was not the job of a king to offer sacrifice. It was not his place to do that, but he thought he knew better than the word of God. And so he offered the sacrifice, and right on time, here comes Samuel down the road, and says, "What is this is that have you done?" *I offered the sacrifice!* The words that Samuel spoke to him rang loud and clear back then, and they still ring loud and clear today: *To obey is better than sacrifice, and to listen is better than the fat of rams!*

To listen and obey: two of the most difficult things for people to do right from the time we're born. Ask any parent, and they'll tell you, listen and obey are two things their children do not know how to do. I remember a comedian who said all children have brain damage because they cannot seem to listen and obey. They'll repeat right back to you what you just told them **not** to do, and then they will go right ahead and do it! It does seem like a form of brain damage, but with my apologies to the comedian, it is not just restricted to children: I think we've all got a little bit of it, because God tells us very plainly what He wants us to do, and we very clearly ignore Him and do what we want, and then wonder why we're in trouble all the time!

I have so many comics. I love to cut out comics from the newspaper and save them. I've got so many comics of Dennis the Menace, sitting in his little rocking chair in the corner. He spends half his life in time-out in that corner. Or Calvin, banished to his room again. He spends half his life in there for doing something wrong.

I think the church is sitting in the corner. I think from time to time God puts us in the corner as a little bit of punishment, to get our attention because we're not listening to Him, we're not obeying Him. How do I know? Because I can see the condition of the church! If we were doing what we're supposed to be doing, if we were in complete obedience to the Spirit of God and the will of God right now, we would have a full Apostolic church with full Apostolic power tearing this world apart. We don't have it. We would have miracles and healings. We would have the dead being raised. It would be happening all over the place, all the time and it's not. And it's not God's fault!

It's so easy to blame him and say, Well, when God sends the end-time revival... when God sends the end-time revival... **God already sent it!** He already gave it to us, back in 1901, when the Holy Ghost was outpoured. That was all we needed right there to do the work. They proved it in the first 14 years of the century. They proved it with powerful miracles, the powerful moving of God. They proved it in Indonesia when the Holy Ghost fell there, and in one year, they duplicated every miracle in the Bible. They proved that all you needed to have the Revival was the Holy Ghost. We've got the Holy Ghost. We don't have the Revival. It's not because God didn't give us something. It's because we're doing it wrong! It's because we're not following the pattern. It's because we're not listening, we're not obeying.

God said that He would not always strive with a man. He said, "My Spirit will not always strive with a man." There's a limit to His patience. He'll try and try and try, but when He runs out of options, then there's no choice left. If he can't get through to us with messengers, whether prophets or punishments, if He can't get through to us any other way, then there's no way but this: Prepare to meet thy God.

Prepare to meet thy God! *Oh well, that wouldn't happen to Apostolic people.* It **does** happen to Apostolic people! It happened to Ananias and Sapphira in the first century, because God couldn't get through to them any other way. They had to have a face-to-face meeting with God, in the throne room of God, because He couldn't get through to them any other way. They didn't want to hear that. There was something wrong with the way they were living. So they lived the way they wanted to. God got their attention.

There was a Brother in this area back in the 1980s, an Apostolic minister. He publicly opposed the work that God was doing through us in this area, and without bothering to investigate it, without bothering to check for facts, he told the newspapers things that were not true. God could not get his attention. That minister, who was not an old man, only in his 30s, is dead now, killed in a head-on crash. And his church couldn't understand. *Why would God allow this to happen? Oh, it must be the devil.* No, it wasn't the devil. It was just that God had run out of options to get hold of this Brother, to get his attention. And finally there was no choice left but to tell him *Prepare to meet thy God. I can't leave you down here anymore, because you're no longer building the kingdom. You're starting to tear it down. You've done all the good you can, and now all you're doing is harm. Prepare to meet thy God.*

We've got a lot of work to do and if we don't do it, then He'll give it to somebody else. But if He can't get our attention, then the message to us is going to be the same thing: Prepare to meet thy God, Israel. Prepare to meet thy God, church. We've had two thousand years to do this work.

His Spirit won't strive forever. We're going to run out of time. *We're going to run out of time!* We need to learn to listen, to hear the voice of God now, and not just to hear what He says, but to obey it, no matter what that means sacrificing, no matter what it means giving up, because nothing is more important than the will of God.

It doesn't matter what pet doctrines we might have to give up. Over the years, the past 20 some odd years, I have had to give up 90% of the things that I was taught were true, because they weren't true. I could have been stubborn like some in my family who were shown truth, but chose to hold on to tradition, but then I would have lost out.

Sometimes the things that we think are so important to God aren't important. His ways are not our ways. His priorities are not our priorities. And whether we realize it or not, He's going to change His ways or His priorities for us. So, if there's any changing to be done, we have to do the changing. If any ways and priorities are going to change, it's got to be ours, so that our ways *do* match His, and our priorities *do* match His. But the only way for that to happen is for Him to tell us what his ways and priorities are. We sang it: *Show me Thy ways. Teach me Thy paths.* I want to know what's important to You. I want to know the way to go, and not decide for myself.

Too much of the church is praying *Thy will be done, and this is what Thy will is!* Too many people want to define God's will for Him. He's never allowed anyone to do that, and He never will. He's sovereign. He's God. And lest Israel have any doubts about that, He closed that chapter by pointing out exactly who he was: *For, lo, he that formeth the mountains, and createth the wind, and declareth unto man what is his thought, that maketh the morning darkness, and treadeth upon the high places of the earth, The Lord, The God of hosts, is his name.* Just in case you don't know who I am, I'm the One who created you. I'm the one who tells you what My thoughts are, what My ways are, not the other way around!

The Lord, the God of hosts: He knows what His will is. We don't have to tell Him. But we do have to ask Him: *What is Your will?* Thy will be done on Earth, as it is in heaven. In heaven, they don't question His will; they do it. It's got to be the same here. It's got to be the same in our life.

Some people pointed out that in the wording of the Lord's Prayer, in Greek, says thy will be done ἐπὶ *(epi)* **in, on, for** or **over** earth, as it is in heaven, reminding us that we are created from the earth, from the dust of the Earth. Let Your will be done in earth, in me, just it is in heaven.

Thy will be done, not mine. Even Jesus, in the garden of Gethsemane, was able to pray that prayer: *Not my will,* even though he knew that the will of God was something that he wanted no part of, that he was terrified of, that scared him to death. He had to surrender his own human will to it.

And we must do the same, to surrender our will and obey His. If we do anything less, we are not the church. We are not *any* church; we're not an Apostolic church.

The only time I ever want to hear God say the words *Prepare to meet thy God* to me are at the rapture. That's the only time I ever want to hear that, because I don't want to hear it as His last resort, because He can't get through to me any other way. I don't want to hear it because I was so stubborn that I wouldn't obey His will, because I'm so spiritually deaf, that I don't know what He wants. I don't want to be that way. I need ears that hear, and a heart that's willing to obey. And that's something that we all need. It's something we all need.

Lord Jesus, give us ears to hear. Let us hear Your word. Teach us Your will, show us Your paths, Your ways that are far above our ways. Teach us Your ways. Teach us obedience. Teach us what it really means to be the Church of God. For the sake of Your kingdom, You people. We ask this in the name of Jesus. Amen!

Redeeming the Time

I'm turning to the book of Ephesians. You know, just as we were finishing our prayer, Brother Mark quoted scripture while he was praying: *Why do you look for the living among the dead?* And it occurred to me, it's so sad that some Christians can only celebrate the resurrection one day a year. And they have to have a season to build up for it that they call Lent, and then they have Easter. We've got the resurrection inside of us every day of our lives, because He is the resurrection and the life, and the one who believes in Him will never die. We've already got resurrection and it's every day! Hallelujah! Thank the Lord!

Ephesians, chapter 5. This is something that came to me yesterday, while we were visiting with Brother Lombard, and I warned Brother Curley that I might just preach this today. And then God gave me a little more of it before I went to sleep last night, and then a little more in the car this morning just as we were pulling into Burger King in East Greenbush. There was a song on the the tape player, and just as we were about to get out of the car, they sang something that confirmed again what God had for me today and what God has for us.

Ephesians, chapter 5, beginning at verse 15.

See then that ye walk circumspectly, not as fools, but as wise, redeeming the time, because the days are evil. Wherefore be ye not unwise, but understanding what the will of the Lord is.

Hallelujah! Thank the Lord!

You know, there are games that Christians play. Games really isn't the right word, but I don't really know any other word for it. In fact, there was a book written about it called **Games Christians Play**. And it's some of the ruts that Christians fall into. They fall into these ruts, and they repeat the same actions over and over again. They don't deliberately intend to play games; they've just gotten so used to living a certain way and acting a certain way, that they don't even realize what they're saying, and I'm sure we're familiar with most of them.

I'm sure we've all heard somebody who, in an attempt to show off their spiritual superiority, gave you a line like this: *"Well, when you've been a Christian as long as I have..."* And of course, they'll put on some false humility so they don't look too conceited. But they're about to tell you some wonderful little piece of news, like when you've been a Christian as long as they have, you're no longer tempted by the devil, or you long no longer need to pray or read your Bible or fast, or some other line of hogwash.

When you've been a Christian as long as I have... Now, I could preach a whole sermon just on that attitude, but I'm going to turn it around backwards and preach on the opposite: When you've walked in sin as long as I have, when you've wasted as many years as I have playing around with the world and the things of the devil, turning my back on the things of God... When you've walked in sin as long as I have... I've wasted so many years that I could have been dedicating to the kingdom. More years than others, and not as many as some.

The number of years isn't important. The point is that I've wasted time, and time is a precious commodity. In life-threatening circumstances, God has allowed time to go backwards only once. That was in the days of King Hezekiah, when the king was dying, and the prophet brought him the message that he wouldn't die. And Hezekiah wanted a sign, and the prophet offered to have the shadow of the sundial go ahead a little bit. That is, time would jump ahead. And the king said, "That's nothing for it to go ahead. Let's see it go backwards. Then I'll know!" God did it, and time went backwards. That's the only time time ever went backwards. Once before, it stopped for almost a day in the days of Joshua, but it didn't go backwards.

I have no way to turn the hands of the clock back. Now, I've got a clock that I just love. I've wanted one of those since I was a little kid. All the numbers are backwards, and the hands move backwards. People look at that and they're absolutely confused. It actually does keep correct time. You just have to think about it, and turn it around in your head. But I don't have a clock that will make time actually go backwards.

I wish that I did have one. There are so many things I'd like to do over again, to do differently next time. You know, they say hindsight's 20/20. When I look back and see what I did, I know exactly what I should have done. I know how I should have lived. I know how I should have walked. I also know what I should *not* have done. All the years that I've wasted: If only I could reclaim them! If only I could change the things I did: All the years I spent drinking, all the years I spent with no morality whatsoever, years I spent messing with drugs. I wasted a lot of years chasing after the pleasures of the world, only to find out that the roads I was following, all of them, were dead ends. Oh, if I could only have back the time I spent on those roads, if I could only have back those years. If only there was a way. If only I could turn back the hands of time, make it go backwards. Not just 20 minutes or 40 minutes, but 20 years. Even 30 years. To change it all, to make it different.

If I had spent every year of my life, since the day I received the Holy Ghost, living for God, where would I be now? If I had spent every waking moment from the day that I got the Holy Ghost when I was 14 years old, if I had spent every waking moment working for the kingdom of God, how much could I have accomplished? But I can't turn it back.

You know, we've heard the scripture that we read preached many, many times over the years. *Redeeming the time because the days are evil.* A secretary I used to work with, a dear lady, Sister H.: She used to quote that a lot, but we always misunderstood what it meant. We always missed 90% of the meaning of that scripture, because we're locked into time, and we can't think of any possibility other than time is going to go forward. And as we mentioned at the beginning of the service, we have very little time left and a tremendous amount of work to do.

And so we always looked at the scripture as saying *take the little bit of time you've got left and make the most of it.* Well that's part of it, but only a very small part of it. We've overlooked the meaning of the word *redeem*.

Redeem! If you redeem something, don't you get it back? If somebody is in prison and you redeem them, don't you get them out? We were lost in sin and Jesus redeemed us. Doesn't that mean He gets us back? Isn't that the prize? He got us! You get something back when you redeem. If you take your empty soda cans and bottles to the store and redeem them, you get your money back. You get the deposit; you get something back.

Redeeming the time: You mean all the years that I wasted in sin? There's a chance to redeem them? There must be, or it wouldn't be written there. And it must not be in the way that I said before, turning the hands of a clock back, because we don't have any way to do that. There must be another way to redeem the time. There must be another way.

Going to jump off on a tangent here. We bought our first computer for the church in the early 1980s, and it was, for its time, not a bad computer. It did a lot for us. And yet, today it is so obsolete that I couldn't sell it if my life depended on it. It's up in a box in the closet. A few years after we bought that one, we upgraded to a better model, and it's still in there and I still have it hooked up, but I only use it for playing music because it is also so obsolete that I can't do anything else with it. Nobody would buy that! Maybe in another 20 years, it'll be an antique and somebody will buy it and think it's just, you know, wonderful.

And when we first started using computers, and I typed out our Bible School lessons, and I typed out correspondence, and we saved things, we didn't have any discs to save them on. We saved them on cassette tapes, the kind we listen to music on. And it would take an incredible amount of room on a tape just to store one document. And if I wanted to retrieve it, I'd have to play through the whole tape until it got to the place where that document was. I'd have to sit there and wait for the computer to search for it on the tape. That's archaic! Then we got our first disc drive. It could only read one side of the disc, and it could only store an incredibly small amount of information, but I was just thrilled. This was just, this was just wonderful: We could do so much more with so much less!

And then we got a new computer, an XT, and we got a drive that could actually read both sides of a disc, and store 360 kilobytes on one disc. And I thought that was just great. That's wonderful. And then we upgraded that disk drive and got another one that could store even more on a disk that looked exactly the same. Then we got smaller discs that stored even more data than the bigger discs. And then we got high density, small discs that stored even more. We just got our new hard drive: Our old hard drive was 42 megabytes, and it was always full. I was always getting the notification that there wasn't any more room to save anything. Now, we've got four hundred and twenty megabytes, and it's small by today's standards. And yet it's no bigger in physical size than the old one. It's no bigger. Somehow they've managed to put more information into a space. Hey, that's great.

I think God is giving us the opportunity to do that with time. Time can't go backward for us, and He can't increase the amount of time we have left, as everything's fixed: He already knows the hour and the day. There's no way to push it ahead anymore. We've got a fixed amount of time.

But God's technology is far beyond ours, and He knows how to fit more into that time than ordinarily would have fit. He's going to give us back the years that we wasted if we're willing to make amends for them by doing something with them. All the years that I wasted, I can have a chance to do it again, not to waste them again, but to do something with them this time. Not by turning back the clock, but by fitting twice as much into the time that's left. He'll make the way, if I'm willing.

But in order for that to happen, it says that I have to walk circumspectly, not as a fool, but as wise, in order to redeem these years, to redeem the time, to get back the time that I wasted and lost.

You know, Paul wrote this letter to the Ephesians. Paul had wasted an awful lot of years. He didn't know he was wasting them; he was a religious scholar. He was a respected Jewish scholar, trained up at the feet of one of the greatest teachers Israel had ever known. He knew the law of Moses inside and out. He thought he was doing God's will when he persecuted the church, dragging men, women and children out of their houses and throwing them into jail for being Christians. He thought he was doing good, and when he finally saw the light, as it were, after being struck blind on the road to Damascus, he realized what a terrible thing he'd done. But there was no way to turn back the clock.

And yet, here he wrote there was a way to redeem the time. He must have found a way to make up, to make amends for all the years that he'd wasted, for all the harm that he done.

And I'll be the first to admit, not only have I wasted time, but there have been times that I've actually done harm to the kingdom of God, through my own negligence, through my own failures, through my own sin. And yet, here's a chance to undo it, to make up for it, to redeem the time.

But I've got to walk wisely, understanding what the will of the Lord is. That's so important. So important. You know, when the Jewish people said to Jesus, *Lord, teach us to pray.* Teach us to pray! You know, it was a legitimate request. I mean what the Pharisees were doing as far as prayer was just unbelievable. It just took hours to say all that stuff.

There is a Jewish story, a beautiful story, about a herdsman who didn't know how to pray. No one had ever taught him. He was a Jewish man, and you know, when he was a child, they should have taught him how to say, the Sh'ma: *Hear O Israel...* And they should have taught him all the benedictions: *Blessed art Thou, O Lord our God, King of the universe...* etc. All the different benedictions begin that way, all the prayers in order, he should have learned, but he never learned them.

But he loved God with all his heart. And so, every day he would say, *"Lord of the universe, You know that if I had one sheep to my name, if it was all I had, I would give it to You, because I love You."* And one day, a Jewish scholar came along that way and heard him praying, and said, "What are you doing?" And he said, "Well, I'm praying." And the scholar said, "Fool! Don't pray like that!" And he taught him the Sh'ma. He taught him all the benedictions in order, and and he taught him all the prayers he needed to know, and then he went on his way. Well, as soon as he was gone, the herdsman forgot all those things. That was too much to remember! And he was afraid to say the prayer he used to pray, because the the wise man had told him not to, and so he didn't pray at all.

And one night, the Lord spoke to that wise man in a dream. He said, "I want you to know that if you don't go back and tell that herdsmen to pray the way he used to, something terrible is going to happen to you. You've robbed me of one who belongs to the world to come!" And the wise man went right back to the herdsman and said, "Tell me, what prayer are you praying?" And he said, "I'm not praying any. I forgot what you taught me, and you told me I shouldn't say what I used to say." And the wise man told him, "Pray the way you use to." *He* knew how to pray, rather then the wise man.

The Jewish people had watched the Pharisees pray. They couldn't help it: On every street corner, there was a Pharisee going into long, repetitious prayers of the top of his lungs so everyone could hear, and see how holy he was. And something inside the common people said *That's not the way to pray. That's not how to do it.* Now, here was a chance to learn something, because here was Jesus. And the one thing they noticed about Him was something about the way He taught. You see, when the scribes and the Pharisees used to teach them, they always taught, *Well, it should be this way,* or *I think it's that way* or *Maybe it's that other way,* or *Maybe it means this.* Jesus didn't do that. They said, *He teaches like he knows what he's talking about! He talks with authority! He doesn't say 'maybe 'anything!* He says, *This is the way it is,* and they saw that He knew what He was talking about. He had wisdom; He had knowledge; He had authority. So we'll ask Him; he'll know the answer: *How do we pray?* And He didn't give them any enormous prayer. He gave them a simple pattern to follow. Not necessarily words to repeat, but a pattern to follow.

Part of that pattern was *Thy will be done.* Four simple words. And yet, four of the most difficult words for any human being to live, because our will is so strong. And so many of us in our lives are not content to say, *O Lord, Thy will be done.* Instead, we say, *My will be done,* or, if we're willing to go a step further, we'll say, "Lord, Thy will be done, but let me tell Thee what Thy will is!"

Well, that doesn't work either. It says here in Ephesians "...knowing what the will of the Lord is." Well, I'm no mind reader. I can't even tell you what *your* will is, let alone with God's will is. He's got to reveal that through His word. And yes, there are other ways He reveals it too: Tongues and interpretation, prophecy, dreams, visions. And as long as they match up with the word of God, they can be revelations of His will for us.

We have to be open to those things: Willing to hear, willing to see. Not so much with the ears and the eyes, but with the heart... with the heart.

If we can know what the will of God is for our life, for our ministry, for the church, for the whole body of Christ... If we can know that, and be willing to do that, we can win back every wasted minute we ever had in our lives. We can win back all the time we've lost. And it's every bit as good as turning back the clock, and we won't have to live those nasty years over again.

You see, one disadvantage of turning back the clock and doing it all over again would be we're that much further from the coming of the Lord. I don't want to go back that far from it. I want Him to come. And yet, I want to redeem the time. I want to undo all the wasted years. I want a chance to make it right.

The key then is in walking wisely, and knowing the will of the Lord: To walk as a wise man and not as a fool. The word of God says, "The fool says in his heart: There is no God." That's easy for us to understand. The atheist is a fool because he says there's no God. And yet, sometimes in the life of Christians, their very life says there is no God, because of the way they live it. When a Christian lives according to *my will be done,* they're living like an atheist, because their life is saying, *There is no God.* They've made themselves the highest authority, and we can't do that. That's not the life of a Christian; that's the life of a fool.

You know, *fool* isn't a word you throw around lightly. That's a very dangerous word. Very dangerous. Don't ever call anybody a fool. That's a dangerous word. A Brother in the church, years ago, was kidding around with me. He was kind of new in the church, and we used to call each other silly names and stuff. We'd kid around. But he called me a fool one day, and he was very taken aback when he saw the change in me, how my facial expression changed, and how shocked I was. And he said, "What's the matter?" I said, "Don't ever call anybody a fool." Don't ever call anybody a fool. That's a very powerful word. We think it's a very light word, but it's a powerful word. The scripture says the one who calls his brother a fool is in danger of hell fire.

Well, why? What's so special about a fool? It's not the same simply as being dumb or stupid. A fool lives his life as if there is no God. A fool puts himself in the driver's seat, and leaves God out in the trunk, if in the car at all. A fool lives according to *my will be done,* and a fool has no chance of redeeming the lost years, but instead is busy making more lost years, wasting more time.

Who builds his house on the sand? The wise man builds his house on the rock, on the will of God, and walks according to the will of God. *Lord, what do you want me to do? Lord, where do you want me to go? Lord, show me what I should do today.*

I love reading through the book of Acts to watch the the apostles following the direction of the Holy Ghost. One place that said "We just we tried to go into such and such a place." They had fully intended to go there. That was on their agenda. *We're going there!* But it said the Holy Ghost would not allow us. Well, what did He do? Put up a roadblock? No, He just said, "Don't go."

And they were in tune enough with the Spirit of God to feel that, to know that, to hear that. And they were humble enough to obey and not go. They could have argued with Him. *"But God, those people need the gospel too!"* Well, sure they did. But it wasn't time. Someplace else needed it more. And so God spoke to them in a dream and showed them a man of Macedonia who said "Come over and help us!" And they knew that's where God wanted them to go. They were willing to go where God said to go, and not go where God said not to go.

And then there were some that were even more yielded than that, like Philip. God didn't even have to say go. God was able to pick him up and put him where he wanted him, because Philip was yielded enough that he didn't have to ask *What's Thy will?* He was already surrendered to it, so God could just do it. That's the perfect ideal. That's what I really want to see. That's what I want my life, that I don't have to say "God, where should I go?" I want to *find* myself there.

Philip was *found* at Azotus. Why? Because God wanted Philip at Azotus. God wanted him there, and He was able to put him there. God wanted Peter outside the prison, so He put him there. Peter thought he was having a vision or dreaming. It wasn't until he was outside the prison, in the street, all by himself, that it suddenly hit him: *Hey, this really happened!* How did it happen? He didn't stand there trying to figure out how it happened. He didn't go back to the prison and say, "Is my cell still locked?" He went on his way to where the church folks were praying, because he knew God had set him free. He knew it must be God's will for him to be on the outside of the prison. After all, it was God's will that got him on the inside of it, in the first place, for being willing to obey the will of God.

But you can't obey it till you know it. That's the hardest part, knowing the will of God. Don't ever deviate from this Book, folks. Don't ever deviate from it. If you think you've got a revelation from God, I don't care if it comes with trumpets and angels and stars falling all over the place and a marching band, and a chorus rising up out of nowhere and singing it to you. If it's not in the word of God, if it contradicts this, it's not from God. It's not. But if it matches up with this, then go with it.

You know, it's saddens me when I watch Christians who are praying for something, because they want to do something. And they're praying and praying and praying. But what they are praying that God would allow them to do is expressly forbidden in [the Bible.] And I keep thinking, why are you wasting your time and God's time? God's not going to change His word for us. He can't. It's forever settled in heaven. Forever settled in heaven! And yet, these are Christian people that I've seen do this.

And I think we all fall into this sometimes. God, I want this so much, please let me do this. I want to do this, I want to do this, I want to do this. But the word says don't do it. He's not going to give you permission. Well, they pray that often enough and long enough till the they finally think God gave them permission. They talk themselves into it. *Well, **of course** it's the will of God: I prayed for six weeks asking to be allowed to do it!* But God's word said don't, and He won't contradict His word. He won't contradict His word.

I told a brother that one time, because he was trying to place his personal revelations on par with the word of God. And I said, "God has magnified His word even above His name." And he said to me, "But God has not magnified His word above His Spirit." And he felt that's where the revelations were coming from. Then we'll have God's word and God's Spirit disagreeing with each other. That tells me that we've got a house divided, and a house divided against itself cannot stand. No, the word of God and the Spirit of God will not contradict each other. So if there's a spirit telling you something and it contradicts [the Bible], it's not the Spirit of God. It's not the Spirit of God! It's what we call a lying spirit. They come around now and then.

There were times in the scripture when God deliberately wanted to deceive somebody. It was necessary because they fell into so much sin it didn't much matter anyway. And God asked one time, "Now, how are we going to do this?" And this one particular spirit stepped forward and said. "I'll do it." And God said, "How?" The spirit said, "I will be a lying spirit in the mouth of his prophets, and I'll go to deceive the king through his prophets by lying to them."

And a lying spirit comes along and whisper something to you, and tells you something that doesn't match up with the word of God, but acts like it's from God. They know how to say *Thus saith the Lord.*

You have a word from the Lord? Don't deviate from the Book. Don't deviate from the road plan. You follow this pattern and you'll make it. You search the word for His will. Pray about His will. Keep your eyes and ears, these eyes and ears, the ones in your heart, keep those open. Keep them functioning. Listen to Him and obey Him.

You can redeem the time, whether you've wasted days, months, years or decades. It doesn't matter if you've wasted 99% of your life. That could be true with any of us: We don't know if we could die tomorrow. We could have wasted 99% of our life, and yet, in that 1% that's left, if we will walk wisely, knowing what His will is and doing it, we can redeem that 99%. We can win it back. We can undo the damage we've done. And we can make a difference for the kingdom. There's a chance to do it. And I have to be honest and say if I didn't, I would be a fool. I spent too many years walking as a fool. I want to walk in a little bit of wisdom now. Wisely, circumspectly, as Paul said, as wise, understanding what the will of the Lord is.

One of the scriptures I use a lot because I love it is Proverbs 23:23. *Buy the truth and sell it not...* The second half of that is *also wisdom and instruction and understanding.* Understanding what the will of the Lord is: Knowing it, understanding it. I want to do that, because if I do, if I'm willing to understand the will of God, and live according to it, and walk in that wisdom, then and all

160

those years that I wasted, all those opportunities that I lost, all that time that I just let fall through my fingers, I can redeem it, and I can still do something for the kingdom of God by redeeming the days, redeeming the time. All those years! Redeeming the time, because the days are evil. Not necessarily the present ones or the ones to come, but the days I lived before were evil. I need to redeem them. I need to redeem them.

It's not a complicated thing, but it's a powerful thing. It's so simple that we could almost overlook it. And yet, there it is a chance to regain what was lost, a chance to redeem wasted years. No point crying over them. Let's redeem them! Let's redeem them! Hallelujah!

Lord Jesus, help us to know Your will, to see and understand, to believe and obey, to walk in Your wisdom and not our own, to follow You, and redeem the time that we've wasted. For the sake of Your kingdom, for the sake of all those who still have not heard, for the sake of the lost, help us to redeem the years that we've wasted, to reclaim them as time spent for the kingdom.

Remember Me

1-15-95

Lighthouse Apostolic Church

Schenectady, New York

I'm going to preach a sermon in two parts. Starting off first in Genesis chapter 3. This is actually a message I preached many years ago, and the other night it was on my heart again, so I decided I'm going to preach it again. Genesis chapter 3 and verse 19:

In the sweat of thy face shalt thou eat bread, till thou return unto the ground; for out of it wast thou taken: for dust thou art, and unto dust shalt thou return.

Turning now to the book of Nehemiah, chapter 5. I love reading the reading the book of Nehemiah, also Ezra. I love reading about restoration. Restoration is a theme that is very close to my heart, and both of those books are concerned with the restoration of Jerusalem. One mentions that the that the work was completed because the people had a mind to work. And someday, God willing, they'll to be able to say that about the kingdom of God: The work was completed because the people had a mind to work. Hallelujah!

Nehemiah, chapter 5, and I'm going to read the last verse of the chapter, verse 19:

Think upon me, my God, for good, according to all that I have done for this people.

In the same book, chapter 13, verse 31, and I'm going to read only the last sentence of the verse:

Remember me, O my God, for good.

I have other scriptures we are going to read afterwards, but I want to preach the first half of the message from these. There is something about the third chapter of Genesis that has always fascinated me. The downfall of the human race, and the curses that were placed by God in the garden: the curse upon the serpent, the curse upon the woman, and the curse upon the ground for Adam's sake. And all those things were terrible, and the words of God came to pass, because He had told them that they would die if they ate from that tree. And spiritually, they died that day, and all their descendants died with them. And that was certainly a terrible thing. There's no question about it, it was shocking. Adam and Eve had never had to deal with the punishment of God before. This was an aspect of God they'd never seen. In the past, they had walked with Him in the garden. They had a good relationship. They were on good terms with their Creator. And they'd never seen this side of Him before, because they'd never disobeyed Him before.

And the punishments came to pass, the curse that was placed, and I know that they were devastated by what had happened, that they'd lost favor with God. So much had happened in just one day: Their eyes were opened and they saw good from evil. They knew for the first time that they were naked, and they were ashamed, not just that God should see them, but that they should see each other. So much had happened, and then the curses. But something that was far more terrible than the new knowledge they just obtained, and the curses that God had placed on them: To me, I think the most terrible thing was what he told them in verse 19, because there was something there that they had not realized. Up until this point, Adam and Eve were the rulers of their world. They had dominion over all the animals. They were in charge. They were important. They had position there. They had something that no other creature on Earth had: They had the special favor of God. They were created in His image, and the animals weren't. They were special! They were important! And there was something in all of that they never realized, and that was what God told them in verse 19: *You're dust, and you will return to dust. You will return to the ground, because I took you out of it.* I don't think they knew that! I don't think they understood that before, that they were created from dust. They hadn't seen it. Adam certainly didn't witness his own creation. None of us remembers our own birth, do we? Do you remember they day you were born? No, we just don't remember that. We know basically what happened. They told us, more or less. We know the story of how babies are born. Adam didn't witness his own creation, so he didn't know he was created from the dust of the earth. His wife was created from his rib, but he didn't even remember that, because he was sound asleep when she was created. He didn't see that either.

To them, they thought the serpent was telling the truth when he told them that they would be like God, because, in a way they thought they already were like God. They were omnipotent! They could not be defeated! They were important and powerful and strong, and God told them 'You're nothing but dirt! You will return unto the earth, because you are dust, and you will return to dust.'

There's something that the Catholic Church does every year on Ash Wednesday which is kind of interesting. They take some ashes made from burnt palm, and they smear it on the head of the people, and with each person that the priest smears them on, he says to them, "Remember man that you are dust, and unto dust you shall return." I'm not overly fond of the rituals of the Catholic church, but there's something profound in that, and that's a reminder that we do need, especially when we start to think we're too important, or indispensable, or the center of the universe. We're dust... and unto dust we shall return. If it's necessary to smear ashes on our head once a year to remember that, maybe we ought to do it, if that's what it takes remember. And that, I think, was the most awful part of what happened that day. Their bubble was burst. Their dream was shattered. Their illusion of who they were was destroyed. And they learned the awful truth of what death mean, that this flesh that we hold so important would no longer exist, and would just decay and turn to dust. They'd never seen death before.

Lest they should lose sight of it, God killed animals that same day to pay for their sin, and forced them to wear the skins of those animals, lest they should forget that something had to die because of sin.

It's not recorded here in Scripture, but it's kind of between the lines, and if you listen carefully, you can hear it: the cry of Adam and Eve when God told them that they were dust, and that they would return to dust. *"My God, don't forget me! Don't forget who I am!"* There is something inside each one of us that has come right from that very moment, that we don't want to be forgotten, that even if we must return to dust, there must be a way that we can continue, in people's minds.

I love to read about ancient Egypt and all the beautiful tombs that they built for their pharaohs so that they could live on through eternity. Everybody knows the names of the ancient pharaohs, even though they've been dead for thousands of years, because their tombs stand as monuments so that no one will ever forget. We don't forget them because we see their tombs, the pyramids, the underground tombs. We don't forget because they left something behind, so they wouldn't be forgotten. And I don't think it's carved anywhere in the tombs, or written in the hieroglyphics, but the message nevertheless is there, just as it was in the Garden of Eden: *My God, don't forget me! When I'm dust, when there's nothing left, don't forget who I was! Somebody please remember me!*

And we go through the cemeteries, and there are beautiful mausoleums with the family name on there. And then there are stones with information about the dead people carved on them. I remember a stone that I saw when I was in high school. It was a high school girl who died, and they put her picture on the tombstone so that anyone who would pass by would know who she was. They could see not only her name, but also her face, so that nobody would ever forget who she was, so that she would be remembered.

There's a terrible fear that was born in Genesis 3:19, that has been passed on to every one of us, when Adam and Eve discovered that they were dust and would not exist forever, would not live forever. And that is the fear that we would be forgotten, that we would no longer be. Nehemiah said it twice; we read the scriptures, that he was afraid that God would forget him: Remember me, my God, for good. Don't forget me and the things that I've done. Remember me! He closed the book with those words: Remember me, my God!

If we could only hear the tones of voice of people in the scriptures... Sometimes it's hard because we only have the printed word, and Nehemiah is long dead. We can't hear the way he said that, but I think there was a note of despair in his voice: the fear that he would be forgotten, the fear that no one would remember what he'd done, that the name of Nehemiah would be wiped off the earth... Just as Adam was afraid, and the Pharaohs were afraid, and the family of that high school girl who died was afraid. They're all afraid that the names will cease to exist and that nobody will remember. Somebody remember me! Somebody remember me!

That's the first half of the message: *Remember me!* We're turning to the book of Isaiah for the second half of the message. Isaiah chapter 49, beginning at verse 14:

But Zion said, The Lord hath forsaken me, and my Lord hath forgotten me. Can a woman forget her sucking child, that she should not have compassion on the son of her womb? Yea, they may forget, yet will I not forget thee. Behold, I have graven thee upon the palms of my hands; thy walls are continually before me.

I'm turning to the book of Hebrews, chapter 13, verse 5, just the last part of the verse:

I will never leave thee, nor forsake thee.

The cry of the human heart, the cry of the human spirit does not fall upon deaf ears. The scripture tells us that the eyes of the Lord roam to and fro throughout the earth, so that there's nothing hidden from Him. He sees everything. I have to believe, then, that His ears do the same thing; that there's nothing whispered in secret that God doesn't hear, that there's no cry in the night that God doesn't know about. He knows if a sparrow falls from the sky. He knows if a hair falls from your head. He knows the cry of the human heart. I believe He heard it there in Genesis, even though Adam and Eve didn't say it: He heard the cry of *"Remember me!"* He heard the cry of it. He heard the cry of Zion, who thought that God had forgotten her. And He asked, "Is it possible that a woman would forget her nursing child?" And then He acknowledged, "Yes, it's possible, and yet, I won't forget you." The bond was even closer than that of a woman and her nursing child! That's about as close as you can get. And yet, the bond between Him and His people is even closer! He said, "I have carved you on the palms of My hands. Your walls are ever before Me." Everywhere He turned, in front of His eyes were His people. He could not possibly forget, because we were before Him at all times. He said, "I will never leave you nor forsake you." We will not be forgotten! We won't be forgotten! It doesn't matter, the fact that this old body is dust. It doesn't matter that it may return to dust. It doesn't matter, because that wasn't the end of it all. That wasn't the end of it. There was a remembrance. Even after death, He still knows... He still knows who we are.

At the end of all time, death and hell give up their dead. The sea gives up the dead, and all of them stand before God for judgment. He still knows who they are! Not one of them has been forgotten. No one has been forgotten. Death has no more power!

One of my favorite stories from the whole Bible is the story of Lazarus. To me, that is one of the most powerful examples of the love of God. Jesus wept at the tomb of Lazarus. And the sister of Lazarus said to Him, "Lord, if You'd only been here, my brother would not have died." She knew that Jesus had the power to heal the sick. But there was something she hadn't quite learned yet. "Your brother will live again." "Oh, I know, Lord. At the resurrection, at the end, he will rise again." She understood that up here [in her mind]. And the words that Jesus spoke to her were some of the most powerful anywhere in the scripture: "I *am* the resurrection, and the life." *I AM THE RESURRECTION AND THE LIFE!* And He walked up to the tomb of that dead man who had been there for days, in that heat, decaying, and told him, "Come out!" And he did. Not forgotten, not left to decay, not left just to turn to dust. Remembered... and Restored.

Death isn't the end anymore. It's not the end. It doesn't matter if this old body collapses in a heap somewhere, and they put it in a box and stick it in the earth. It doesn't matter if that old box caves in. My family has always been very poor, at least in the past three generations. We have one burial plot that we have been using since the 1930s [before vaults were required]. It's just one plot, meant for one person, and we keep putting people in it. The last time was just about four years ago, when my Aunt S. died. They did a sonogram of the grave, and said, yes, she could go in there because the grave had "settled." And I said to the woman from the cemetery, "Is that a polite way of saying that the caskets have all collapsed on top of each other?" And she said, "Yes." (Some years later, her daughter was buried in the very same

167

plot.) It doesn't matter though! It doesn't matter! Let the casket collapse! Let worms crawl in! I don't care! It doesn't matter! Because those ears that have decayed and turned to dust and disappeared entirely are going to hear a sound someday of a trumpet, and a voice that says, "*Arise, My love, My fair one, and come away!*" He still remembers me!

Not only does He still remember, but He still loves. The grave couldn't take away that love; it could not separate us. And He comes to claim His own. He wept when Lazarus died. And yet, He knows when everyone every one of us falls, when one of us becomes ill, or dies. He knows. And I imagine He weeps, because He loves us, too. For every trial that we face, for every obstacle, for every time we stumble, I think He cries for us. He cried over the city of Jerusalem that wouldn't give two cents for Him. How more for those who love Him, for those who know who He is and look for His return?

Adam! You need to know this! He won't forget you! Eve! Do you hear me? He's not going to forget! Nehemiah! He has remembered! Zion! He cannot forget you: You're carved on the palms of his hands! There's no way He can escape from us, because every time He turns around, there we are, and He remembers us, that He loves us! His people! It says it so many times in the scripture, that He will see say "It is my people!" and we will say, "It is the Lord; He's our God!"

Recognition! Remembrance! *Yes, I remember you! You're My people!* And, *Yes, Lord, we remember You! You're our God!* I don't want to forget, and I know He won't. Our souls cry out in the night, "Lord, remember me!" And He answers back, "I cannot forget you. I cannot forget you." At the times when we feel at our lowest and our most alone, we need to remember: He's carved us on the palms of His hands. He cannot forget forget us! He cannot forget us! We're fond of saying that the only things God can't do are lie and fail, but there's another thing He cannot do: He cannot forget His people, because love never fails, and that love is just too powerful, and it will not let Him forget.

Did you ever see somebody walk down the street with his girlfriend's name tattooed on his arm, or 'Mom' or something like that? He can't forget! My father and mother have been divorced since the early 1960s, but Dad's got my mother's name tattooed on his arm. Not only can't he forget, his second wife can't! He won't forget. The love that he had for my mother drove him to have her name written on his arm. The love that God has for us moved Him to carve us on His hands! That's a lot more than a tattoo! It's not a matter of just putting it in ink that can be removed. He carved us on the palm of His hand! That scar will be there forever! In fact, He's got one on each hand: scars to help Him remember us. And when that trumpet blows, and that voice calls, and we rise up to meet Him in the air, whether we were among the dead in Christ who go first, or those of us who remain and are caught up afterwards, there's not going to be any problem of recognition. He's going to know who we are right away. Yes, it's My people! It's My people! And we can say, Yes, this is our God! He has come! We have waited for Him, and He has come to save us! This is the Lord! We waited for Him! We will rejoice and be glad in His salvation!

Dead and decayed in the ground, it doesn't matter. Locked in a tomb three days and rotting, it doesn't matter. Collapsed underneath three or four other caskets, it doesn't matter. Burned in an oven and turned to ashes and scattered to the wind, and it doesn't matter. The ears will hear the sound, because He remembers us. He remembers us. Remember me, O my God! *I cannot forget you, My people!* Hallelujah!

Lord Jesus, thank You for the assurance that we are not forgotten! We are not forsaken, we are not alone. And that no matter what happens to us, where we go, where we wind up, we are not forgotten, and we will live again. Death can't hold us, because You have the keys of hell and of death. It couldn't hold You, and now it cannot hold us. We are not forgotten! Thank You, Jesus! Hallelujah! Thank the Lord!

Resurrection

1st Corinthians chapter 15, and beginning at verse 12:

Now if Christ be preached that he rose from the dead, how say some among you that there is no resurrection of the dead?

But if there be no resurrection of the dead, then is Christ not risen:

And if Christ be not risen, then is our preaching vain, and your faith is also vain.

Yea, and we are found false witnesses of God; because we have testified of God that he raised up Christ: whom he raised not up, if so be that the dead rise not.

For if the dead rise not, then is not Christ raised:

And if Christ be not raised, your faith is vain; ye are yet in your sins.

Then they also which are fallen asleep in Christ are perished.

If in this life only we have hope in Christ, we are of all men most miserable.

But now is Christ risen from the dead, and become the firstfruits of them that slept.

For since by man came death, by man came also the resurrection of the dead.

For as in Adam all die, even so in Christ shall all be made alive.

Hallelujah! I think we've probably all heard people who say they don't really believe that Jesus rose from the dead. Or some will say, well, He rose, but it wasn't a physical rising; it was only a spiritual rising. There are religions the preach that He did not physically rise. But they, at least, believe in a spiritual resurrection. But there are many people who say that He just didn't rise at all, and they have all sorts of theories that His disciples smuggled Him away during the night, or that He wasn't really dead, that He was just kind of in shock, and revived in the tomb and and walked away. They have all sorts of

170

theories built up, that He married Mary Magdalene, and settle down, raised a family.

And we can excuse people who don't know the power of God, who are not Christians, who say things like that, because they just don't know any better, but it becomes a frightening thing when people who profess to know God deny the resurrection. And this is somewhat the situation that Paul ran into in the Corinthian Church.

We've probably all heard of the Pharisees and the Sadducees. These were the two religious groups in the time of Jesus. And generally, when we speak of Pharisees, we think of hypocrites. But actually, what the Pharisees were all about was their particular doctrine in regard to the Jewish religion, which was the opposite of what the Sadducees believed. The Pharisees believed in angels, they believed in spirits, and they believed that the dead would some day be raised up. The Sadducees didn't believe in any of that. They didn't believe in angels, they didn't believe in spirits, and they didn't believe that the dead would ever rise. If you want an easy way to remember which is which: if I didn't believe in the resurrection of the dead, I'd be 'sad, you see.'

The doctrine of the Pharisees and the doctrine of the Sadducees had found their way even into the Gentile churches such as Corinth. And so within the Corinthian Church we had Pharisees, who believed that the dead would rise, and Sadducees, who said the dead would not rise.

Now Paul was a Pharisee. He believed in the resurrection of the dead. Jesus was also doctrinally a Pharisee and believed in the resurrection of the dead. The division between the Pharisees and Sadducees was something that the early church often took advantage of. When a Jewish mob cornered Paul, they were trying to accuse him of speaking blasphemy. He took advantage of the fact that the group was divided between Pharisees and Sadducees and he started an argument with them on the resurrection of the dead. They started fighting each other and they didn't fight him anymore.

And Jesus did similar things like that, he would say to the Sadducees, "You call your God *the God of Abraham, Isaac, and Jacob.* Is He the God of the dead, or is He the God of the living?" They had to rethink their position on the resurrection. If Abraham, Isaac and Jacob were just perished, and were never going to rise again, then how could God be the God of Abraham, Isaac, and Jacob? If there was no Abraham Isaac and Jacob anymore, how could He be their God?

But the most significant thing that Paul pointed out to the Corinthian Church was that if they chose not to believe in a literal resurrection of the dead, that meant Jesus never rose from the dead. What they were believing was undermining their entire faith by denying the resurrection of Jesus. If Jesus didn't rise from the dead, your faith is in vain: You're still in your sins. If our faith in Jesus is only for this life now, we're more miserable than the people out there who have never heard of Him. We will be the most miserable of all people if Jesus didn't rise from the dead.

We talked about this, I think about two weeks ago, a little bit about the resurrection, and how impossible it would have been for the disciples to fake the resurrection, to steal the body away. You know that the tomb was sealed, and that there was a guard outside. Now, it's not a simple matter of bribing guards, like you might be able to do today, because in the Roman Empire, if a prisoner escaped, the person in charge of keeping that prisoner was put to death. And therefore, those soldiers, if they had allowed themselves to be bribed, would have had to surrender their lives. They were not about to let anybody steal that body away. They made the tomb extra secure because they remembered that Jesus had said He would rise. And they were sure that His followers would try to take him out of the tomb.

Was he really dead? You know, He only hung on the cross for a few hours. Prisoners usually hung for days before they died. Passover was coming, and they didn't want those bodies hanging on the cross during the holiday. So they had the soldiers break the legs of the prisoners that were still alive on the crosses. When their legs were broken, they could no longer push themselves up to get a breath of air. You see, when you're hanging on a cross, all your weight is on your diaphragm. If you want to breathe, you have to push yourself up with your legs to get a breath. Once their legs were broken, they would suffocate.

The soldiers came to Jesus and saw that He was already dead. Well, how could that be? His injuries were not severe enough to kill Him. Well, this is very simple: He said, "I lay My life down." He said, "Nobody has the power to take it from Me. I lay it down and I pick it up again." He gave up the ghost; He surrendered His life of His own will. Even Pilate was amazed that He was dead. When Joseph of Arimathea came to Pilate and asked for the body of Jesus, Pilate was surprised to hear that He was dead already. He wasn't going to take Joseph's word for it, even though Joseph was a member of the Sanhedrin, a higher Jewish religious leader. He was not going to take Joseph's word for it. He sent for the centurion who was in charge of the crucifixion and asked, "Is he dead already? How long has he been dead?" They were amazed that He was dead, but the Centurion verified that Jesus was dead. Absolutely dead.

And they sealed Him in that tomb. But it couldn't hold Him. Couldn't keep Him in there.

Not only is there a resurrection, but there was something about it that they had overlooked, that He had tried to tell them all during His ministry on earth. During the three years that He walked around in Galilee and Judea, telling them about the kingdom of God, they had overlooked something about the resurrection.

His friend Lazarus was sick. They sent word that Lazarus was sick, and asked if Jesus would come and heal him. They knew He could, because He healed so many others. And yet, Jesus didn't seem to be in any hurry to get to Bethany to the house of Lazarus and his sisters, Mary and Martha. He was in no hurry. He stopped to heal someone else along the way, and He went very slowly. The apostles were wondering why, and they asked Him about it. He said, "Oh, Lazarus is asleep." And they said, "Oh, well if he's sleeping, then maybe he's getting better!" But Jesus said, "No, Lazarus is dead."

He's dead. There was no need to hurry. Lazarus was dead by the time Jesus got to Bethany. He had been in the tomb for three days already, sealed in there. And his sisters came out to meet Jesus and each said, "Lord, if You'd only been here, my brother wouldn't have died."

It was almost like a rebuke! *Why did You take so long? You knew he was sick. You could have stopped this from happening.*

And Jesus said,"Your brother will rise again." Well, they'd been trained up in the teachings of the Pharisees. They knew. *Oh yes, at the resurrection. At the last day, my brother will rise.* Again, that's not a lot of comfort. When their brother is laying in the tomb, that wasn't what they wanted to hear.

This was not going the way they had planned it. They had expected that Jesus would get there before their brother died, and would heal him, and everybody would have lived happily ever after. Instead, He delayed His coming, and waited until Lazarus had been dead a few days, and then showed up. And what did He offer? His hopes, some reference to the teaching of the Pharisees: Your brother will rise again. Yeah, we know that, Lord, we know, we know: In the resurrection, at the last day.

And Jesus spoke to the sisters of Lazarus some of the most powerful words in the scripture: ***I am the resurrection and the life! The one who believes in Me will never die.*** Never die! "Do you believe this?" The sister of Lazarus said, "Yes, I do. I believe that You're the Messiah!" If He said it, it must be true. She still didn't know what it meant, but she was willing to accept it if He said it. You've seen those bumper stickers that say *God said it. I believe it. That settles it.* It was kind of like that. Jesus said it, and she believed it, even though she did not understand it.

And Jesus asked them to show Him the tomb. So they took Him to the place where they had the tomb sealed up. And He saw the people standing there, a whole crowd of people there who had come to be with Mary and Martha in their sorrow. He said, "Roll that stone away!" And one of the sisters said, "Lord, he's been in there a few days. It's going to stink!" She was quite blunt about it: He's going to smell!

They didn't embalm the dead. They washed them, perhaps anointed with some oil or perfume, and that was the best they could do. But it was a hot climate, you know. They had to get them into a tomb and seal them up. It's going to stink!

And Jesus said, "Didn't I tell you that if you'd only believe, you'd see the power of God?" It comes down to this again: Jesus said it, you'd better believe it. And so they rolled that stone away. It says here that Jesus cried. He cried, and the people standing by said, "See how much He loved him?" I'm not sure that that's the reason Jesus was crying. Maybe it was really because after all this time that He been walking around preaching to these people, they still didn't have a clue of what He was all about, who He was, why He was there, and because they didn't have the faith that they should have had, because they didn't understand who He was.

And so He had to demonstrate who He was, to prove it to them, and He said, "Lazarus! Come out of there!" And he did, because Jesus **IS** the resurrection. It's not a future event that you have to wait for. He **was** the resurrection. He **is** the resurrection.

In the first chapter of the Book of Revelation, Jesus appeared to John. John wasn't quite sure who He was, so Jesus identified Himself by saying, *"I am He that liveth and was dead. Now, I am alive forevermore. I have the keys of hell and of death."* The last possible victory was over death, and He won it because He was the resurrection, He was the life.

Death couldn't hold Lazarus in that tomb. And because He was the resurrection, death couldn't hold a lot of other people. There was a man whose daughter was very ill. He went to find Jesus, and said, "My daughter is dying. Will you come and heal her?" And Jesus said, "Yes." But again, He didn't hurry. And finally, some men came from from the man's house and said, "Don't bother the teacher any more. Your daughter is dead." Jesus told him, "Don't worry; just keep believing." They got to the house and there's this girl, twelve or thirteen years old, lying on the bed. They'd already washed her and prepared her for burial. She was dead. Everybody was standing around her, crying and mourning. Jesus walks in and says, "She's not dead. She's asleep!"

Excuse us? She's what? She's asleep? And they laughed. They ridiculed Him because He couldn't tell the difference between dead and asleep. But it wasn't Jesus who couldn't tell the difference. It was them, because to Jesus, death was nothing more than sleep, and He put them all outside except for the parents, and he took the little girl by the hand and said, "Little girl, get up." She got up!

In the city of Nain, He passed by a funeral procession and there was an old woman there whose only son had died. He was her sole source of support. Without her son, she would have had to resort to begging to stay alive. Her son was all she had. And Jesus walked up to the bier that they were carrying the young man on, and He took him by the hand and raised him up. and gave him back to his mother.

Death had no more power. It's something we overlook sometimes. At Easter and Passover, we talk about the resurrection. We know that there was a great earthquake when Jesus died. It tells us also that the tombs of many of the saints opened up at the moment that Jesus died. The rocks rolled away from those tombs. And three days later, when Jesus rose, so did many of those people! Many of the Old Testament saints rose up when Jesus did, and it said they appeared to many, because death couldn't hold them anymore either.

I'll tell you what, the devil thought he had this thing all sewed up. He thought he had the victory. He'd had all the people who had ever lived locked up in death... secure. And then, finally, the One that God sends to straighten the whole thing out, the Messiah, the devil killed Him too, and he's got Him too! Except the next thing you know, Jesus is having a victory party and leading them all out, and there wasn't a single thing the devil could do about it! There wasn't anything he could do about it anymore!

Death had no more victory! It lost its sting! There was nothing that anybody could do about it. He was the resurrection! He was the life!

It tells me here that if the princes of this world... speaking in the spiritual sense, the devils... if they had known anything about this, they never would have crucified Him because if He hadn't died, He couldn't rise and conquer death! But they didn't know. They didn't know.

What incredible power! The stone rolled away, soldiers fleeing in horror, or falling as dead men. Mary Magdalene comes and looks into the tomb. Brother Mark, you quoted it a couple of weeks ago during service: **Why do you look for the living among the dead?** Angels sitting in there, two of them: *He's not here. He got up and He walked out.*

He's not dead. There's no more death, no such thing anymore. Oh, this old body may fall to the ground, and it may crumble into dust. But it rises again, because the death to sin, repentance, is the only death a Christian should ever see. That's the only death.

They had a lot of dissension in the early church about what was going to happen to the dead. When they died, was that the end of it? Would they just cease to exist? How are they all going to live forever with God? They didn't know. And so Paul told them. He wrote to the Thessalonian church, because he wanted them to understand that because Jesus rose, we rise also.

He told them that those of us who were still alive and remaining when Jesus returned for His church would not go ahead of those who had already died, that those who had died would rise first. The Lord will descend from heaven with a shout, and the voice of the archangel, and the trumpet of God, and the dead in Christ will rise. And then we who are alive and remain will be caught up with them to meet the Lord in the air. And he said, that's how we will always be with the Lord. He said, "Comfort each other with those words."

And it is a comfort to know that it doesn't matter whether I'm alive or dead physically when He comes, because I've got a spiritual life that can't end. This old corruptible body.... Corruptible.... That's an old word for something that will decay... will be exchanged for one that will never decay, just as His was when He arose.

Oh yeah, they could still touch Him. He was still physical. He said that they could see that He had flesh and bones. A spirit doesn't have those things. This is really Me, He was telling them: A physical resurrection, but a change, as the old body that could decay changes into one that will never decay, that will never grow old.

That sounds like good news to me. Paul said, "Comfort one another with these words." That's a comfort. Death was the thing people feared most, and often, it still is. People are terrified of dying, because they can't see what's on the other side of it. Well, I've got the word of One who's been there and come back. I have nothing to be afraid of, because I'll come back too: Because He lives, we live also!

That's part of the heritage, the birthright, of the church. Don't let anybody steal that from you. Don't let anybody diminish the power of the story of the resurrection, because it's truth! Don't let them tell you it wasn't a physical resurrection! Don't let them tell you the dead don't rise! People who say that the dead don't rise lose all their faith, because there's nothing left to base it on. Because that means that Jesus didn't rise. And if Jesus didn't rise, there's no hope for any of us. But Jesus rose and we do too. Hallelujah!

Death has no more power. It has been swallowed up in victory! Swallowed up in victory! It has no more power. It's lost it forever. Hallelujah! Thank the Lord!

Paul spoke about the change. He said, *"I show you a mystery: We shall not all sleep, but we shall all be changed. In a moment, in the twinkling of an eye, at the last trump, for the trumpet shall sound, and the dead shall be raised incorruptible, and we shall be changed. This corruptible must put on incorruption. This mortal must put on immortality. So when this corruptible shall have put on incorruption, and this mortal shall have put on immortality, then shall be brought to pass the saying that is written: Death is swallowed up in victory. Death, where is thy sting? Grave, where is thy victory? The sting of death is sin, and the strength of sin is the Law. Thanks be to God, which gives us the victory through our Lord Jesus Christ. Therefore, my beloved brethren, be steadfast, unmovable, always abounding in the work of the Lord, forasmuch as you know that your labor is not in vain."* Hallelujah!

One last word from Paul: *"The last enemy that shall be destroyed is death."* And it seems to me that the death knell for death is already ringing! He destroyed it, just as it says, He led captivity captive. He killed death and it has no more power. Hallelujah!

You know, the resurrection is not something we should celebrate just one day a year. Rather, it's something that should live in us every day of the year. It's *not* a once-a-year affair, but it's something that we need to be renewed in every day. Because He rose, we live. We live every day. Therefore, He is risen every day. Hallelujah! Thank the Lord!

I'm not afraid to say when it comes to doctrine, I'm a Pharisee. Yes, I believe in angels. Yes, I believe in spirits, and most importantly, I believe in the resurrection of the Dead! Amen! Hallelujah! Hallelujah! Thank the Lord! He lives! He lives! Hallelujah!

Lord Jesus, we thank you for the knowledge of Your resurrection that has given us the power over death, so that just as You did, we can walk up to the lifeless bodies and say "Get up!" Because in Your name, we can do anything, and nothing is impossible if we believe. We thank You for the promise that if this old mortal body shall fall and die, it shall rise again, and what was mortal shall become immortal, what was corruptible shall become incorruptible, and we who were once under the curse of death shall live forever by Your power. We thank You for this, Lord. Don't ever let us lose sight of it. In the name of Jesus. Amen.

Thank the Lord. Thank you, Jesus. Hallelujah! The Lord is good!

The Ark of God is Taken

We're taking a story from the book of 1st Samuel. We're going back to the time when Eli was the High Priest over Israel and we find that Eli's sons, Hophni and Phineas, were engaged in temple prostitution in the doorway of the Tabernacle of the congregation. Temple prostitution was originally found in the worship of the Babylonian fertility goddess, and had been adopted by many other nations, using different names for the goddess. But the way it worked was the same: In the temple of the goddess, men and women lived and worked as prostitutes. Unlike ordinary prostitution, money wasn't paid to the prostitutes, but was paid into the temple treasury. Both men and women would come to the temple and have sex with one of the prostitutes as a form of worship. Because of the association with fertility, temple prostitution was always heterosexual, that is, male worshipers with female prostitutes, and vice versa. In the Law of Moses, temple prostitution was forbidden to the people of Israel.

And yet, we will see today that Israel not only engaged in temple prostitution, but it was the sons of the High Priest, who were themselves priests, who were engaged in it. We're reading from the book of 1st Samuel, chapter 2, verses 22 through 25.

Now Eli was very old, and heard all that his sons did unto all Israel; and how they lay with the women that assembled at the door of the tabernacle of the congregation. And he said unto them, Why do ye such things? for I hear of your evil dealings by all this people. Nay, my sons; for it is no good report that I hear: ye make the Lord's people to transgress. If one man sin against another, the judge

shall judge him: but if a man sin against the Lord, who shall entreat for him?
Notwithstanding they hearkened not unto the voice of their father, because the
Lord would slay them. Now because of the fact that Hophni and Phineas, Eli's
sons, refused to repent of the wicked thing they were doing, God prophesied
against them and in the 34th verse, we read:

And this shall be a sign unto thee, that shall come upon thy two sons, on Hophni
and Phinehas; in one day they shall die both of them.

Now, if I find it interesting at this point that Eli was High Priest, and Eli
knew what was going on, and he did speak to his sons about it, but as High
Priest, he had the authority to put a stop to it. And yet, he did not. For some
reason, he allowed it to continue to the point where God was forced to move
against his sons, to the point where God was forced to prophesy, to say that
your sons will both die. On the same day, they will die.

And there came a time, not too long afterward, that the Philistines came to
battle against Israel. The Philistines were one of the nations that previously
lived in the land where Israel now was. And it was one of the nations that
Israel was supposed to defeat and conquer when they took over the land
of Canaan. However, they did not completely destroy the Philistines. The
place where the Philistines lived was along the seacoast of the Mediterranean
Sea, and they were a constant source of trouble and turmoil for the Israelites.
We're all familiar with the story of David and Goliath. Goliath was a Philistine
giant, and it was during just such a battle as the one we're about to look at
that the Philistines sent out Goliath to fight, and David slew him.

In this particular battle, we read in chapter 4 and verse 2.

And the Philistines put themselves in array against Israel: and when they joined
battle, Israel was smitten before the Philistines: and they slew of the army in the
field about four thousand men.

At the very beginning of the battle, already four thousand of the Israelites
have fallen. Now, this caused a lot of confusion among the elders. Let me
read the beginning of the next verse:

And when the people were come into the camp, the elders of Israel said,
Wherefore hath the Lord smitten us today before the Philistines?

This was unheard of! In all the battles that Israel had fought before, with maybe one or two small exceptions, Israel had always prevailed against their enemies, and now for some reason God wasn't fighting for them. God had always fought for Israel. In fact, sometimes when Israel went out to fight against their enemies, Israel didn't even have to fight, because when they got there, God had already fought against their enemies. No doubt they remembered Jericho, how God fought for them at Jericho and some of the other cities, and in fact, the only time that I can recall when God did not fight was the battle right after Jericho: Israel went out to battle, and they lost, and they didn't understand why they lost then, either. But the Lord spoke to Joshua and said it was because somebody in Israel sinned. One of the people sinned. And they searched out who it was that sinned, and they found that it was a man named Aiken.

Now, when the walls of Jericho had fallen, God had instructed, the people of Israel that they were not to take any spoil from the city of Jericho. There were not to take anything. They were told to leave it all behind. Aiken disobeyed, and he stole a wedge of gold and a garment from Jericho, and he hid these in his tent. And this one sin caused many in Israel, to die in their next battle, because God wouldn't fight because there was sin in the camp.

And the result was that they took Aiken, and they took his wife and his children, and his animals and everything that belonged to Aiken. And they put them all together in one area, and all the people of Israel stood in a huge circle around Aiken and his family, and they picked up stones and stoned them all to death. The whole family had to die because of Aiken's sin. And many others died in the battle because of Aiken's sin. Sin separates people from God and when there's sin in the camp, God will not fight for Israel.

Now it would seem logical that, at this point, when Israel went out to fight against the Philistines and they lost the battle, that the priests and the elders would realize that something was wrong: There must be sin in the camp, because God's not fighting for us! But it didn't click. Perhaps they didn't believe what they were doing was wrong, or perhaps they just didn't care. Eli had warned his sons about the sin that they were committing, and how they were causing the other people in Israel to sin by committing prostitution in the Tabernacle. Apparently, they didn't care. So what did the elders do?

Looking at verse 3, the middle of the verse:

Let us fetch the Ark of the covenant of the Lord out of Shiloh unto us, that, when it cometh among us, it may save us out of the hand of our enemies.

They called for the Ark of the Covenant! There's been a lot of publicity about the Ark of the Covenant... even a popular movie being made about the Ark of the Covenant. Just briefly, the Ark of the Covenant was a large box covered with gold, and on top was a cover called The Mercy Seat with two angels on top of it whose wings spread over the seat. Inside the box were the original Ten Commandments and a few other things: Some manna from the wilderness, Aaron's rod that budded. But the most important thing about the Ark was not what it contained: It was the seat itself, the cover, the Mercy Seat with the two angels, because it was between those two angels that the very presence of God, the Spirit of God, what they called the Shekinah glory of God, lived in between the cherubim. Right in between those two angels is where the presence of God lived. And it was always in the history of Israel, that everywhere the Ark went, when it went before them, Israel was victorious.

No doubt they were remembering walking through the wilderness, how the Ark went before them and led them to the promised land. And they remembered crossing over Jordan: When they crossed over, the Ark went before them, and the River Jordan opened for them. They remembered marching around Jericho, they marched around Jericho once a day for six days. And on the seventh day, they marched around it seven times with The Ark of God ahead of them. And when the time time came, the walls of the city fell.

They remembered all the glorious times that God had fought for Israel, when the Ark of God went on ahead of them, and they thought, *Let us bring the Ark now, and the Ark will go ahead of us.* Now, for a carnal thought, this was marvelous, but for a spiritual thought, it was lousy. They should have realized that the reason God was not fighting for them was not because the Ark of God was in Shiloh, away from the battle, but because there was sin in the camp,

The elders called for the Ark, not realizing, or not wanting to believe, that God was angry with Israel because of sin, because of the sin that Hophni and Phineas committed, and because of the sin that they caused others to commit, right in the doorway of the Tabernacle. They had brought shame upon Israel and nobody seemed to care.

So they brought the Ark out. Verses 4 and 5 of the same 4th chapter:

So the people sent to Shiloh, that they might bring from thence the Ark of the Covenant of the Lord of hosts, which dwelleth between the cherubim: and the two sons of Eli, Hophni and Phineas, were there with the Ark of the Covenant of God. And when the Ark of the Covenant of the Lord came into the camp, all Israel shouted with a great shout, so that the earth rang again.

Well, they just had themselves a grand old time! I'm telling you, they had church! They shouted and they danced and they just had a grand time: The Ark of the Covenant's come; we're going to have victory. Now it's gonna fight for us! Well, you can shout and dance all you want, but when God's angry, when there's sin in the camp, God's not going to fight! God's not going to fight! You'll be destroyed! You know, the scripture tells us be sure your sin will find you out.

Maybe Hophni and Phineas thought they could hide their sin from God, but you can't hide your sin from God. You can't do it. Be sure your sin will find you out. God was angry with Hophni and Phineas, and God was angry with Israel, and it didn't matter how close the Ark of God was. It didn't matter that the Ark of God went before them into battle. God was angry with them. They didn't realize what they had with them. They were taking advantage of God here. They had something that no other nation had. It was the Ark of God, with the presence of the one true Living God, that set Israel apart from every other nation around, and they didn't understand that. They took that for granted. They didn't appreciate what they had.

Sure, they brought out the Ark, and they went into battle against the Philistines. And you know, when the Philistines heard the noise, it scared them. They heard all the rejoicing down in the camp of the Hebrews. They heard all the shouting and jumping and dancing and singing. In verses 6 through 8:

And when the Philistines heard the noise of the shout, they said, What meaneth the noise of this great shout in the camp of the Hebrews? And they understood that the Ark of the Lord was come into the camp. And the Philistines were afraid, for they said, God is come into the camp. And they said, Woe unto us! for there hath not been such a thing heretofore. Woe unto us! who shall deliver us out of the hand of these mighty Gods? these are the Gods that smote the Egyptians with all the plagues in the wilderness.

The God of Israel had a reputation. The Philistines were afraid of the God of Israel. They weren't afraid of the Israelites. They weren't afraid to face the Israelites alone, but they knew the power of the God of Israel, and they were afraid. But that fear didn't last long. They pulled themselves together and they built up their courage. In verse 9, they said:

Be strong and quit yourselves like men, O ye Philistines, that ye be not servants unto the Hebrews, as they have been to you: quit yourselves like men, and fight.

And that's what they did:

And the Philistines fought, and Israel was smitten, and they fled every man into his tent: and there was a very great slaughter; for there fell of Israel thirty thousand footmen.

What a terrible thing! Thirty thousand to die in one battle! But worst of all, the worst thing of all was not that Israel lost the battle, not that the Philistines won, and not that thirty thousand were slain. Verse 11 tells us the worst thing:

And the Ark of God was taken; and the two sons of Eli, Hophni and Phineas, were slain.

The two sons of Eli, Hophni and Phineas, were slain, in fulfillment of the prophecy that God had given. But the worst thing, the Ark of God had been taken by the Philistines, by these pagans. The Philistines worshipped Dagon. Dagon was a fish god; he had the head of a fish. These people who worship this fish god had the Ark of God, the Ark of the one true God. They had the presence of God! What a terrible thing! Verse 12:

And there ran a man of Benjamin out of the army, and came to Shiloh the same day with his clothes rent, and with earth upon his head.

He had ripped his clothes and put dirt on his head, traditional Jewish signs of mourning. Verse 13:

And when he came, lo, Eli sat upon a seat by the wayside watching: for his heart trembled for the Ark of God.

Oh, *now* his heart trembled for the Ark of God? What happened when those men came to Shiloh in the first place to take it? Where was the High Priest then? Why wasn't he worried about the Ark of God then? He knew Israel had sinned. He knew that God was angry with Israel. He heard the prophecy against his sons. Why wasn't he worried about the Ark of God then? Why did he wait until it was already gone into battle to worry about the Ark of God? He worried too late. He should have known better. And how many of us worry too late, when it's too late to worry? How many of us wait till the last minute? And then worry about what we should have done in the beginning about what God wanted us to do before. We wait until it's too late and then we worry about what we should have done.

Verses 16 and 17:

And the man said unto Eli, I am he that came out of the army, and I fled today out of the army. And he said, What is there done, my son? And the messenger answered and said, Israel is fled before the Philistines, and there hath been also a great slaughter among the people, and thy two sons also, Hophni and Phineas, are dead...

Now, up to this point, Eli handled the news all right. There was no great outburst from Eli at that point. And then the messenger continued:

and the Ark of God is taken. And it came to pass, when he made mention of the Ark of God, that he fell from off the seat backward by the side of the gate, and his neck brake, and he died.

It's too late to worry about the Ark now, Eli! It's too late now! The shock was too great, when he heard that the Ark of God was taken. He waited too long to worry about the things of God. He was the High Priest. He was the ruler in Israel. He was the judge. He should have known better. It was his responsibility to protect the things of God. It was his responsibility to defend the people of Israel, to know what was right and what was wrong. It was his responsibility, right from the beginning, to put a stop to the sin in the Tabernacle, but he didn't do it. He waited until it was too late. And *then* he worried. And *then* he worried! And what was the result? Ten thousand Israelites dead, the Israelites have fled from the Philistines, his sons Hophni and Phineas are dead. And worst of all, the worst thing that could possibly happen, the Ark of God is taken. That one thing that set Israel apart from every other nation. The very Shekinah Glory of God. The Spirit of God. That which made Israel great was gone, and it was in the hands of the heathens.

How late we realize how much we needed God. How late Eli realized that he needed God, and how important the Ark of God was to Israel. We can only say that his ministry as High Priest, his job as Judge of Israel, was a failure, because it was not until the day he died, it was not until it was too late, that he realized how important it was, how much he needed God, how much the things of God meant to him and to the people around him.

We go on to read about his daughter-in-law. His son, Phineas had a wife who was pregnant. We read in the 19th verse:

And his daughter in law, Phineas' wife, was with child, near to be delivered: and when she heard the tidings that the Ark of God was taken, and that her father in law and her husband were dead, she bowed herself and travailed; for her pains came upon her.

All of a sudden, she realized. Phineas' wife suddenly began to realize. Why did she wait so long to realize? Why did she wait? She knew what Phineas was doing in the Tabernacle. She know what his brother Hophni was doing in the Tabernacle. She knew that they were leading the people into sin. Why didn't she say something sooner? Why didn't she stand up sooner? Now, it's too late. Now her father-in-law is dead, her husband is dead, her brother-in-law is dead, and the Ark of God has been taken.

And you know, not only did she go into labor, but she died. Verse 20:

And about the time of her death, the women that stood by her said unto her, Fear not; for thou hast born a son. But she answered not, neither did she regard it.

She would not even look at the child! Can you imagine how broken in spirit she was? All her life, she had been used to having the presence of God near. All her life, she had taken it for granted. And now, it was gone. Now she realized how important it had been. Now she realized what it meant to have God so close to her. Verse 21:

And she named the child Ichabod...

What an awful name to give a baby: Ichabod. It means *there is no glory.* What a horrible name! Can you imagine the despair she must have felt to name her son *There is no glory?*

...saying, The glory is departed from Israel: because the ark of God was taken, and because of her father in law and her husband. And she said, The glory is departed from Israel: for the ark of God is taken.

Too late, then, Phineas' wife realized just what she had. If all of us could take the time to realize the opportunity that we have before us. We are living in a time unlike any other in all of history. We read in the scripture that the people in the Old Testament, the prophets, how much they wanted to know, and to experience, the things that are available to the church today and they could not, because in their time it was not available. All they could see were shadows of it, far off. They realized it wasn't for them. They prophesied that it would come in a future time. But **this** is that time! This is the time! The prophet spoke of Jesus, said He came to preach the acceptable year of the Lord. I'm here to say **this** is the acceptable year of the Lord, now is the time of salvation. Now is **always** the time of salvation. Now is the time, because now the Spirit of God is here. Now there is the opportunity, because the Spirit of God is near.

If we could realize the opportunity we have... We take for granted what we have. We take for granted the country we live in. how many countries are there today, where it is illegal to preach the Gospel of Jesus Christ. How blessed we are to live in a country where not only can we stand anywhere we want to and preach the Gospel of Jesus Christ, but we can go on television and preach the Gospel. We can go on radio and preach the Gospel. We can open up a church building and preach the Gospel. We can, if we want to, stand on the street corner, preach the Gospel of Jesus Christ, and there are so many places on earth where we can't do that. If we only realized how blessed we are! We're too much like Eli. We're too much like Phineas' wife. We take for granted the great things that we have, that God has given us. We take for granted the fact that the Spirit of God is so close to us, and we ignore it. We're going to wait until it's too late.

How many times have people said, *I don't have to serve God now. I'm young.*

There's time yet for me to serve God, only to be killed in some fatal accident? How many times has a middle-aged person said, *Well, when I'm old, I'll serve God*, only to die of some fatal disease? We don't have tomorrow promised to us. Not one of us has ever been promised tomorrow. If you're familiar with the program of Alcoholics Anonymous, their basic premise is *I can't worry about tomorrow; for today, I will be sober.*

Today is all we have promised to us. We don't know what tomorrow will bring. We don't know if we will wake up tomorrow, Every breath comes from God. I could not take another breath if it was not given to me by God. He has given us now, and now is the time for us to seek God. The scripture tells us in the Book of Ecclesiastes chapter 3, verse 1, a very familiar portion of scripture:

To every thing there is a season, and a time to every purpose under the heaven:

There is a time to seek the Lord, and that time is now. It is **always** time to seek the Lord. *There is no time like the present* is an old saying, and this is the time to seek the Lord. There's no reason to put it off. To put it off can only be dangerous.

I wonder how many times Phineas' wife thought, *Well, maybe I should talk to my husband about what he's doing, and ask him to stop. Maybe I should go to the Tabernacle and pray. Maybe I should repent.* But she put it off. I wonder how many times Eli thought, *I need to put a stop to the sin that's going on there. Not just to speak to my sons, but to actually put a stop to it.* But he put it off.

There is a time to seek God, and it is time now for us to turn with all our hearts to Him. He said that if we would come to Him, He would accept us. He said, *"Behold, I stand at the door and I knock. And if any man opened to me, I will come unto him and I will sup with him, and he with me."* Jesus is knocking at that door, and when you open it, it doesn't matter who you are: If you open the door, Jesus will come in.

The Fourth Man in the Furnace

Praise the Lord! I'm reading from the book of Daniel, chapter 3:

Nebuchadnezzar the king made an image of gold, whose height was threescore cubits, and the breadth thereof six cubits: he set it up in the plain of Dura, in the province of Babylon.

Then Nebuchadnezzar the king sent to gather together the princes, the governors, and the captains, the judges, the treasurers, the counselors, the sheriffs, and all the rulers of the provinces, to come to the dedication of the image which Nebuchadnezzar the king had set up.

Then the princes, the governors, and captains, the judges, the treasurers, the counselors, the sheriffs, and all the rulers of the provinces, were gathered together unto the dedication of the image that Nebuchadnezzar the king had set up; and they stood before the image that Nebuchadnezzar had set up.

Then an herald cried aloud, To you it is commanded, O people, nations, and languages,

That at what time ye hear the sound of the cornet, flute, harp, sackbut, psaltery, dulcimer, and all kinds of music, ye fall down and worship the golden image that Nebuchadnezzar the king hath set up:

And whoso falleth not down and worshippeth shall the same hour be cast into the midst of a burning fiery furnace.

Therefore at that time, when all the people heard the sound of the cornet, flute, harp, sackbut, psaltery, and all kinds of music, all the people, the nations, and the languages, fell down and worshipped the golden image that Nebuchadnezzar the king had set up.

Wherefore at that time certain Chaldeans came near, and accused the Jews.

They spake and said to the king Nebuchadnezzar, O king, live for ever.

Thou, O king, hast made a decree, that every man that shall hear the sound of the cornet, flute, harp, sackbut, psaltery, and dulcimer, and all kinds of music, shall fall down and worship the golden image:

And whoso falleth not down and worshippeth, that he should be cast into the midst of a burning fiery furnace.

There are certain Jews whom thou hast set over the affairs of the province of Babylon, Shadrach, Meshach, and Abednego; these men, O king, have not regarded thee: they serve not thy gods, nor worship the golden image which thou hast set up.

Then Nebuchadnezzar in his rage and fury commanded to bring Shadrach, Meshach, and Abednego. Then they brought these men before the king.

Nebuchadnezzar spake and said unto them, Is it true, O Shadrach, Meshach, and Abednego, do not ye serve my gods, nor worship the golden image which I have set up?

Now if ye be ready that at what time ye hear the sound of the cornet, flute, harp, sackbut, psaltery, and dulcimer, and all kinds of music, ye fall down and worship the image which I have made; well: but if ye worship not, ye shall be cast the same hour into the midst of a burning fiery furnace; and who is that God that shall deliver you out of my hands?

Shadrach, Meshach, and Abednego, answered and said to the king, O Nebuchad-nezzar, we are not careful to answer thee in this matter.

If it be so, our God whom we serve is able to deliver us from the burning fiery furnace, and he will deliver us out of thine hand, O king.

But if not, be it known unto thee, O king, that we will not serve thy gods, nor worship the golden image which thou hast set up.

Then was Nebuchadnezzar full of fury, and the form of his visage was changed against Shadrach, Meshach, and Abednego: therefore he spake, and commanded that they should heat the furnace one seven times more than it was wont to be heated.

And he commanded the most mighty men that were in his army to bind Shadrach, Meshach, and Abednego, and to cast them into the burning fiery furnace.

Then these men were bound in their coats, their hosen, and their hats, and their other garments, and were cast into the midst of the burning fiery furnace.

Therefore because the king's commandment was urgent, and the furnace exceeding hot, the flames of the fire slew those men that took up Shadrach, Meshach, and Abednego.

And these three men, Shadrach, Meshach, and Abednego, fell down bound into the midst of the burning fiery furnace.

Then Nebuchadnezzar the king was astonished, and rose up in haste, and spake, and said unto his counselors, Did not we cast three men bound into the midst of the fire? They answered and said unto the king, True, O king.

He answered and said, Lo, I see four men loose, walking in the midst of the fire, and they have no hurt; and the form of the fourth is like the Son of God.

Then Nebuchadnezzar came near to the mouth of the burning fiery furnace, and spake, and said, Shadrach, Meshach, and Abednego, ye servants of the most high God, come forth, and come hither. Then Shadrach, Meshach, and Abednego, came forth of the midst of the fire.

And the princes, governors, and captains, and the king's counselors, being gathered together, saw these men, upon whose bodies the fire had no power, nor was an hair of their head singed, neither were their coats changed, nor the smell of fire had passed on them.

That's a beautiful story story from the history of when Judah was carried away into Babylon, a true story of a great miracle that God did, because people refuse to worship an idol, because they stood for His truth.

Shadrach, Meshach and Abednego, if they had still been living in Judah, would probably have been princes or nobles. Many years before, one of the prophets had predicted that Judah would be carried away into Babylon and her chief princes would be made eunuchs in the palace of the king of Babylon. And so it was that Shadrach, Meshach and Abednego, as well as the prophet Daniel in whose book we find the story, were all eunuchs in the palace of the king.

We remember the story of how when Daniel first was taken there and was first made a eunuch, he was supposed to be eating the food that the king had provided, but he didn't want it. He asked instead for plain food, and asked that these young men who were with him, Shadrach, Meshach and Abednego, be given plain food, and not the fancy food that the king had ordered. And the prince of the eunuchs was a little worried. He said, *But what happens if the king sees that you're getting thinner from not eating his good food? You know, he's going to take it out on me.* And so they had a little trial period, and it turned out that Daniel and Shadrach, Meshach, and Abednego, eating the plain food, fared better than those who were eating the king's food. They looked healthier.

Right from the very beginning, Daniel was given favor with the king of Babylon, with Nebuchadnezzar. And Shadrach, Meshach and Abednego also were given favor. They were given some authority in the province of Babylon. They were important people, which was a considerable honor, since they were Jews and were also captives. They were not really citizens of Babylon, but yet they were given this authority. And yet, in spite of the allure of all things Babylon had to offer, they would not give up their love of the one true God. Everything that they had known in the past, Jerusalem and Judah, all of it was gone. Their families were probably killed, and they had nothing left. And they were even made eunuchs in the palace of the king. And yet, when they were given this authority, rather than adopting the ways of Babylon and becoming Babylonians and worshipping the Babylonian gods, they held true to what they still had: And that was the Holy One of Israel, the God of Judah, the one true God, and they trusted this God so much that they were willing to place their life in His hand.

Of course, we know that it's against the law of God to worship another god, and when Nebuchadnezzar set up the statue and said everyone's going to worship it, I'm sure there were other Jews in Babylon who did not worship the statue. They knew it was wrong. But these people, these Chaldeans, who were actually astrologers, who turned in Shadrach, Meshach and Abednego, were trying to get them in trouble. They didn't like them. They resented the fact that these Jews were rising in authority, that they had been given some power in Babylon. Here, they thought, is the perfect chance for us to get rid of them. Here's the chance to have them killed because we know that they won't worship the statue.

Now, the king might have overlooked it if no one had called it to his attention. He may never have known that Shadrach, Meshach, and Abednego were not worshipping his golden statue, but these people called it to his attention, and that made him angry. But he gave them a second chance: *Is it true that you didn't worship the statue? Well, if you're willing to fall down now and worship, that's fine. We'll forget the whole thing. But you have to know the penalty if you don't is that you'll go into the furnace.* Up to this point, the king was fairly friendly to them, but they were very blunt and honest with the king. *We are not careful to answer you in this matter. We don't have to defend ourselves before you in this matter. We don't even have to think ahead of time about where we're going to say. We already know that no matter what happens. We're not going to worship your God. We're not going to worship this golden image. We will only worship Our God and if you throw us in the furnace, He is able to deliver us from it, and even if He chooses not to, we still aren't going to worship your god.*

Now that was almost a slap in the face to the king of Babylon. He was not used to being spoken to that way. The king of Babylon was a man of very, very great authority. The rules of his kingdom were very strict, and you did not do anything to offend him. In fact, you didn't even go into the king's presence without being asked. Anybody who dared to go before the king of Babylon without being asked could be killed on the spot. That was the law. You didn't dare go into his presence unasked, but then when you were asked in, and then spoke to him that way, they were definitely asking for a death sentence here. Nebuchadnezzar was furious with them and his attitude toward them changed. All of a sudden, he wasn't trying to save them anymore. All of a sudden, he wasn't trying to help them. Now, he was furious with them. How dare they speak to him that way? How dare they insult his gods and his statue? How dare they think that their invisible Hebrew God that nobody could see and whose name they weren't even allowed to pronounce, how dare they think that they could worship that God and not the gods of Babylon?

Nebuchadnezzar was furious and he made that furnace seven times hotter than it usually was. He insisted on that, and then he had his soldiers tie up those three Jewish men who refused to worship His statue, and he had his soldiers throw them in. The fire was so hot that it killed the soldiers that were throwing them in.

But God was in there with the three young men. King Nebuchadnezzar said, *I see* **four** *men walking around in the fire, unbound; the ropes are gone.* He knew his soldiers had tied them up: He told them to do it. He told his soldiers to tie them tightly, and throw them in there, and yet the ropes were gone. That's the only thing they lost in that fire. Their clothes were not burned. There was no smell of smoke on them. The only thing Shadrach, Meshach and Abednego lost in that fire was the ropes... The things that held them bound. And God walked in that fire with them. Nebuchadnezzar said the fourth man is like the son of God.

Now, who was he talking about? The son of one of his gods? All he knew was that what he was seeing was something divine. It wasn't an ordinary human. It wasn't just a human being he saw. He saw something that, to him, said, this is the son of God. This is the son of a God. What God? He didn't say, but it was the son of a God. He saw him in there.

What is the lesson for us in this? We, too, go through fiery trials. If we try to live for God, Jesus told us that we would suffer persecution. In the New Testament, it tells us that all, not some, not a few, but **all** who live godly in Christ Jesus shall suffer persecution. That's a promise to us. In one place, Simon Peter said to Jesus, *"Lord, we've left everything to follow You."* And Jesus said to him, *There's nobody among you who left fathers or mothers, or brothers, or sisters, or children, or wives, or husbands, or houses, or lands, who will not receive in this life, now, a hundredfold: Mothers and sisters and brothers and houses and lands and persecutions, and in the life to come, eternal life.*

He included persecutions in the list of blessings they were going to receive for following Him! He promised persecution. There's no way to escape it. If you're not being persecuted in some way for your Christian faith, you must not be living it, right? Because they said all who live Godly in Christ Jesus shall suffer persecution. There's no way to escape that. We will go through fiery trials. There will be times when it seems that we just can't go on anymore, when it just seems that the flames of this furnace can't get any hotter.

The pressure is coming in from every side: The family is on my case because I go to church too much. The boss is on my case because I won't lie for him, or I won't do dishonest things at work. People are on my case for being a

Christian. I can't take the pressure anymore! Everything's going wrong at once! All these trials have come in at once. I can't take the fire! But what are you going to lose in the fire? Are you going to lose your house? No. Are you going to lose your clothes? No. Are you going to lose your salvation? No. You're going to lose the things that tie you down! You're going to lose the ropes that bind you, and you're not walking through the fire alone, because with you, there's another One who in His form is like the son of God.

Just like when Shadrach, Meshach and Abednego were in that furnace they were not alone. They did not go into that fire alone because they trusted their God. They knew He was able to deliver them. They said, No matter what happens, we're not going to worship your gods. We're not going to worship that golden statue. We're going to worship Our God. He lives, and He is able to deliver us out of any fire you can build, no matter how hot it is.

Nebuchadnezzar made that fire seven times hotter than usual. The normal temperature would have been enough to kill them, but he made it seven times hotter. But it couldn't hurt them, and they weren't alone in it. God was in there with them. He walked with them, and all they lost was the ropes. All they lost was the ropes!

We're going to go through some terrible trials, and even some of the little trials seem like they're more than enough, more than we can bear. And yet, they're going to get worse. Some of them are going to be almost unbearable, but we're not going through them alone. We're not going through them alone! The Bible promises us that God won't put anything more on us than we're able to bear, but with each thing that He puts on his, He makes a way out, a way to escape. He is in there with us. He can go through with us. You don't have to go through it alone. When you're in the midst of your trial, when it seems that everything has gone wrong and everything is dark around you, and you're sure that the valley of the shadow of death couldn't be any darker than where you are right now, you are not alone. And even when it seems that God is the farthest from you, you just can't seem to get hold of Him, and it seems like He's deserted you, you are not alone.

Shadrach, Meshach and Abednego did not see God before they were thrown into the furnace. Nobody saw God with them before they went into the furnace. Those three knew they were going into that furnace. They must have thought they might really be about to die. They felt the heat from that furnace. They felt it, and saw that it killed the soldiers who were throwing them in. And yet, they didn't give up. God was with them, even though they couldn't see Him. But when they got into the middle of that fire, they did see Him and even King Nebuchadnezzar saw Him. He saw that they were not alone in there. They had a God who was protecting them. And when we are in the middle of our trials, if we do not lose our faith, if we can hold on, and recognize the fact that we are not alone, that God is with us, and if we can hold up our head, and continue on and continue walking the Christian life, then those around us will see God with us too. But if we fall apart and say, well, God let me down or God failed me, they're not going to see God. But if we can say no matter how bad it gets, I know God is still with me, I know God is still on my side, I know God hasn't left me, they will see God too. They will know that He's with us. They'll know that we've been with Him. They'll know that we have something. They'll know that we have a God.

Nebuchadnezzar did not believe in the God of Israel. He said to them what God is that who's going to be able to rescue you from my hand? No God that you think is better than my statue is going to be able to save you! But after he saw them in the fire, he knew they had a God! He knew they had a God who was able to protect them! He knew it!

Going back to Daniel 3, starting at the 28th verse:

Then Nebuchadnezzar spake, and said, Blessed be the God of Shadrach, Meshach, and Abednego, who hath sent his angel, and delivered his servants that trusted in him...

He recognized the power of the one true God. He gave glory to the God that, a few minutes ago, he didn't think existed, because he saw that God with Shadrach, Meshach, and Abednego, and it wasn't just because he saw a physical presence, but because he saw the salvation of that God. He saw that God was able to deliver them from his furnace. He didn't think any God could. He knew his own gods didn't have the power to protect anybody from a fiery furnace. He didn't think any God could, but he knew now that the God of Israel, the God of Shadrach, Meshach, and Abednego, did have that kind of power. He knew that this God had power. He said, "*Blessed be the God of Shadrach, Meshach, and Abednego, who hath sent his angel, and delivered his servants that trusted in him, and have changed the king's word, and yielded their bodies, that they might not serve nor worship any god, except their own God. Therefore I make a decree, That every people, nation, and language, which speak any thing amiss against the God of Shadrach, Meshach, and Abednego, shall be cut in pieces, and their houses shall be made a dunghill: because there is no other God that can deliver after this sort.*"

Amen! No other God can save like this! No other God can do that! What other God can rescue people from a firm fiery furnace? Who else can do it? And not just rescue them, but be in there in the middle of it with them?

If you had taken the idols of Babylon, and the golden statue that was 90 feet tall, and put that in the fiery furnace, they would have melted. The gods of wood burn. The gods of stone would crumble. The gods of gold and silver would melt, but the God of Israel can stand in their fiery furnace with you! The one true God, the Living God, He's not affected by a fiery furnace. He can go through your trials with you. No other God can do that! No other God can deliver like that! No other God! And there is no other God. The gods of the nations were nothing. They were stone. They were metal.

Nebuchadnezzar's image, his big statue of himself, 90 feet high, it wasn't alive. It had eyes, but it couldn't see; it had ears but it couldn't hear, it had a mouth but it couldn't speak, because it was dead. It was nothing! But the God of Israel, the invisible God that Nebuchadnezzar thought couldn't help them, delivered Shadrach, Meshach and Abednego out of that furnace.

That's the same God who delivered Daniel from the lions' den. The king who threw Daniel into the lions' den, King Darius: He didn't want to throw Daniel in there. He didn't want to, but he had to. The law compelled him to. But he had a little bit of faith. Maybe he remembered what had happened to his predecessor with Shadrach, Meshach and Abednego, and how he had realized that the God of Israel was powerful, as Daniel was thrown into the lions' den. The king said to him, "May your God, whom you serve continually, rescue you!" May your God rescue you! May He save you! Your God whom you serve faithfully day and night, may He rescue you from the lions' den.

He must have known! He must have known that the God of Israel could, that Daniel's God could! He knew his own gods couldn't. He wouldn't have wasted time saying, *May the gods of Babylon rescue you*, because he knew none of his gods had any power against the lions. Those lions were hungry, but perhaps the God of Israel, the God who is not afraid of a fiery furnace, perhaps He could rescue from a den of lions too.

And the next morning, the king went to the lions' den, and he called out and said, *Daniel, servant of the Living God! Has your God, whom you serve continually, been able to rescue you from the lions?* I know he was just wanting to hear *Yes*, not just because he loved Daniel, but because he really wanted to believe that this living God did have this power. He had something in his heart that knew that the God of Israel was alive. He knew that, he sensed it. And the God of Israel **was** alive, because Daniel answered him and said, *"O King, live forever! My God sent His angels and He shut the mouths of the lions. They have not hurt me because I was found innocent in His sight. Nor have I ever done any wrong before you, O King."* The King was overjoyed. No other God could do that! King Darius issued a proclamation. He said, *"I issue a decree that in every part of my kingdom people must fear and reverence the god of Daniel, for he is the Living God and He endures forever. His kingdom will not be destroyed. His Dominion will never end. He rescues and He saves. He performs signs and wonders in the heavens and on the Earth. He has rescued Daniel from the power of the Lions."*

He who rescued Shadrach, Meshach and Abednego from the fiery furnace, who walked right in there with them, was the same One who walked right into the lions' den and shut the mouths of the lions! He can save, and there is no terrible trouble you can be in that is so bad that God can't walk in there with you and rescue you from it. He is right there with you in your trials. He won't make you go through them alone.

We're all familiar with the story Footprints. We've seen the posters with Footprints, about the man who had a dream that he was walking on the beach and he saw the footprints of his life. And, you know, he saw that in many places there were two sets of footprints, where the Lord had walked with him. But it seemed like during the hard times there was only one set of footprints, and he didn't understand, and said, "Lord, You said You'd always be with me. How come during the hard times, when I was going through the most difficult times of my life, there's only one set of footprints, and I walked alone? You left me!" And God said, "No, I didn't leave you during those times. When you needed Me most, I carried you."

He won't leave you in your time of trouble. He's not going to leave you in your affliction. He's not going to leave you in your trials. He won't leave you to die alone in a fiery furnace: He'll be right in there with you, and He will bring you out. There will not even be the smell of smoke on your clothes when you come out. He's not going to leave you to die in a lion's den, but He'll be in there to shut the mouths of the lions when they would destroy you. When your enemies rise up against you, and curse you, and persecute you because of Him, he's right there. You will not go through that persecution alone, but He is going through it with you. You don't have to suffer alone.

Our God is a God who has felt affliction. He knows what it's like and He will go through it with you. You don't ever have to be alone. You don't have to be alone. One of the last promises He made to his disciples, just after He gave them the Great Commission, was *Surely I will be with you always, even to the very end of the age.* To the very end of time, I will be with you. He said I will not leave you. In another place, I will not leave you or forsake you. I will never leave you. He promised that! And even in the furnaces, even in the lions' den, even in the valley of the shadow of death, He will not leave you. We all know the 23rd Psalm. Such a beautiful Psalm, probably quoted more than any other portion of scripture. *Yea, though I walk through the valley of the shadow of death, I will fear no evil, for Thou art with me.*

Here with me! I'm not walking through that dark valley alone! God, You're with me! I'm so thankful to know that I don't have to walk that dark valley alone, but that He's walking right by my side, and if it does get tough, He will carry me. He will not leave me alone there. He will not! He will not abandon me. We have abandoned God many times, but God has never abandoned us. He will never abandon you. He will always be with you. Even when it seems like He's far away, He is right there by your side and He will not leave you. He will not leave you in the valley of the shadow of death. He will not leave you in the lions' den. He will not leave you in the fiery furnace. He will stay with you; He will hold your hand. And the only thing that you will lose are the things that bind you!

I remember a song from a few years back: I don't remember the whole song, but I remember one part that said that "the chains that seem to bind you serve only to remind you that they drop powerless behind you when you praise Him!"

You know, you walk into that fiery furnace, and worship, and you're going to come out with no chains binding you! All you'll lose is the ropes; all you lose is the bondage. You don't lose the freedom, you don't lose your life, you don't lose your clothes, you don't come out with a smell of smoke on you. You don't get eaten by lions, and you don't get lost in the valley of the shadow of death, because you're not alone in there. We have a God that can do something that no other god can do!

All over the world, people worship many different gods, but none of them can deliver like our God can. None of them will walk through your trials with you. Many of the gods of other religions teach that you have to walk through it by yourself. And if you do it right, you get to go to heaven. If you do it wrong, you have to come back and do it over again. But our God didn't say you had to do it alone. He said He'd go with you all the way, every inch of the way. He'd walk with you and He'd never make you walk alone. Never! He'll walk every inch with you, and every time you're in trouble, He'll be right there, sticking closer to you than you can imagine. The Bible tells me there's a Friend who sticks closer than a brother. That's close, and that's Jesus! He sticks closer than a brother. *"I will never leave you nor forsake you."* *"Yea, though I walk through the valley of the shadow of death, I will fear no evil."* I don't have to be afraid! You don't have to be afraid, because He's with us, and He promised never to leave us.

Our God can't break a promise. He's not like us that He can lie, and He's not like us that He can fail. If He says He'll be with us, He'll be with us. He promised that! He won't go back on His word.

Thank God, we have a King who can save! I'm so thankful that our God is not like the gods of the nations, with ears that don't hear and a heart that doesn't care, a mouth but can't speak, but we have a God who can be touched by our infirmities! We have a God who knows what it is to suffer, because He walks through it with us. And we have a God who won't leave us, who has the power to save us. Unlike any other god in all of creation, we have a God who can save, who can deliver, who can quench the flames of a furnace. He can shut the mouths of lions, and He can be a light where there is no light. That's our God! That's Jesus!

It's good to know that we have a God who loves us, that we have a God who cares, and that when we're in trouble, we don't have to go to the foot of some stone or golden idol and pray to it, expecting an answer, when actually, it can't hear us and it doesn't care. Even if it *could* hear, it doesn't care, because it has no heart. Our God loves us! He loves us so much that He was willing to sacrifice Himself for us, and He loves us enough that He promised that no matter where we went, He would go with us, He would walk with us.

I'm thankful for that! I'm so thankful for that! It would be an awfully rough journey without Him. I don't think I'd ever make it to the end. I'd never get out of that valley, never get out of that furnace, and never get out of that lions' den, if I didn't have the son of God walking there with me. Thank the Lord!

The Idols of Pentecost

We're turning to the book of Jeremiah, the weeping prophet. Jeremiah the 7th chapter, beginning at the beginning of the chapter:

The word that came to Jeremiah from the Lord, saying, Stand in the gate of the Lord's house, and proclaim there this word, and say, Hear the word of the Lord, all ye of Judah, that enter in at these gates to worship the Lord. Thus saith the Lord of hosts, the God of Israel, Amend your ways and your doings, and I will cause you to dwell in this place. Trust ye not in lying words, saying, The temple of the Lord, The temple of the Lord, The temple of the Lord, are these. For if ye thoroughly amend your ways and your doings; if ye thoroughly execute judgment between a man and his neighbor; If ye oppress not the stranger, the fatherless, and the widow, and shed not innocent blood in this place, neither walk after other gods to your hurt: Then will I cause you to dwell in this place, in the land that I gave to your fathers, for ever and ever. Behold, ye trust in lying words, that cannot profit. Will ye steal, murder, and commit adultery, and swear falsely, and burn incense unto Baal, and walk after other gods whom ye know not; And come and stand before me in this house, which is called by my name, and say, We are delivered to do all these abominations? Is this house, which is called by my name, become a den of robbers in your eyes? Behold, even I have seen it, saith the Lord. But go ye now unto my place which was in Shiloh, where I set my name at the first, and see what I did to it for the wickedness of my people Israel. And now, because ye have done all these works, saith the Lord, and I spake unto you, rising up early and speaking, but ye heard not; and I called you, but ye answered not; Therefore will I do unto this house, which is called by my name, wherein ye trust, and unto the place which I gave to you and to your fathers, as I have done to Shiloh. And I will cast you out of my sight, as I have cast out all your brethren, even the whole seed of Ephraim.

Turn now to the book of Isaiah, and chapter 29, the very end of the chapter, verse 24:

They also that erred in spirit shall come to understanding, and they that murmured shall learn doctrine.

Going on to the next chapter:

Woe to the rebellious children, saith the Lord, that take counsel, but not of me; and that cover with a covering, but not of my Spirit, that they may add sin to sin: That walk to go down into Egypt, and have not asked at my mouth; to strengthen themselves in the strength of Pharaoh, and to trust in the shadow of Egypt! Therefore shall the strength of Pharaoh be your shame, and the trust in the shadow of Egypt your confusion.

I don't know what to promise you from my message today, because I really don't know what it's going to be. This was one of those days when, just before service, God finally gave me the scriptures I was to preach from. So we'll have to wait and see where He's going with it, so we know where we're going with it.

The people of Judah in the days of Jeremiah had a certain self-righteousness about them that is, unfortunately, all too common, and has been all through the ages. Anytime God does something with a group of people, or for a group of people, there's the danger of becoming self-righteous. Jesus ran into it in His day when He began to preach to the Jewish people, and talk to them about their sin. And they were offended, they were insulted, they were incensed, and they self-righteously informed Him, just in case He didn't know, that they were the children of Abraham.

He had talked to them about being set free, and they said "We're the children of Abraham; we have never been in bondage to any man." Now, that was a pretty funny statement coming from people who spent 300 years in slavery in Egypt, from a people have been carried away into Babylon and held captive there. and who are now enslaved to the Romans. That was a pretty funny statement. *We've never been in bondage to any man.* Not only had they been in bondage physically, but they were still in bondage spiritually!

But there was that self-righteous about the whole thing: *We are the children of Abraham! Obviously, you don't realize who you're talking to, Jesus of Nazareth. We're the Jewish people; we are the chosen people!*

It wasn't just unique to His generation, because Jeremiah had the same problem in his day because of the presence of God in Judah. They thought, *We're really it!* And they'd walk into the beautiful temple building. *This is the temple. We have nothing to fear. We are the chosen people of God. For we are in His Temple that's called by His name and we can do anything we please!*

He said, You're going to do all these things like burning incense to Baal, and murdering, and being greedy, cheating each other? All these terrible, terrible things you're going to do to each other, and then walk into this Temple and say, *We've been set free in order to do all these things?*

Not understanding that the freedom that comes with being the people of God is not freedom **to,** but freedom **from.** There's a difference. It's not freedom to go out and do anything we please, to live any way we want because we have forgiveness. You find that kind of thing sometimes among people who preach eternal security, that there's no way to lose your salvation. So they live anyway they please, because they figure they've already accepted Jesus. Now they're safe forever, and they can live however they want. It doesn't work that way. We're not saved so that we can go out and commit abomination. We're not saved so we can burn incense to other gods, or live for other things. We're saved **from** those things. We are set free **from** them.

But there they were walking into the temple trusting in the building itself, and ignoring the God whose name was called there. And Jeremiah warned them, speaking the word of the Lord to them: *Don't trust lying words, saying the Temple of the Lord, the Temple of the Lord, the Temple of the Lord are these.* That's not going to save you!

They were under the mistaken impression that belonging to the right church was going to get them to heaven. And there they were in the Temple. You couldn't beat that as far as belonging to the right Church. There was the Temple of the Most High God, and they thought that was all they needed. They could walk into the Temple and it really didn't much matter what else they did. That self-righteousness again!

Now, Pentecostal people understand... Let me back up: Pentecostal people are *supposed to* understand that belonging to a particular church or denomination is not going to get anybody to heaven. That was something that was revealed along around the 1700s, or restored, I should say, when the Revival period began, because that was something that the Protestant Reformation didn't quite catch on to. The Catholics had always taught, of course, that belonging to the right church, belonging to their one true church... Catholic means Universal, so it was supposed to be the one true church... belonging to that was going to get you into heaven. You had to be baptized as a Catholic to get into heaven. Well, along came the Protestant Reformation. They didn't quite figure out that belonging to a particular denomination wasn't going to get anybody anywhere.

But the Revival period came in the 1700s. Preachers would stand up in places like England and Scotland and Ireland, and they'd say, You know, it does not matter what church you belong to you. You've got to be right with God. It's not a matter of making your peace with the church, but making your peace with God. It's not a matter of belonging to the church, but belonging to God. And they preached that each person had a personal responsibility between him or herself and God, and that was unheard of, because the churches before that time, the Protestant churches and the Catholic churches and the Orthodox Churches, had not stressed the fact that a human being could go directly to God. *In fact, you weren't supposed to!* That was what the whole idea of the sacrament of confession. You go to the priest and tell him your sins, so he can forgive you or you pray to the Saints or you can pray to Mary. You pray to angels. I saw one Catholic prayer book that had people praying to the Ark of the Covenant! No one even knows where it is, and they're praying to it, and to every angel they knew by name, and some that they invented, because they couldn't go directly to God.

The church had made God inaccessible to the people, that God was so far away and distant from everything, that there was no way to approach Him directly. The Revival period came: The preachers said not only **can** you approach Him directly, but you **have to** approach him directly! The church cannot intercede for you. The Saints cannot intercede for you. The Virgin

Mary is not up there working on your salvation. It's up to you! Which is exactly what the scripture said, that every man had to work out his own salvation with fear and trembling. It's up to us to read the word. It's up to us to know what it says. It's up to us to get right with God, and not trust in lying words saying this is the true church, this is the true church, this is the true church. It doesn't work that way. But there was that self-righteousness. There was that pride in the building that they had built, and today in the denominations that we've built. We can't do it that way.

They that erred in spirit will come to understanding. That's what this is about, actually. It's a mistake in spirit, not so much a mistake in doctrine, because the Jewish people in the days of Jeremiah knew the law of Moses. They just thought they didn't have to adhere to it because they were the people of God. It wasn't that they didn't know the truth. It was that they thought they didn't have to stick to it. It was that they were putting too much faith in who *they* were, and not enough on who God was. They made a mistake in spirit; they had the wrong spirit.

There was a time when a group of people opposed the preaching of Jesus. Well, that happened a lot to Jesus. He was kind of used to that. A lot of times people wouldn't listen to what He had to say, or else they'd ridicule. When He went into the house where the little girl had died, and said "She's not dead. She's asleep," the scripture says they laughed him to scorn. They thought that was the most ridiculous thing they'd ever heard. And they made fun of Him and ridiculed Him. But He raised that little girl. He didn't get bent out of shape. He just put them all out, and told the little girl to get up.

But the apostles were more easily offended than that, so that when people oppose their teachings before the day of Pentecost, they wanted to get revenge. *Who do they think they are, not listening to us? Don't they understand who we are? We're the chosen twelve! We follow Jesus.*

One particular time, they said to Jesus, "Lord, do you want us to call fire down out of heaven on their heads to consume them?" Why? Had they committed some horrible offense? No, they just rejected the teaching of Jesus. They just weren't interested in hearing it at that time. It wasn't the end of the world, but the apostles wanted to kill them! They wanted instantaneous judgment to fall. There was that self-righteousness there: *Well, if you don't want it, then we're just going to wipe you off the face of the earth!* And Jesus told them, now get this, "You don't know what Spirit you're of." They erred in spirit.

But Isaiah said those who erred in spirit will come to understanding. They will begin to understand what Spirit they're of. Eventually the apostles did. They began to understand what Spirit they were of, but it took a while. It wasn't until they actually received that Spirit, that they understood that Spirit. Because even after the resurrection, they still didn't understand what the whole thing was about. They still didn't understand what Spirit they were of, what the purpose of Jesus on the earth was. *Will you at this time restore the kingdom to Israel?*

Talk about feeling like you're beating your head against the wall! That's how Jesus must have felt at that point: They still didn't get it.

But He was patient. He didn't get offended and say, *Forget it! You people are hopeless. I'm going to start over with another bunch. You people can't get the hang of anything!*

He's probably wondering, is this group mentally slow? There's something wrong with these people! They don't get it! But He said, "It's not for you to know the times and the seasons. You just go back to Jerusalem and wait." *You'll understand it in time.* "You'll receive power after the Holy Ghost is come upon you, and you will be witnesses." *You'll know then what Spirit you're of!*

But now, what's our excuse? Because here we are, in an Apostolic Pentecostal church with the spirit of God. And all too often, we don't know what Spirit we're of. I haven't tried to call down fire from heaven on anybody's head lately, but we still err in spirit too many times. We put our faith in the denomination, instead of in the Spirit of the Lord.

I find it too much: Too much of the self-righteousness that existed in the days of Jeremiah. Too much of the self-righteousness that existed in the days of Jesus. Too many people too proud of who they are.

I like to go through the songbook and see some of the songs that were written by people who understood exactly who we really are. Songs like *Don't Let Me Walk Too Far From Calvary*, or *Tell me how much I owe; I want to repay!*

Songs that remind us that we're not as important as we think we are.

I listened to a tape one time, and it's actually a very good teaching tape by a person at one of the churches of another Apostolic denomination. She spent a considerable amount of time at the beginning of that tape praising the denomination she belongs to, calling it glorious and wonderful. I don't know how else to explain it, but all the glory was going to the organization. And I heard not one word of praise for the God was behind the whole thing! And it was frightening. It was frightening! It didn't detract from the eventual message she had, because it's one of the best I've ever heard. But there was an error in spirit there. Not an error in doctrine, because she's Apostolic, but there's an error in spirit when the church is getting the credit instead of God,

The same error in spirit can be found throughout the Apostolic church. The same error, the same pride in what we have built. You'll find it in the literature, you'll find it in the books, the history books that they've written. You'll find the error in spirit with the credit going to the organizations. *See what we've built!* And it's no different than the words in the days of Jeremiah: *The Temple of the Lord, the Temple of the Lord, the Temple of the Lord are these. This is the Apostolic church. This is the Apostolic church.*

You can't trust in words like that, because the Apostolic church won't get anybody to heaven. It does not have that power. It never did. That wasn't what it was for. The Apostolic church can't get anybody to heaven because the Apostolic church itself needs to be gotten to heaven! And the only Person who can bring the Apostolic church to heaven is Jesus.

So if we're looking for the church to bring us to heaven, we are in trouble, because only Jesus can bring us to heaven. If we're looking for the church to save us, we're out of luck, because only Jesus can save us. If we're looking for the church to wash away our sins, we are still out of luck: It can't do it. It can't wash away sins. They can't forgive sins. They can't save us. It can't get us to Heaven. It can't make us holy. It can't make us righteous. It can't do any of those things.

Why not? Because the organizations that we create, as far as God's concerned, they don't exist. We created those for our convenience, to make things easy for us to administrate. And there's nothing wrong with that, except when we start to think that those things have power.

When Israel came out of Egypt, Moses went up the mountain, and he was up there an awful long time, because God had a lot of stuff to dictate. Moses was slow of speech and slow of tongue, and at that point, probably slow of hand trying to write it all down.

The people got antsy. Now, I want you to understand something about the Jewish people at that time. There was something about them that was unique in all the world. Well, yes, we know, they were the people of the one true God. But there was something else: They were the only people on the face of the earth who could not see their God! Every other nation had visible representations of their gods. They knew what their god or gods or goddesses looked like, and here are these people who worship a God nobody can see. And up until just before that time, they worshiped a God whose name they didn't even know. You talk about being the laughingstock of the world! They insisted there was only one God, but they didn't know what He looked like or even what His name was. You talk about crazy!

And Israel had gotten just a little bit tired of that kind of a status. God had finally revealed His name to Moses, so the people of Israel finally knew their God's name. But that wasn't enough. They wanted to see Him, too. And so they said to Aaron, "Make us God..." Not *another* God. Not a *different* God. They weren't looking to get into worshiping false gods. Rather, they wanted a visible representation of Jehovah, something to look at and say, *There is our God* to all the nations that would point and say *Where is their God?* There's our God! Well, they had just come out of Egypt, and most of Egypt's gods were at least half animal, if not all animal. They would be half human and half lion, or a jackal, or a cat. They were animals. And so it was only natural that after 300 years in Egypt, Israel would try to represent the God of heaven as an animal.

Now, you want to talk about excuses that don't hold water: Aaron was just a scream when Moses confronted him: *Well, we put the gold into the fire, and this calf came out... all by itself!* Right! And the ghost of Elvis is living in my microwave, and space aliens fixed my teeth! Just as far-fetched as that.

So they made a golden calf, and the people said "This is the God who brought us up out of Egypt," and they began to worship the calf. But they'd made it with their own hands! How could it possibly have any power?

The calf had four legs, but couldn't walk. It had two eyes, but couldn't see, two ears, but couldn't hear. It had a mouth, but couldn't speak. How could it possibly do anything? It was something they'd made with their own hands, and it had no power, and yet they wanted to trust in it.

And they had a grand old worship service around that calf. This is the God that brought us up out of Egypt! Praise be to the name of the Lord! Calling that calf Jehovah!

We read that story, and we are just incensed, and horrified that they could do something so idolatrous. But we've done exactly the same thing by elevating our denominations to the status of God. *You have to belong to the church to be saved. The church will get you to heaven. You got to go to the right Church.*

And yet, *we* created the denomination. We created it. God didn't sit down in heaven one day, and make an alphabet soup list of names: UPC, ALJC, PAW and so on. He didn't do it. He didn't create a United Pentecostal church or a Pentecostal Assemblies of the World. He never conceived of an Assemblies of the Lord Jesus Christ. He never conceived of those things. We did that. It's not that there's anything wrong with them, although there's too many: there needs to be only one.

There's nothing wrong with denominations, because governments were put into the church to help us to administer group of people. But the danger comes when we take this organization that we have created, and claim that it is the Church of the Living God. It's exactly the same thing the Catholic Church did. It's exactly the same thing the Jewish people did in the days of Jeremiah. It's exactly what they did with the golden calf in the wilderness, and it's nothing short of idolatry.

It's not that we've tried to create a new God. But we've erred in spirit, and have not understood what we've done, and we need understanding. We need to understand that we have created the denominations and not God. And anything that we create, and actually, we shouldn't use that word, because the word create does not actually belong to us. It's not something we have the power to do. King Solomon said, "There's no new thing under the sun." Anything we could make is created from something that existed before in one form or another.

The Hebrew verb for create is *bará*, and it means to create something, to make something, out of nothing. To create from something that did not exist before, to actually speak matter into existence. We can't do that! We can't actually create, but we can make things, and organize things. But anything we make is going to be flawed, because we're flawed. When God created the world, it says that on each of the six days, when He saw what He had created, He saw that it was good. It was good!

But we can't say that about the things that we make, because they're flawed, because we're human beings. We try to do things our way and we make mistakes. So we make a denomination and it may look great, but it's got flaws.

And one of the most dangerous of those flaws is the self-righteousness that creeps in when we start to think that we've created the Church of the Living God. Foolish people! We **are** the Church of the Living God! We didn't create it!

We're supposed to **be** the church, not belong to the church. We're supposed to **be** the church, not organize the church. The church isn't the piece of paper that the government likes to see. The church isn't the initials that we throw around like they're in the Bible somewhere. That's not the church! We are! We are!

When we get to heaven, he's not going to divide us up by denominations. You know, there's an old joke about that, about the man who goes to heaven, and he's getting the grand tour. And St. Peter was showing him all the different places in heaven: Well, over there, those people, those are the Presbyterians. And those are the Jews. And this is this group, and this is that group. And then there's this really high wall; it's a big enclosed area and you can't see over the top of it. And the man said to St. Peter, "What's in there?" And Peter said. "Shh! That's the..." And that's where you fill in the name of a denomination. You can fill in the Pentecostals, or you can fill in the Catholics, because they both fit real well. "They think they're the only ones up here!"

You know, we joke about that, about heaven being segregated by denomination, but it's not. You won't get up there and find the UPC section, and the ALJC section. It doesn't work that way, because those things aren't the church. We're the church! The people: one body, one group, whether we try to divide it up or not, whether we try to split into groups or not, it's one body, one group of people. And He won't divide us by denomination. He disregards those things. And yet, we have majored on them. We have placed so much importance, so much stock, in something we created ourselves, that we have created an idol, that we have created a god.

It's a frightening thing, that there are people in the Apostolic church who, if given the choice between obeying the word of God or obeying the church, would choose the church. And by doing so, they have made the church their god. They have turned it into an idol. And they've jeopardized their salvation because there's no place for idolaters in the kingdom of God. Idolatry is not allowed.

You know, it was odd, one of the things that John said in one of his epistles: He told the church to keep themselves safe from idols. It's odd because, other than a few problems in the Corinthian church, the first century church didn't have any idols. That was one thing the people who had come in... Well, first of all, the Jewish Christians had never had idols because the Jewish religion didn't permit any type of statues of any of any sort, and so they didn't have them. The Gentile Christians were all too happy to trade away their statues of gold and silver and wood that had eyes and couldn't see and ears and couldn't hear. They were all too happy to trade it away for a God who could actually make a difference in their lives. So the early church didn't have any statues of any kind, and here's John telling the people to keep themselves safe from idols!

Flee from idols. What was he talking about? There are more kinds of idols than statues. We've become so narrow in our focus that, when we think of idols, all we can think about is Buddha or the Virgin Mary, these big statues of plaster or wood or gold, or silver idols. Idols, idols.

And yet, we have idols in our own churches, we have idols in our own homes, because we're putting things in the place of God, and we put our trust in things other than God,

We read Isaiah 30: The rebellious children, the Lord said, take counsel, they get advice, but not from God. Asking everybody's opinion but God's. And they cover themselves with a covering, that is, they protect themselves with something, but not the Spirit of God. Their trust is in something else. They go down to Egypt, symbolic of the world. They don't ask God for help, but they go to the world for help. And strengthen themselves at the hand of Pharaoh, and they trust in the shadow of Egypt. And therefore, that strength will be their shame. And their trust in the world will be their confusion.

So who is He talking about, the heathen? No, he's talking about us. He's talking about us, we who have allowed idols to come into the church, His church. We've allowed idols to take the place of God. We've put our trust in all the wrong things. It's not a matter of incorrect doctrine here, but a matter of error in spirit, a matter of lack of understanding, not seeing what we're doing. Like Laodicea, so easy to see everybody else, but we can't see ourselves. We can't see what we've allowed ourselves to become, what we've allowed to creep into the church.

Do you really think that the people of Israel would have built a golden calf if they knew it was an idol? If they understood that it was a false god, and that they couldn't have it? No, they would not have. They were not trying to replace Jehovah, just visualize Him. Just give Him an image. We've done the same thing by equating the church with God, by making the church out to be something divine when it's not. When all it is, is a bunch of people saved by grace. Sinners saved by grace, that's all.

The church has no power of itself. Any power we have, any righteousness we have does not come from the organizations we've made. It comes from Him. It comes from Him.

And yet, we've made idols, and we've trusted in the wrong things. What have we allowed ourselves to become? What have we turned the church into? What have we done with the Holy One of Israel?

Oh, it's the Church of God! It's the Church of God! It's the Apostolic Church! No. **We** are supposed to **be** the Apostolic Church.

We cannot have anything else in the church that we trust in. Not in people, but in God. There are some people in this country today who have made the United States their god. They've made this country their god. And it's idolatry, because the United States can't wash away our sins. The United States can't get us to heaven. The United States is not the object of God's special favor; it's just as doomed as the rest of the world. The United States is not the church.

We are the church. Not the building, not the organization or denomination, not the different government positions in the church that we give ourselves. None of that is the church. The people are the church. And people can't get us to heaven. They need to be **gotten** to heaven.

What are we going to trust in? Where we going to put our faith? Are we going to stand around glorifying the denominations we've built? Or are we going to realize that those divisions don't mean a thing to God, and that we're one people, whether we like it or not, whether we admit it or not, whether we choose to fellowship with each other or not.

The painful truth is that I'm not welcome in that church on Brandywine Avenue. I'm not welcome in that building. But I'm a part of them. And they wouldn't feel comfortable coming in here. But they are part of us, whether they like it or not.

What holds us apart? The idols do. That's what separates us. It's the idols. The idols of our denominations, the idols of our ideologies, the idols of our prejudices, our preconceived notions, the idols that we have allowed to judge us and to judge others, the idols that we have made gods, that we have surrendered ourselves to.

When we surrender ourselves to the will of a church, we are in bondage to idols, because we're supposed to be surrendered only to God. Only God paid the price.

Paul told the people, *I wasn't crucified for you. I didn't die for you. I don't forgive your sins. You belong to Christ.*

That's who we belong to. It's the only God we can acknowledge because it's the only God who can save us. Our denominations may have political power, but they have no spiritual power, because they aren't the church. The people are! If there's spiritual power in a denomination, it's in the people, and not in the organization.

We're looking for the uniting of the apostolic churches into one, but the honest truth, whether we see it or not, is that it has already happened because we have the same Spirit. We've been baptized by the same Holy Ghost. And we are one people. We are one body, whether we choose to acknowledge it or not.

If I look at the foot and say, it's not part of the body, it doesn't disconnect it. My right hand may say to my left hand, "Well, I'm the right hand. Therefore, I'm more important. You're not part of the body!" But it doesn't make the left hand not part of the body.

UPC may look down their nose at ALJC or at us, or vice versa, but it doesn't separate anybody from the body, because there is only one Apostolic Church. There is only one body and it's not any organization. It's the people. It's those people who have repented of their sins, been baptized in Jesus' name, and are full of the Holy Ghost and living for God. You can hang any name you want over the door. It doesn't matter.

It doesn't matter. And some of the names people have given their churches are pretty ridiculous, but it doesn't matter. You want to hang a sign outside that says *Church of Dishwater,* you go right ahead. It doesn't make any difference, because the church can't get you anywhere. That building won't help you. The organization won't help. They can't do it.

But if Jesus Christ is in there, then you've got the church. If Jesus Christ is in the midst of a group of people, that's the Church of the Living God. And it's one body, one people.

Folks, we've erred in spirit, and it's time we learn understanding. It's time we learn not to rebel against the Lord and to go looking to the world or to our own idols for our salvation. It's time we stopped looking to the denominations for our help. It's time we stopped looking to man-made things to save us. Because if we do, the strength of those things will be our shame, and our trust in those things will be our confusion.

Confusion is not of God. His people should never be put to shame. When we trust in Him, when He is the only God we acknowledge, when it's only in Him that we've put our faith, when it's only to Him that we have surrendered, we'll never be put to shame. We'll never be confused. Then we'll be one body, leaning on our Lord, exactly like Solomon said: *Leaning on her Beloved.*

It's time to put the idols out of the church. To put away the false gods that we've created. It's time to get Baal out of Pentecost.

Baal in the Old Testament is often plural, Baalim with *im* on the end, because there wasn't just one thing called Baal. One preacher I heard described it as a whole galaxy of gods. And we think we're above that. And yet, Baal's alive and well, all of them, in the Church of the Living God, because we've made idols, And we've fallen down and worshiped them, saying *these are the things that save us. This is what saves us from sin: Our church, our organization.*

I tell you, we've got more golden calves than Israel ever dreamed of. We've got more statues than the Canaanites ever imagined.

We listen in horror to the stories of the different gods the Canaanites worshiped. We listen in horror to the stories of Molech, the big statue with his arms outstretched, and they'd burn their children alive in the arms of that statue. But haven't we done the same thing? Haven't we killed so many in the church? Haven't we driven the children out?

Do you know there are more people who have been thrown out of the church than there are inside the church? More people have been cast out than are still in, for whatever stupid reason, as if we had authority to put somebody out. We burned our children alive to the god that we created.

Yes, we've got idols, alive and well, living in the church, ruling our lives, making our decisions for us. And we bow down and we worship them, all the while claiming to be Christians, saying T*his is what we've been set free to do: Set free to put ourselves in bondage to idols.*

No, I don't think so. I think it's time the church put the idols away. I think it's time we did a thorough house cleaning of the Church of the Living God. Not the organizations, but the people, every one of us, to look and see what idols we've created or what idols we've adopted.

It's an incredible thing that the people of Israel would go through the wilderness victorious in all their battles against the Canaanites, where the gods of the Canaanites could not defend their people, and the God of Israel brought victory after victory after victory. Yet, no sooner did Israel get into the land than they adopted the Canaanite gods that couldn't protect their own people! What in heaven's name was wrong with them? They had freedom, and they put themselves back into bondage to idols that couldn't even protect their own nations.

And yet, I watch the Church of the Living God, set free from the sin of the world, putting themselves into bondage to new idols. Just set free from one slavery, and put ourselves into another. To serve things that cannot save. To serve organizations, to serve denominations, to serve ideologies, to serve prejudices. And it all comes down to serving the flesh.

We read the Old Testament so self-righteously, when the prophets got on the case of Israel and Judah because they were in an idolatrous people, and a rebellious people. All the idolatry! Oh, how terrible! Oh, how terrible! Thank God we're not like that. No different than the Pharisee at the altar: *Thank God, I'm not like that sinner over there.* Thank God, I'm not like him.

And yet we are. And yet we're just as idolatrous as Israel, just as idolatrous as Judah. Just as much in bondage. And we wonder why we can't fulfill the Great Commission. We wonder why we haven't made much progress.

He told us we'd be witnesses in all the world, and yet we seem to have so much trouble. So much of this nation that we keep thinking is so wonderfully spiritual, so wonderfully Christian, so much of this nation is in complete darkness, blindness, bondage, when it comes to the things of God. So much so that the nations we thought we had to rescue are sending us missionaries because we're such a mess!

While we sit comfortably on padded pews. The Church of God, the Church of God, the Church of God is this. We used to sing it: *The Church of the Living God is moving through the land.* These songs we used to sing, so proud of being the Church of God, and all the while putting our faith in the denomination and not in the God himself. Worshiping the idols that we created.

Church, put the idols away! We need to put the idols out of our hearts out of our lives. We need to do a thorough search for anything that might be hidden. There are times in the Old Testament where you can read about people who claim to have put away the idols, and yet they had little statues buried in their tents. Hidden, thinking nobody sees. And here, we've got little statues buried in our hearts. Thinking, nobody knows. Nobody sees. And we're even worse than those who openly worship a statue, because we've added the sin of deceit to our idolatry.

It's time for the church to repent, and be converted, converted from idolatry to monotheism, to the worship of the one true God. That's a frightening message to have to preach in an Apostolic church, and yet it needs to be preached from every Apostolic pulpit in this country! It's time for the Apostolic Church to repent and be converted from idolatry, to put aside and leave behind the idols that we served as slaves. To abandon our faith and hope in things that we have created, thinking that somehow we could make our own way to heaven, because we can't do it.

And if we trust in anything other than the Living God to get us to heaven, then we're not an Apostolic Church. Then we're idolaters. I don't want to be part of an idolatrous church. I don't want idols ruling my life. I don't want it! I don't want anything other than the Living God sitting on the throne in my heart!

We've got to make a search throughout our heart, to every dark corner, and find out where we put our trust, find out where our faith is, where our hope is. What are we looking to? What's going to save us? And if it's anything other than Jesus Christ, **anything** other than Jesus Christ, then we're idolaters. No wonder John said flee from idols! No wonder he said we had to keep ourselves safe from them, because they creep in, the items that we have created.

When we try to get rid of them, it's no different than Ephesus, where the silversmiths got the whole city going for hours on end: *Great is Diana of the Ephesians! Great is Diana of the Ephesians!* because they were afraid of losing what made their living. They were creators of idols. And we're afraid to give up our idols. Something inside of us is screaming that our idols are great: Great are our own ideas! Great is our own will! Great are our denominations!

What's the difference? Between a preacher spending all kinds of time telling how glorious a particular denomination is before preaching or teaching... What's the difference between that, and the silversmiths standing up and saying *Great is Diana of the Ephesians* for hours? Where's the difference?

They're both things we've created; neither one has power to save. The difference is that it's more frightening when it's someone who is supposed to be Apostolic giving the power and praise and glory to the denomination. We can excuse the silversmiths of Ephesus, because they didn't know any better. But we can't excuse an Apostolic preacher who puts the denomination above God.

We need to clean it out. We need to destroy the Dianas in our lives, the Molechs, the Dagons, the Baals. We need to destroy them, no matter what names they go by today.

The false gods and goddesses of the other nations, centuries earlier, had other names. It wasn't that they were anything different, people just changed their names. The Greek and Roman gods and goddesses, they're the same people, just different names. And many of them can be traced back to Egypt and to Babylon. They just changed their names. So what did we do? Change Diana and call it UPC? Did we change Dagon to PAW? Do we change Baal to our own will? It doesn't matter what we call it. It doesn't matter; it's exactly the same thing. All the gods, and goddesses of the nations are alive and well and living in the Apostolic Church!

[Earlier, this Brother] talked about needing to get an exterminator... I've got news: We are infested with idols, and it's time we do something about it. For too long we've been content to live in the shadow of the gods and goddesses we created, of the idols that we've made.

We can't remain an Apostolic church if we're going to live in the shadow of idols. The Dianas have to go! The Baals have to go! Dagon has got to fall on his face before the Living God, just as he did in the Old Testament! And we've got to destroy the valley where we've burned our children to Molech, where we've destroyed and driven people out of the church. And it's time we go out and bring them back. It's time we undo some of the damage that we've done in the names of our idols.

There was no way Israel could bring back the children they burned alive, but we've got a chance. Maybe we can rescue some. But it won't happen until we put away our idols. Because if we try to bring them back first, we'll just sacrifice them all on the altar of our idolatry again.

I'm not willing to sacrifice anything on the altar of idolatry. I'm not going to sacrifice the lost who come in looking for hope. I'm not going to sacrifice the word of God, and I'm not going to sacrifice my salvation on the altar of idolatry. We've done that for too long. We've done it for too long.

It's time to break down that altar, and find the stones of an old altar of the Lord, where once upon a time we knew how to worship. And it's time we sacrifice ourselves on that altar. It's time we crucify the flesh and live in the Spirit. It's time we prove once and for all that there's only one God who answers by fire, and it's not Baal. It's Jesus!

Joshua said to the people, "Choose today whom you're going to serve." Who're you going to worship? Who're you going to trust? I can't answer for anybody else in the church. But I can answer for me. The same answer Joshua gave. You people can worship your idols if you want to; I won't have any part of them. I worship the Lord. Him only will I serve.

Pentecost, put away your idols! Apostolic Church, worship only one God, and let it be Jesus! Hallelujah!

Lord, open our eyes that we might see our hearts. Show us ourselves as You see us, that we might know what idols we have allowed to be set up in our lives, that we might see what we have put before You, that we might tear them down. We will never know peace until we've torn down the idols in our hearts, and Lord, We want peace. We need peace. We need peace in our lives. A peace the statues cannot give us, a piece that denominations cannot give us. But it's a peace that comes from the Prince of Peace. We want to be a people with one God, Trusting only in You, and in nothing else. Sure in our faith, solid on a foundation that cannot crumble, knowing that You are our only source, our only refuge, our only hope, our only salvation. Teach us, Lord, to lean completely on You, and on no one and nothing else. Help us to live up to the name of Apostolic, to no longer err in spirit, but to have understanding. In the name of Jesus. Amen!

The Urgency

I'm turning to the book of Matthew. This is going to be a rare occasion for you. I'm actually going to preach from the New Testament instead of the Old Testament! Every once in awhile, I have to do that to keep you off your guard!

Matthew chapter 24, and beginning at the beginning of the chapter:

And Jesus went out, and departed from the temple: and his disciples came to him for to shew him the buildings of the temple.

And Jesus said unto them, See ye not all these things? verily I say unto you, There shall not be left here one stone upon another, that shall not be thrown down.

And as he sat upon the mount of Olives, the disciples came unto him privately, saying, Tell us, when shall these things be? and what shall be the sign of thy coming, and of the end of the world?

And Jesus answered and said unto them, Take heed that no man deceive you.

For many shall come in my name, saying, I am Christ; and shall deceive many.

And ye shall hear of wars and rumors of wars: see that ye be not troubled: for all these things must come to pass, but the end is not yet.

For nation shall rise against nation, and kingdom against kingdom: and there shall be famines, and pestilences, and earthquakes, in divers places.

All these are the beginning of sorrows.

Then shall they deliver you up to be afflicted, and shall kill you: and ye shall be hated of all nations for my name's sake.

And then shall many be offended, and shall betray one another, and shall hate one another.

And many false prophets shall rise, and shall deceive many.

And because iniquity shall abound, the love of many shall wax cold.

But he that shall endure unto the end, the same shall be saved.

And this gospel of the kingdom shall be preached in all the world for a witness unto all nations; and then shall the end come.

When ye therefore shall see the abomination of desolation, spoken of by Daniel the prophet, stand in the holy place, (whoso readeth, let him understand:)

Then let them which be in Judaea flee into the mountains:

Let him which is on the housetop not come down to take any thing out of his house:

Neither let him which is in the field return back to take his clothes.

And woe unto them that are with child, and to them that give suck in those days!

But pray ye that your flight be not in the winter, neither on the sabbath day:

For then shall be great tribulation, such as was not since the beginning of the world to this time, no, nor ever shall be.

And except those days should be shortened, there should no flesh be saved: but for the elect's sake those days shall be shortened.

Then if any man shall say unto you, Lo, here is Christ, or there; believe it not.

For there shall arise false Christs, and false prophets, and shall shew great signs and wonders; insomuch that, if it were possible, they shall deceive the very elect.

Behold, I have told you before.

Wherefore if they shall say unto you, Behold, he is in the desert; go not forth: behold, he is in the secret chambers; believe it not.

For as the lightning cometh out of the east, and shineth even unto the west; so shall also the coming of the Son of man be.

For wheresoever the carcass is, there will the eagles be gathered together.

Immediately after the tribulation of those days shall the sun be darkened, and the moon shall not give her light, and the stars shall fall from heaven, and the powers of the heavens shall be shaken:

And then shall appear the sign of the Son of man in heaven: and then shall all the tribes of the earth mourn, and they shall see the Son of man coming in the clouds of heaven with power and great glory.

And he shall send his angels with a great sound of a trumpet, and they shall *gather together his elect from the four winds, from one end of heaven to the other.*

Now learn a parable of the fig tree; When his branch is yet tender, and putteth forth leaves, ye know that summer is nigh:

So likewise ye, when ye shall see all these things, know that it is near, even at the doors.

Verily I say unto you, This generation shall not pass, till all these things be fulfilled.

Heaven and earth shall pass away, but my words shall not pass away.

But of that day and hour knoweth no man, no, not the angels of heaven, but my Father only.

But as the days of Noah were, so shall also the coming of the Son of man be.

For as in the days that were before the flood they were eating and drinking, marrying and giving in marriage, until the day that Noe entered into the ark,

And knew not until the flood came, and took them all away; so shall also the coming of the Son of man be.

Then shall two be in the field; the one shall be taken, and the other left.

Two women shall be grinding at the mill; the one shall be taken, and the other left.

Watch therefore: for ye know not what hour your Lord doth come.

But know this, that if the goodman of the house had known in what watch the thief would come, he would have watched, and would not have suffered his house to be broken up.

Therefore be ye also ready: for in such an hour as ye think not the Son of man cometh.

[Buzzing sound heard.] I assume that was just static, but it scared me because I thought it was a wasp. I think you all know how I feel about wasps. I was preaching in the Tucson church one time, and they had the back door open because it was July and very hot. And just as I stood up to preach, a wasp came in the back door of the church, and flew all the way up to the front and then stopped there in front of me, hovering in the air, looking at me. I thought, well, I have two choices: I can panic, or I can preach. And I remembered years before, Brother Hanby telling me the story of when he was preaching a Tent

Revival. A man had come in the back of the tent with a brick in his hand, and told Brother Hanby to sit down and shut up, or he was going to hit him with the brick. But Brother Hanby kept right on preaching. The man dropped the brick and ran up front and repented.

And I thought of that story, and I looked at the wasp, and I began to preach. And the wasp flew up and sat on the ceiling, and stayed there till I was done!

Okay, we're turning now to 1st Thessalonians, chapter 4. I'm going to begin at verse 13. Before I read this, though, I need to mention that there's one word in here that has changed meaning. Remember, every once in a while we come across a word that meant something else back in 1611, but means something else now. Today, the word *prevent* means to stop something from happening. But it used to mean *precede, go ahead of, go before*. That's what *prevent* meant.

But I would not have you to be ignorant, brethren, concerning them which are asleep, that ye sorrow not, even as others which have no hope.

For if we believe that Jesus died and rose again, even so them also which sleep in Jesus will God bring with him.

For this we say unto you by the word of the Lord, that we which are alive and remain unto the coming of the Lord shall not prevent them which are asleep.

For the Lord himself shall descend from heaven with a shout, with the voice of the archangel, and with the trump of God: and the dead in Christ shall rise first:

Then we which are alive and remain shall be caught up together with them in the clouds, to meet the Lord in the air: and so shall we ever be with the Lord.

Wherefore comfort one another with these words.

The other night, I had a dream that fascinated me, intrigued me, and scared me all at once. The dream started off at some kind of a camp meeting, a church camp meeting. I don't know what the building was, but it wasn't any building I'd been in before. The place was packed. There were brothers and sisters from all over the country, possibly all over the world, and we'd all gathered together for several days of camp meeting. There was a lot of excitement in the air. We were all excited about being with each.

The place was just so crowded, and every room had like three or floor people sleeping on the floor, because they were just so many people. And even though there were three or four bathrooms in the place, it wasn't enough. But it was great to have so many people together. It was nighttime, and most folks were asleep, but I was awake. A lot of times when that happens, when I'm awake when I'm supposed to be sleeping, it usually means that God is trying to tell me something. He is not about to let me go to sleep until I finish listening regardless of how much I fight it and say I want to go to sleep. I remember feeling a sense of urgency in this dream, and thinking that I needed to get all these people together and tell them about this. I was apparently scheduled to preach at the first service, but the first service wasn't scheduled until the next evening. And here it was, the night before, and I kept thinking, *I'm not sure this can wait; this is something they've got to hear.*

Now, it was an interesting collection of people. Some were young, some were old. I didn't actually know anybody there personally, but I knew who some of them were. I knew that some of the older people were Pentecostal preachers who had been preaching for a long time, for generations practically. They'd been in it a long time, and we were all gathered there for the same purpose. And yet, I had this urgency, and I talked with some of the Brothers, and they were feeling something similar, that we needed to have service before the first service was scheduled, so that we could preach, so that this message could come forth.

And I began to think about that feeling of urgency that I was feeling, and remembering that from time to time in my life, I've felt it. And yet, I've always let go of it. I've always let it go. I never held on to that urgency.

We've had 90-some years of Pentecost in the 20th century, and there have been some glorious times. If you ever get a chance, read Sister Goss' book, **The Winds of God.** It's about the first 14 years of the 20th century, and it's just incredible. The miracles that were recorded were just phenomenal. The exciting things that happened, things that we haven't even seen since. Variations on a theme, you could call it. I mean, we're used to hearing people speak in tongues, but there was an example, and I think it was in that book, of somebody writing in tongues! The person called for a pen and paper, and began to write in fluent Chinese without ever having studied the language, just by the Spirit of God. Just powerful things, happening all over the country, and then spreading around the world, and that's wonderful. We've had 90-some odd years of that, but you know, we fallen into a rut, the rut that I call *Pentecost as usual*, because we've gotten used to it. We're not the first generation from those who receive the Holy Ghost back in 1901. That first generation, they never lost their fervor. They never lost it! The early church, the first generation, those who were there on the day of Pentecost, those who were converted on the day of Pentecost, those who were converted in that first generation, they never lost that fervor either.

It was the next generation, and then the following generation that began to lose it. They began to lose that fervor to the point where 66 years after the whole thing began, it began to backslide. Jude wrote his epistle because the church was backsliding after just 66 years.

Well, it's been more than 90 years now. And I'm afraid that the same thing that happened in the first century church has crept into our own, and that is complacency. We've come to take it for granted. We've come to accept Pentecost as something usual, something ordinary. You go to church two or three times a week, you worship, you clap your hands, you shout and dance, you speak in tongues; whatever it is that you do. And then you just go on with your life. Day after day, week after week, month after month, year after year, ignoring the words of our own preachers, ignoring the words of our own songwriters, all of whom have tried, year after year, to convey the urgency to us.

Some of you may remember Lanny Wolfe's song that started off by saying *What if this would be the year that Jesus comes, the year that we've waited for so long? We'd have so little time to get our lost world won, if this would be the year when Jesus comes.* But then he said, *"What if this would be the day that Jesus comes?"* And then finally asks, *"What if this would be the moment that Jesus comes,"* trying to convey to us that we are not given the rest of eternity to do this work, that there is a limited amount of time, and we don't know how much time that is. But I'm feeling that sense of urgency again, that we're running out of time to do the work. And we've barely started. We've barely started.

When we were down at the conference in Birmingham, the first night there,

I had preached something, and I threw in a little anecdote that I'm going to throw in again. Now, I spend a lot of my time waiting for people to come pick me up, whether it's a cab or a friend, because I can't drive. I'm the type that's usually a little early. I'm very rarely late. On the other hand, most people are usually late, and so I spend half my life waiting. But for me, nothing is as frustrating as somebody being late: Half hour late, an hour late sometimes. My brother and his wife: three hours late, and I'll call their house, and they haven't left yet. Really, my brother and sister-in-law were once three hours late, coming to my house for dinner, and they had not even left home yet! And they never picked up the phone to say they were running late! Now that's frustrating!

Can you imagine God looking down at the church to see how far we've progressed with the work we have to do, and finding out we've barely started? Or maybe we haven't started... We haven't left home! We haven't taken it outside the walls of the church. We haven't taken it out to the people who need us. And the time is short.

90-some odd years of Pentecost as usual, where it didn't really matter that the kingdom of God was supposed to be the first priority in our lives. We could get away with what we wanted, and we did. We did! Oh, we were faithful, went to church regularly, often were out on the streets witnessing. I can remember Sister Lily K. and I getting so excited while witnessing: We danced up and down State Street in front of Proctor's Theater! I mean, that's great. We were doing some of the work.

We can't have any other concerns at this point. Time is short enough, and I can't tell you exactly how short, because like Jesus said, in the verses we read in Matthew, we don't know the hour or the day. We can't know exactly when He's coming back, but He gave us the signs to look for, so that we would know the time and the season, so that we would not be caught unaware... So we would not just suddenly find ourselves standing before Him empty-handed saying, *Well, we didn't know You were coming back!* He gave us enough signs to look for so that we would know.

The signs have come to pass. Now I know that there have been other generations that thought, *Well, this is it! We're the last generation!* But this generation, now, is where **all** the signs have come to pass.

Oh, but there have always been all those things, haven't there? No, there haven't always been all those things. Did you know that before the year 1700 there were far fewer earthquakes in the world? They were so infrequent that they were almost unheard of. There may have been one earthquake a year someplace. But now, there's not a day that goes by when we don't have a major quake someplace. Scientists tell us it's because the earth is cooling. The Bible says it's because Jesus is coming back. It's a sign.

All the things we were told to look for have come to pass, and Jesus said that the generation that saw them would not pass away till it was all fulfilled. He told us to take a lesson from the fig tree: We're smart enough to know that when the tree puts forth buds, and then gets leaves, summer is coming.

We need to be smart enough to realize that we've got the signs coming to pass in this world. They tell us our time is running out. The clock is ticking, and since we can't see the clock, we don't know exactly how much time we've got. What if this would be the year when Jesus comes? What if this would be the day? What if this would be the moment?

We've barely started the work. We've barely begun. But there may not be more time. We've got an awful lot of work to do, and if we are going to have any chance at all of reaching this world with the Gospel, it's going to mean that every single Christian man, woman and child is going to have to be sold out to the Kingdom of God, 100%. It's going to mean that we're going to have to take everything else in our life that we think is important, and throw it on the back burner, and keep our attention on the Kingdom of God.

It's so easy to get caught up in all the other things we worry about: What are we going to eat? What are we going to wear? How am I going to pay the bills? What are we going to do? Where we going to go? What are we... When are we... Where will we... *You don't worry about those things!* You let the the non-Christians worry about those things! Let them worry about it! You seek first the Kingdom of God and His righteousness, and all those things will be added unto you. But you've got to make the Kingdom of God your first priority.

Have ever had the experience that you find what you're looking for when you stopped looking for it? That's true of all the things you need in your life. You stop seeking after them, and they'll come to you when you start seeking for the Kingdom of God. That's got to be our first priority, because there is so much work to do for the Kingdom.

And over the years, the preachers have told us, and over the years, the songwriters have told us, and even God Himself has told us, speaking in prophecy. One beautiful, powerful prophecy that came forth, and Lanny Wolfe wrote it into a song. Church service was going on, everybody having a grand old time, but just Pentecost as usual, when the Lord interrupted them and said, *"My house is full, but My field is empty! All My children want to sit around the table, nobody wants to work in the field."*

That's where the work is. It's not in here. This is just a refueling station. Wouldn't do much good if you took your car to the gas station, filled it up, and then just sat there in the gas station till it ran empty, and then filled it up again. You've got to go somewhere with it. You come here and get your refilling. Then take it out there and do something with it! Bring it out there!

You can call this medical school if you want to. Sister Phyllis M. used to call this the Holy Ghost hospital. She said church was the Holy Ghost hospital. This is medical school. You're learning how to take care of the sick, because all those people out there, they're really sick spiritually, and they need a physician. But they may not come in here, so you go to them, like Jesus did, because they need it. They have got to know. We've got a responsibility to see that there's a world out there that's in chains, chains of sin. They are in bondage, they are in darkness.

We could just shake our heads and say, *oh, what a shame,* or we could look down our noses at them, because we've been set free, but that's not what the first century church would have done. When they came across people in bondage, what did they do? They set them free. Freely you have received, freely give.

That's our responsibility: Set them free. What good is our freedom if we can't share it with somebody else? What good is the liberty that the Spirit of God gives us if we can't set somebody else free with it too, if the people we love have to perish in bondage? That's not the way it's supposed to be.

We've got a responsibility to them. They need us, whether they like us or not. Jesus was right when He said that we would be hated by all nations for His name's sake. The scripture says all who live godly in Christ Jesus shall suffer persecution. But he also counted persecution on the list of blessings we'd get. So maybe it's not such a bad thing. Maybe if we really are being persecuted for His name's sake, it means we're doing something right. And if they're leaving us alone, or praising us, maybe we're doing something wrong. But regardless of what they think of us, we've got a responsibility to them.

You know, a lot of times when we go to the doctor or the dentist, the things they do to us hurt, don't they? Oh yeah, they hurt. The last time I had a filling done, he must have given me five or six shots of Novocaine, because it just wasn't working. And each time, he'd start drilling. He'd say, "That still hurts?" I know he wasn't trying to hurt me. He was doing something that was good for me. But it didn't endear him to my heart at that particular moment. People may not appreciate what we're trying to do, but it is for their own good.

We need to take it out to them. and give it to them in love. That's important. The word says "...speaking the truth in love." You don't catch any flies with vinegar, do you? You go out there and take a king-sized King James Bible, and whack them upside the head with it, and tell them they're going to burn in hell if they don't get the Holy Ghost. Have you helped anyone get saved that day? Obviously, no. If you pry open their mouth and stick the corner of the Bible in and try to shove it down their throat sideways, have you won anybody? No. But if you love them unconditionally, and show them the love of Jesus, then you got a chance. Then you've got a chance, when you show them the fruit of the Spirit in your life. That's how you know Christians, you know, not by how much they dance, how much they shout or how much they speak in tongues. Jesus said, "By this shall all men know that you're My disciples, if you love one another."

If you have love one for another... That's part of being sold out to the Kingdom of God, being sold out to each other... So that we no longer matter, but our brothers and sisters do. Doesn't matter what happens to me, it only matters what happens to you: You need to be so sold out to your brothers and sisters that you'd be willing to sacrifice your own salvation for them. There's no way that would ever happen, of course, because if you're that dedicated, you won't lose your salvation. But that's how dedicated you need to be, that you would be willing to sacrifice yourself if it meant that your brother or sister could make it in. Whatever it takes to get them in...

We're building an ark, folks. And we know the sky is getting dark and the rain is coming. We've seen the signs. Noah had a hundred years to preach. We've already preached more than 90. The time is growing short. And I promise you, the minute the rain began to fall, the people knew that they should have listened to Noah, and they knocked on the door of that ark. But Noah couldn't let them in, because Noah hadn't shut that door. The Bible says **God** shut the door. When God shuts a door, nobody opens it.

The time to get into this ark is now, because God's going to shut the door. We won't be able to get anybody else in then. For that hundred years, Noah served as a preacher of righteousness. That's not easy to do while you're building a giant boat, but he did it. And he managed to get the message out to the people of the world. In that time, one man, in a hundred years, managed to preach to the whole world. We've got more than one man. We got a whole bunch of men and women, and they know the message.

It's our responsibility: Apostolic folks all over this world. It's our responsibility to take it outside of the doors of our churches, out into the highways and the byways, to find the castoffs of the earth, to find the ones no one else wants: the poor, the homeless, the sick, those that are in bondage. Set them free, and share with them what you found.

We don't know how much time we've got. It could be a year; it could be twenty years. It could be a month, or a day, or an hour. But however much time we've got left, it's up to us to make the most of that time, to use it wisely.

We often hear people tell us how we have to be good stewards with the things that God gives us. And we usually talk about being good stewards of our money. But we also need to be good stewards of our time: A minimum of 10% of our time belongs to God. When we talk about tithing, it's not just your money God's interested in. 10% of your time also belongs to Him. That's not a lot to ask, considering that He gave His whole life for us.

The time needs to be spent wisely because we don't know how much of it there is. Only He knows. And when that trumpet finally blows, and we find ourselves standing before Him, I don't want to have to be ashamed and say that I didn't do any of the work, or that I didn't do my share of the work, or that I have nothing to show for it.

Sister Joan Ewing wrote a song about how she didn't want to stand before Him without a star in her crown. What she was saying is *I don't want to get there and find out I have nothing to show for my efforts.* She wanted to make sure she accomplished something while she was here, that not only was she getting in, but she was bringing people with her.

Most places, it's considered rude if you arrive bringing extra guests. But not the Kingdom of God: We've got to bring as many with us as we can. The more we can get in, the better. No one's going to be turned away at the door. But we've got to get them in now, before the door closes. We've got to get them in now, while there's still time.

The Bible tells us to work while there is still light, while it's daytime, because the night is coming, and you can't work then. The night's coming. The work has to be done now, while there's still a chance to do it.

Maybe our problem is we haven't been persecuted enough. Historically, the church has done so much better in places where it was persecuted, where it was illegal. Those are the places where the church really grows. Those are the places where they really have revival, where they take their lives in their hands if they go inside a Pentecostal church, or where they're not even allowed to have church buildings. That was where it really grew, was when it was persecuted.

We've had it a little too easy here. We've had it a little too easy, and the fact that we haven't suffered any persecution suggests mostly to me that we haven't done the job, because Jesus promised we'd suffer persecution. That was part of the package deal. That's part of it. There's no escaping from that. If you're living godly in Christ Jesus, if you're living for God and doing His work, there will be some persecution. It will come. And if it doesn't come, we must be doing something wrong. We must be doing something wrong.

You know, the devil never attacks people who are doing what he wants them to do. He only attacks the people who are doing something for God. He has no need to bother some people, because they're so messed up that they don't need his help to get any more messed up. But when the devil attacks, it's because he's trying to prevent you from doing something for God. That's not a good reason to quit. That's all the more reason to continue on.

That's a good sign, not a bad sign, when the devil attacks. Just take a brief moment, slap him in the face with scripture, and continue on with the work. The devil just has a short memory; he needs reminders. He has no rights in the Kingdom of God. He has no rights in the church. He has no authority over you, but he forgets that. ***Don't you ever forget that!*** And when the devil forgets, remind him! If the devil throws your past at you, do you remember what to do? Remind him of his future! *"The devil was thrown into the Lake of Fire, tormented day and night forever and ever."* He forgets that, too. But I love to remind him. I love to remind him, because he's fond of throwing my past in my face, so I just throw his future in his!

And yes, he attacks from time to time, and yes, he throws stumbling blocks. I can't let that stop me. Neither can you! We've got a job to do. There's work to be done in this Kingdom. God needs workers. He needs us, all of us. Nobody's exempt from the work.

Some of the best preachers the world has ever known have been children. Everybody can do something. Brother Hanby, he started preaching when he was fourteen. Fourteen years old! There have been younger preachers than that. No one told them *Stand up and preach*, but something inside of them said *Stand up and preach!* And they did. If a child can obey, can't we? Can't we?

Whether it's standing up in a pulpit and preaching, or whether it's standing on a street corner, whether it's handing a tract to somebody, or whether it's taking the time to sit and talk with somebody who needs somebody to talk to, just showing the love of Jesus like that. Or whether it's... I like what Brother Mark here did: He went door to door, and left a copy of the Gospel of John at every house! I like that. That's good. That's good.

Planting some seed there, because God's word doesn't come back empty. It accomplishes what He sends it out to do. And the Gospel of John is a powerful book. There's no Gospel that shows just who Jesus was quite the way John did it. He didn't pull any punches. It was in the Gospel of John that Jesus annoyed the Jewish people so much. When He said *"Abraham rejoiced to see My day; he saw it and was glad."* And the people said, 'You're not even 50 years old. Have you seen Abraham?" And I love what He said to them: *"Before Abraham was, I am!"*

That showed exactly who He was. *I am that I am* or *I am who I am.* He showed who He was. They didn't miss that: They picked up stones right away to throw at Him and He walked right through the midst of them! *Hallelujah! That's powerful stuff!*

All right, I'm off on a tangent and I need to draw this to a conclusion. There is an urgency. We need to catch hold of it and not lose it. I don't think we have another 90 years for *Pentecost as usual.* I can't tell you how many years we do have, but I seriously doubt we have another 90 years. We don't have that much. There's no way we could be left to our own devices for another 90 years: We would blow this planet sky high!

We haven't got another 90 years to do it. There's no time for *Pentecost as usual.* No time for playing church. There's only time for building the Kingdom. And it's going to take all of us doing it. They rebuilt the walls of the city of Jerusalem after Babylon destroyed them. The men, the women, the children: Everybody worked. They worked with a sword in one hand, symbolizing the word of God, and bricks in the other. And it said that the work was completed because the people had a mind to work! And that's what we need, a mind to work, with our sword in one hand, and working with the other. *Hallelujah! Hallelujah! Thank the Lord!*

Lord Jesus, mold the hearts of Your people and put an urgency in there. Kindle a flame of urgency to remind us time and again that our time is short, and that there's work that needs to be done. Give us a burden for it, a desire for it. Open our eyes to see the people who need it. Open our ears to hear the cry of the lost, and let it grow ever louder in our ears, until we are driven to do the work, because it needs to be done. In your own words, Lord, let Your kingdom come, and let us work to build it. In the name of Jesus. Amen!

Who Hath Bewitched You?

We're turning to the book of Galatians. Something's been on my heart most of the week. I was over at some friends' house Thursday evening, and I already knew this is what I was preaching Sunday. We were looking through the book of Galatians, and these words began to jump off the page at me. And I said, *"Okay, I get the message."*

Galatians chapter 3, beginning at the beginning of the chapter:

O foolish Galatians, who hath bewitched you, that ye should not obey the truth, before whose eyes Jesus Christ hath been evidently set forth, crucified among you? This only would I learn of you, Received ye the Spirit by the works of the law, or by the hearing of faith? Are ye so foolish? having begun in the Spirit, are ye now made perfect by the flesh? Have ye suffered so many things in vain? if it be yet in vain. He therefore that ministereth to you the Spirit, and worketh miracles among you, doeth he it by the works of the law, or by the hearing of faith?

There are all different kinds of preachers. There are some preachers that I've heard that I really couldn't get much out of what they teach preached. I knew a preacher one time who assumed that volume was equivalent to anointing, and he was under the impression that if he was not absolutely screaming at the top of his lungs that he was not preaching under the anointing of the Holy Ghost. Well, the problem was that he screamed his sermons so loud that I never understood a word he said. I had no idea what he was preaching about. I didn't even know the topic of his sermon because all he did was stand there and scream and pound the pulpit. But he got the whole congregation hollering and shouting. What was that, the Spirit of God, or was that their own flesh? It's easy to whip people up and get them screaming and shouting.

Now, there's nothing wrong with screaming and shouting. I've shouted a lot during sermons myself and there's nothing wrong with shouting when you preach. I do that sometimes too, but that's not generally my style of preaching. I'm a teacher preacher. When I preach something, it's because there's something that needs to be given to the people. There's a message that has to be given, something that has to be taught, a piece of food that has to be served.

You wait for the Evangelist to come to the pulpit, and then they'll preach and get you shouting and hollering and screaming. They can do that. I have to feed. Never yet seen a kid shout happily about spinach coming to the table. I've seen them scream a few times!

I wish sometimes that the Bible came with "tone of voice" markings in it. If you get a copy of the Old Testament in Hebrew, when you look at it, there are extra markings in there that are not actually part of the text. What they are are tone markings for the Cantor in the synagogue, because theoretically, the entire Old Testament can be chanted or sung, and it tells them what tones to use: whether the voice should go up or the voice should go down.

But I wish we had tone of voice markings for the Bible. I would love to hear the tone of voice that people used when they said certain things. But sometimes you can tell by reading between the lines. Like, when Philip said to Jesus, "Lord, just show us the Father, and that will be enough for us." I can hear frustration in his voice, but I can hear amazement in the voice of Jesus when He said, "Have I been with you all this time, Philip, and you still don't know Me?" Tone of voice!

Chapter 3 of Galatians: *Foolish Galatians...* Now, that's not a word to use lightly. Remember Jesus said, "The one who says to his brother 'thou fool' is in danger of hell fire." You don't use the word fool lightly. You'll very rarely hear me use the word fool. I will never call somebody a fool. That's a dangerous thing to say. The scripture tells us that the fool says in his heart, *there is no God.*

And yet, here comes Paul who not just once, but twice, called the Galatians foolish, and then asked who bewitched them. *Who put a spell on you? What happened while I was gone?* You see, when he left, they were doing just fine: A promising church: growing, strong. Everything looks like it's going really well, and then he gets word of what's actually going on there after he leaves, and he wants to know: *Who put a spell on you?* It has to be witchcraft! It has to be some kind of magic, because there is no way, by natural process, that you people could get so far away from what I taught you.

Going back to the first chapter of Galatians, verse 6. *I marvel... I am amazed... I am astonished... that you are so soon removed from him that called you into the grace of Christ unto another gospel.* How did this happen so fast? His only conclusion was that somebody put a spell on them. Somebody had confused them, bewitched them, mesmerized them.

This brings me back to one of the first things I said: There are some preachers who are very persuasive by volume, and they'll shout their sermon at you, and there may be nothing wrong with that. But sometimes they use that: Less than scrupulous preachers have been known to use that to try and get across a message that's not true. They get the people going emotionally, so that they're shouting and hollering. Then they throw a little leaven into the mixture. And the people don't notice it and they swallow it. It only takes a little bit to poison them.

Apparently, somebody did this to the Galatians: Came in, and by some deceitful process, convinced them of things that weren't true. Bewitched them. Confused them. Taught them what Paul first called "another gospel." But then he said that it really isn't another gospel, because there is no other gospel. There's no other good news, he said, but there are some who would pervert the gospel, twist the gospel, confuse the gospel, and preach you a message that has no power to save. But he said that no one had the right to do that, not even an angel from heaven.

I don't care to hear Joseph Smith tell me what the angel Moroni revealed to him, because it's not in the word of God. So if there is somebody running around, some angel named Moroni, I've got news for Joseph Smith: He's a fallen angel. And the book of Galatians says *let him be accursed.*

Could the Galatians be that foolish, to think that beginning in the Spirit, they could now be perfected by the works of the flesh? To be so hung up on the things that are external, the things that don't matter? And evidently they were. Paul said, I only want to know one thing. Just answer me this one question: Did you get the Holy Ghost by the works of the Law, or was it by the hearing of faith?

Did you have to drag a bull to the gate of the temple to get the Holy Ghost? No. Did you have to keep the Sabbath to get the Holy Ghost? No. And remember, now, the Galatians were Gentiles. Did you have to be circumcised to get the Holy Ghost? Well no, they didn't.

Well, if everything was okay before, how come all of a sudden now you need to keep the Law? The One who gave you the Spirit and works miracles among you, does He do it by the Law, or is it by faith?

The Law can be a very dangerous thing to Christians. That's why we weren't put under it. Peter was honest enough to admit that even his own ancestors couldn't keep the law, and said to those that wanted to make the Gentiles keep it, "Why do you want to put a yoke on their neck that even we couldn't carry? Why would you want to do something like that to them? God never gave the Law to the Gentiles.

And yet, even today, 2,000 years later, we get caught up in the things of the flesh and forget about the things of the Spirit. I said all of that to bring me to a point about holiness. So, the Law was our schoolmaster, and children have to be taught things. In a particular way, you tell the child don't touch the stove. Don't go in the street. You may give an explanation of why, but the explanation tends to go over their heads. The part they need to remember is *don't do it.*

They may not understand the reasons, but it doesn't matter. The child may not understand that the stove is hot, but touching it is still going to burn them. He may not understand the dangers of a busy intersection, but if he walks out, he's going to get run over. And so, with little children, you have to do that: *Don't do this.*

The Law was our schoolmaster to bring us to Christ. Under the Law, everything was black and white. There was no gray area under the Law. It was all *Thou shalt not.* Jesus summed up the Law in two commandments. I can sum it up in three words: Thou shalt not! Don't do this! Don't do that! It was just *Thou shalt not* after *Thou shalt not* after *Thou shalt not.* It wasn't left up to people to decide; it wasn't left up to the conscience. The people didn't have the Holy Ghost living inside of them. There was nothing to guide them into truth. They needed the Law.

But the Law was our schoolmaster to bring us to Christ. But after that faith has come, we are no longer under a schoolmaster. And so, these things in the New Testament weren't taught with *Thou shalt not.* They were taught in a different way.

Assuming that the church all is filled with the Holy Ghost, which it's supposed to be... Because if we're not, then we're not the church. Remember what Paul said, "If any man have not the spirit of Christ, he is none of His." No Holy Ghost? No church! It doesn't much matter what they do. But we're supposed to have the Spirit of God that leads us and guides us into all truth. So all Paul needed to do was give a list of people that would not inherit the kingdom of God, and then leave it up to us.

If you've got the Spirit of God inside of you, and you see in the word of God that such and such a group of people aren't going to make it to the kingdom of God, then you'd better realize that if you are one of those people, then something's got to change.

If the scripture tells us that adulterers do not inherit the Kingdom, and you're an adulterer, the Spirit of God is supposed to point that out to you and say, "Hey adulterers, don't make it." You judge yourself, but not somebody else.

One of the legacies left to Pentecost from the 19th century Holiness Movement was a misunderstanding of holiness, embracing Old Testament holiness, with *Thou shalt not.* And with it came an insidious little spirit that we call the spirit of judgment: Judging everybody else, but not ourselves. And judging by the only criteria that we can judge. *Oh well, I'm not judging; it's the word of God judging!* But judging what? Well, judging what we can see: the outward appearance. But is that what God is judging? No.

And so we have the spirit of judgment that has infected the Pentecostal churches, and I say infected because it is a disease that has infected the

Pentecostal churches for all of the 20th century, causing them to teach holiness with *Thou shalt not.* And to actually have the nerve to stand in the pulpit and say that someone's going to go to hell for doing this, that or the other thing. I can't find anywhere in [the Bible] that that's *my* decision to make!

You'll never hear me stand up here and tell somebody they're going to burn in hell because of what they're doing. If Adolf Hitler was sitting there, I'm not going to stand here and tell him he's going to hell. It's not my decision. I'm not the judge, I don't want that job. You'd have to depend on my moods, because some days everybody gets in. Other days, nobody's going!

He didn't leave the decision to us. We're not stable enough to do something like that. We're just too fickle. But the bottom line is that we can't see the heart. We can't see the heart. All we can see is the outward appearance and we can't judge by that. That's how the Pharisees judged. That's how the Old Testament taught people to judge, by the outward appearance.

Jesus threw them a curve ball, and told them to judge righteous judgment, because the outward judgment wasn't righteous; only the inward judgment was righteous. But they couldn't do that.

Well, if you can't judge according to the heart, then don't judge, which is exactly what He went on to say. The New Testament is full of scripture telling us not to judge. And how dare we notice a speck in our brother's eye, when we've got a two-by-four in our own?

But see, that's what the spirit of judgment does: It blinds us so that we can't see ourselves and we can only see others. It blinds us to the one and only person we have the right to judge: ourselves. It focuses on all the human flaws of everybody else, and causes us to judge them.

Now, I know I've taught this here before. There are seven churches mentioned in the Book of Revelation, and there are letters to those churches. The last two, I think, are the most significant, because they symbolize the church in this age: The Apostolic churches of the end time, but there are two of them.

And I've sat in Pentecostal churches, for years, listening to Pentecostal preachers accuse all the rest of Christianity of being Laodicea. You know that God didn't have a good thing to say about Laodicea. Now one, they all want to be Philadelphia and say that the rest of Christianity is Laodicea, but doctrinally, Laodicea was an Apostolic Church.

That's something they don't want to admit, that Laodicea knew the truth. That's what made them the way they were. That's what made them so proud. And we can diagnose their problem by translating the name Laodicea: it means people who judge, or people of judgment. That was their whole problem: The spirit of judgment infected that church, and they saw everybody but themselves. They didn't know they were poor and miserable and blind and naked. All they saw was that nobody else could measure up to them.

They needed to be like Philadelphia. It was only a little church. It knew that it only had a little bit of strength. But its name sums it up: Philadelphia - *brotherly love, or the love between brothers and sisters.* That's what held them together. That's where their strength came from: that love... And that the only people they were judging were themselves and nobody else.

It's a dangerous thing when the spirit of judgment takes control of a church. And we've been praying for the past few years for the spirit of judgment to lose its hold in some of the apostolic churches. And we have indeed begun to see that happen. We've seen a major shake-up, for example, in the United Pentecostal Church, and they lost a good number of their churches, because all of a sudden the spirit of judgment lost its hold there, and the ministers and the people began to look and say, *"Wait a minute, we're teaching things that aren't in the word of God. We're requiring things of people that scripture doesn't. We've put a yoke on the neck of people who are supposed to be free. We put them in more bondage than the world ever had them in."*

And yet, while the spirit of judgment lost its hold in some places, it has strengthened its hold in others. Some churches went absolutely crazy. Preachers who had been stable for years began to preach some off-the-wall things.

The UPC in one upstate NY city was a good example, where a preacher who had been stable for years suddenly stood up and informed the congregation that he was the word of God in that church! And in that same church, for weeks on end the only sermon he could preach was an anti-gay sermon, not even knowing whether there were any gay people in his congregation. For some reason, he couldn't seem to preach anything else.

But I know the reason why, because the only people in that congregation who recognized the presence of the spirit of judgment happened to be gay people, they knew it was there and so it attacked them. The preacher didn't have to know anything; the spirit of judgment knew. We've seen it again: It strengthens its hold in some places, but then it loses its hold in others.

I had a wonderful story told to me by an Assembly of God minister who was seeing the same thing happen. This took place out in California. Now, this Assembly of God minister is gay, and works in the headquarters of the Assemblies of God in Missouri. He went out to California to visit his mother, and he was supposed to preach for the pastor of the church that his mother attends. He came out to his mother while he was there, thinking she could handle it. It turned out she couldn't, and she got very upset. He thought, "Well, I'd better go tell her pastor before she does." So he went over to the church to talk to the pastor, and he said, "There's something I need to tell you." The pastor said, "Well, are you preaching for me tonight or aren't you?" And he said, "Well, yes, but there's something I have to tell you." The pastor said, "I already know." And the minister said, "You already know?" The pastor said, "Yes, you're gay. So are you preaching for me tonight or aren't you?" The spirit of judgment had lost its hold in that congregation, and that's a wonderful thing.

To me, it is a frightening thing that churches that are part of [this organization] would ever have to deal with the spirit of judgment, because that's one of the main reasons we were founded, was to combat that spirit. But unfortunately, we have seen it make inroads [among us]. We have seen it infect us like a cancer. And like a cancer, it had to be removed. If you can't get the spirit out, then you got to cut off the body part, because it only takes a little bit. It only takes a little bit. We cannot allow ourselves to be bewitched.

I don't think Paul was just grasping at straws when he chose the word bewitched. There's a reason for that. Several years ago, I heard a very good teaching on witchcraft. You know, when we think about witchcraft and witches, we think either of the Wicked Witch of the West, or we think of some of these new age, Pagan kind of people who call themselves witches. I don't think that's what scripture was talking about when it spoke about witches. A witch is somebody who rebels against the natural authority, who goes against the established order of the way things were created to be.

The church was created to be a certain way. There are certain things that are supposed to be taught, and certain things that are not supposed to be taught. And anything that goes against that is witchcraft. It's witchcraft. And the people, the church in Galatia, had been bewitched by it. They'd been placed under a spell by a spirit of judgment.

We cannot allow that to happen to us. We cannot allow ourselves to go back into bondage. I don't know about you, but I spent too many years in slavery to sin. I am not about to go back into bondage to anything. The scripture says *Stand fast therefore in the liberty wherewith Christ hath set you free.* Stand in it! Cherish that liberty! Use that liberty, because if you don't cherish that liberty, if you don't prize it, if you don't consider it to be precious and holy, you will lose that liberty!

What man in his right mind, set free from slavery, would go back into it? Usually, that's preached in the context of sin, that if you're set free from sin, why would you go back into it? But it applies to our liberty in the Spirit, as well. We can't sell ourselves into bondage to the things of the flesh, to the Law of Moses or to any earthly law, because there's a different law that we're subject to, and that's the law of the Spirit, the law of faith.

We didn't start out on this walk by the flesh. Nothing our flesh ever did could have gotten us clean from our sins. Nothing our flesh ever did could have gotten us the Holy Ghost, nor could it have brought us this far in our walk with God. We've gotten this far by faith. Let's not switch to trying to do it by the flesh.

Now, I won't stand here and preach *Thou shalt not.* You've got the Holy Ghost inside you to tell you what you shall not do, not me. Not me. The loudest sermon on holiness I'm ever going to preach is going to be my own example, because that's the most effective one, because if I'm not living it, it doesn't much matter what I say anyway. And if I am living it, it'll shine like a light. And that's the same sermon that you need to preach as well: Live it.

Live it! You won't win anybody with *Thou shalt not.*

For thousands of years under the Law of Moses, they tried to win people that way, and all it did was cause death. No wonder Paul called the Law a curse! And Peter called it a yoke. Moses may not have liked to hear those things, but the bottom line is, they were true.

We have freedom. We've been given liberty. *Where the Spirit of the Lord is, there is liberty. And if the Son, therefore, shall set you free, you shall be free indeed.* Don't allow yourselves to be bewitched into giving up that freedom, into putting on any type of a yoke of bondage.

No man is your judge. God is the judge. It's before Him that we stand to give account, not before any minister, not before any church organization or any congregation. And if I judge myself now, then when I stand before Him, I won't need to be judged. But if I judge others now instead of myself, I'll be taking a whole mess load of junk with me when I go before Him. And in that case, I wouldn't want to be in my shoes then!

We've been redeemed from the curse of the Law. Let's not be entangled again with the yoke of bondage. If we put ourselves into debt to any portion of the things of the flesh, then we're in bondage to the whole thing. Sell out a little, and you're sold out completely.

Paul told the Galatians, "You did run well. Who hindered you that you should not obey the truth? This persuasion does not come from Him that called you." This was not from the One who gave you the Holy Ghost. This came from people!

Try the spirits! Check out what people teach you. Look to the word of God. If it isn't in there, it doesn't matter what you feel, or how good it sounds. If it's not in the word of God, it's not of God. If it contradicts the Bible, it's not of God. His word is forever settled in heaven.

Let in a little bit of a lie, and the whole thing will creep in. You know the old saying, give someone an inch, and he'll take a mile? The devil's that way: Give him an inch, he'll take a mile. A little bit of leaven leavens the whole lump.

So many are so worried we're going to fulfill the lust of the flesh, that we're going to be worldly, that we're going to be sinful, that we're not going to shine as a light. Paul said this simply: "Walk in the Spirit, and you shall not fulfill the lust of the flesh." It's that simple. Walk in the Spirit, not in the law. Walk in the Spirit, trust the Spirit. That's what He's there for, to be your guide, to lead you the way you should go, to be your warning around something that isn't good for you. You've all felt that, if you're around some manifestation of something evil, haven't you gotten that horrible, uncomfortable feeling, as the Holy Ghost speaks to you: *Get away from that. It's not good for you!* You know that feeling; that's what it's there for. You don't need the schoolmaster anymore to tell you *Thou shall not.* You don't need the Old Testament to teach you *Thou shalt not.* You've got the Author of it living inside of you. What more could you ask? You got the Author of the world's best-seller living inside of you teaching, preaching.

But I needed warning, because we've already seen the damage that can be done. We lost two congregations this week. We've lost them in the past. We'll probably lose more in the future. It didn't come as a total surprise, because we do have a minister in the office of prophet, Brother Curley, and he saw these things before they happened, and he warned us that things like this were going to happen. He didn't know any of the specifics. He didn't know he'd find himself caught in the middle of it, but he knew it was going to happen.

But any time something like this happens, that an infection creeps in, if it can't be cured, you've got to cut off the body part. Jesus said it's better to enter into heaven without your hand or without your eye, you know, than not make it in at all.

The first congregation we ever opened fell into spiritualism. They were burning black candles. They were taking ritual baths with strange kinds of oil. We couldn't heal the infection and so we had to cut it off. In another one of our early congregations, the pastor began to teach that there was no devil. He ridiculed people's beliefs from the pulpit. He was hurting people. We couldn't cure the infection; we had to cut it off. We were willing to cut off a church. That second congregation was almost a hundred people. That was the largest church we'd ever had. But we had to cut it off rather than let it infect the rest of the body.

And I don't care if it's a church of 10,000 people: If there's an infection in that body that's going to infect the rest of the church, we cannot allow that to happen. We can't let it happen... Not if we want to make it in. I don't know about you, but I want to make it in. I don't care if I get there last; I just want to get there. Amen!

Building With Old Stones

I'm turning to the book of First Kings. *Hallelujah!* You know, I love the LORD today. I love the LORD every day, but every once in a while, I'm just reminded of how much I love Him, and how much I need Him, how much I rely on Him in my life.

I've known for several days that the folks from Rochester [NY] were coming. I really didn't know what I was going to preach about, what I was going to talk about, but it really didn't matter because I knew God did. And then yesterday, while I was sleeping, He kind of kicks me in the side and says, "Wake up! There's something I need to tell you." And he gave me what it was that I was supposed to preach today.

Book of 1 Kings, chapter 18. We're going to be reading three portions of scripture. Of course, I'm famous for that. I'm never satisfied with just one spot; I've got to go for two or three. 1 Kings, chapter 18, beginning at verse 30.

And Elijah said unto all the people, come near unto me, and all the people came near to him. And he repaired the altar of the LORD that was broken down. And Elijah took twelve stones, according to the number of the tribes of the sons of Jacob, and to whom the word of the LORD came, saying, Israel shall be thy name. And with the stones, he built an altar, in the name of the LORD, and he made a trench about the altar, as great as would contain two measures of seed.

Turning now to 1 Corinthians, chapter three. And I'm going to be beginning at verse nine:

For we are laborers together with God: ye are God's husbandry, ye are God's building. According to the grace of God which is given unto me, as a wise masterbuilder, I have laid the foundation, and another buildeth thereon. But let every man take heed how he buildeth thereupon. For other foundation can no man lay than that is laid, which is Jesus Christ.

And finally, I'm turning to Ephesians chapter two, and I'm beginning with verse 19:

Now therefore ye are no more strangers and foreigners, but fellowcitizens with the saints, and of the household of God; And are built upon the foundation of the apostles and prophets, Jesus Christ himself being the chief corner stone; In whom all the building fitly framed together groweth unto an holy temple in the LORD: In whom ye also are builded together for an habitation of God through the Spirit.

I want to lay a little background for parts of the story, especially what I read in 1 Kings. The situation that was going on there is not what I'm preaching about, but I want to have some background for the story. The prophet Elijah lived during a time when most of Israel was worshipping false gods. Most of the 10 northern tribes, the northern kingdom of Israel, they were worshipping the Babylonian goddess Ashtaroth, sometimes called Asherah. They were worshipping Baal. Poor Brother Curley: I'm giving him all these words to spell! (Note: Bro. Curley was providing sign language services for the hearing-impaired, and was trying to quickly finger spell the proper names.) They were worshipping everything but the true God. And the day came when Elijah decided that enough was enough. And he called all the people together and he asked them basically how long they were going to sit on the fence. How long were they not going to make a decision about who God really was? He said, *"Now, if Baal is God, serve Baal. But if the LORD is God, serve the LORD."*

And he set up a contest, a sweepstakes, to determine who is God. He told the prophets of Baal and the prophets of Asherah to set up an altar, and to put a sacrifice on there with wood underneath it, but not to put any fire there to burn it. He said, "Then you call upon your gods." He said, "I'll do the same. And the God who answers by fire, let him be God." Well, they thought that was just fine.

And Elijah sat down under a tree. And he gave them all day to do what they had to do. And they shouted to Baal. And they screamed, and they hollered, and they danced and they cut themselves with knives to get his attention. The Bible tells us there was no response, there was no voice, there wasn't any that paid any attention to them. So Elijah began to mock them, you know, "Maybe he's on a vacation, or he's on a journey. You know, after all, he's a god. He's busy, you know, you better call a little louder." But nothing happened.

And Elijah waited until it was time for the evening sacrifice. And this gets to the point of what I want from this story. You see, there was an altar already set up there. They've been using it all day; there was a sacrifice on it all ready to go. There was no real need, from the physical perspective, for Elijah to build another altar. There was one already there, with an untouched sacrifice that hadn't been burned. And God could just as easily have sent the fire onto that altar. But Elijah wouldn't use that altar. There was something wrong with that altar. Some might say, "It's just a bunch of stones piled on top of each other. What could be wrong with it?"

There was something wrong with that altar; he couldn't use it. The stones of that altar were dedicated to a god who had eyes but couldn't see, and had ears and couldn't hear, hands, but couldn't reach to help. The god that those stones were dedicated to was dead. There was no life there. There was nothing worthy of a sacrifice there. Even the wood and the animal laid on it were polluted by the fact that the whole thing was dedicated to a dead god. That wouldn't do for Elijah or his God. That wouldn't do.

So Elijah did a little archaeology. He did a little archaeology. He went looking for the stones from an old altar from back in the days when Israel knew how to worship the true God. He looked for the ruins of an old altar. And he took twelve of those stones from that old altar and he built a new altar to the LORD. And only then was he ready to offer his sacrifice. Only then was he ready to do anything with it. Only when he'd found the old altar.

Many years later, Babylon invaded Judah, leveled Jerusalem, tore down the temple, tore down the walls of the city, and carried the people away captive into Babylon. Seventy years they were in captivity before they were allowed to come home. But I want you to know that the very first thing they did when they got back to Jerusalem, to the ruins of that city, before they built a house, before they set up a tent, before they tried to put up the walls, or build a temple, they went and repaired the altar. They found the place where the altar belonged, and they rebuilt it. What I want to talk to you tonight is about building a foundation. Now there are people who will hear me say this and they're going to roll their eyes and say, *"Here he goes again: The 'foundation freak' is preaching foundation again!"* I've been preaching foundation for years. *"When is he going to let us build?"* When am I going to let you build? Not till the foundations right. Not till the foundation is right.

A couple of years ago, we had a few people in this church who don't come here anymore. They were all bent out of shape because I wouldn't let them go out and witness to people. I wouldn't let them go out and stand on the streets and hand out literature and they wanted to know why not. Isn't evangelism what the church is for? Yes, yes, it is. But I said, "Until you've got something in here, don't go out there and advertise it!" The things that they were promising people, the love, the joy, the peace, the hope... they didn't have them in here. They didn't have them in their own lives. I said, "How can you go out there?" To demonstrate my point, I put on this hideous red suit jacket and I stood up here like a used car salesman, and I tried to sell them the Brooklyn Bridge and swampland in Florida, and the Statue of Liberty. And they thought it was funny. And I said, "Well, what's so funny?" And they said, "You don't have those things." I said, "That's right, and I can't sell what I don't have, can I? I can't allow us to build until we know the foundation is right."

It won't do to offer a sacrifice on an altar of Baal. We got to do a little bit of archaeology; we have to dig. We've got to dig until we find the old stones. Other people try to lay other foundations. But you know, the scripture says you can't lay any other foundation than that which is laid. So they may get together a whole heap of stones and build on them. But because they don't have a true foundation, what they build is going to fall. It's just sand. It's not a rock. But there is an old foundation. There is a very old foundation, started by the prophets. And then the apostles came and continued building that foundation. And the stone that the builders threw away, that they didn't want, turned out to be the cornerstone. And that's Jesus Christ. Now that's a foundation that you can build on. And the scripture says that each one will build what he can. Some will be building with hay and stubble, others with silver and gold. The important thing is you build on that foundation what you can. And if it's on that foundation, it will stand. But if you build on any other, it's going to fall.

I've always been fascinated by ancient cultures. I love to read about Egypt and the pharaohs and the pyramids. And I love reading about the things they found in King Tut's tomb. That kind of stuff fascinates me. I've always wanted to go to Egypt, to look at the ruins and to go to Rome and to Greece, and to Israel. And to see all the things from ancient civilizations. But we have to do that spiritually too. We've got to dig through 2000 years worth of garbage, and false foundations of men's traditions, of 'this way looks good to me, and that way, it looks good to them, and we'll each do it our own way.' The book of Proverbs says that there's a way that looks right to a man, but the end of that way is death. Oh, it looks good. It looks good.

I've never understood people who thought they could know more than the apostles. And yet the very next generation after them began to replace the things that [the apostles] had taught, thinking they could do it better, and they plunged Church into the dark ages, to the point where people weren't even allowed to have a relationship with God anymore! The church told you that you *couldn't* have a relationship with God. The only way to get to God was through the priest, or through Mary, or the saints; that you couldn't approach to Him and speak directly to Him, or ask Him for help. And all the power and all the glory of the first century church settled into the dust, buried with the foundation. I'm going to dig: I'm going to dig until I find an old foundation. I'm going to check every stone in that foundation, and make sure that every one is the apostles and the prophets. And I'm going to look for the cornerstone. I don't want to see the date the building was made. I want to see the name Jesus written on that cornerstone. I want to know that if I build on this, it's not going to fall.

And it doesn't matter what I build. I told somebody today "I'll be very honest: I am not qualified for this job. But when God called me, He didn't ask, 'Are you qualified for this job?'" God only has one requirement for people to work for him. Good old Isaiah! I love to talk about how Isaiah found himself, with no warning, standing in the throne room of God, knowing full well he didn't belong there, terrified because he was a sinful man. And there's God on his throne, in all His glory and all the angels around Him. And God asked, "Who am I going to send? Who's going to go?" Isaiah didn't even ask what the mission was! *Who's going to go where? Who's going to do what?* He didn't ask. He stepped out, knowing that he didn't even belong there, and said, *"I'll go. Send me. Here am I."* He was willing. That's God's only requirement: Just be willing.

So what I build on this foundation may not be as beautiful as what someone else can offer. I don't have a lot of talents. Nothing wrong with talents, everybody's got some. I won't win any awards for best preacher. God knows I won't win any awards for singing! But if I'm building on the right foundation, it doesn't much matter, because the building will stand. I'm going to dig.

In the book of Jeremiah, it says to stand in the ways, all the different roads, stand in them, and see. See all the different roads there are, that life offers? Well, you can choose any one, you know, you have free will. But then he gave some advice: Ask for the old path. The old one. It says that's the good way. And you'll find rest for your soul. Not the wide one that's paved and beautiful, but the old one, the old dirt road that looks like it can't possibly go anywhere, the one that's narrow and bumpy. That's the one that leads to eternal life. You know, Jesus said that the road that led to destruction was wide. There were many people going in that way. But He said the road that leads to eternal life is narrow. And then He said something that most of us miss. He didn't say that few were going in. He said few even find it! They don't find it. Why? Because it doesn't look like they want it to look. It doesn't look like they want it to look.

If you would gone in the first decade of [the 20th] century, to Los Angeles. You could have found some beautiful, beautiful church buildings there. You could have found church buildings there were four or five floors high, you know, like big caverns with beautiful stained glass windows. But spiritually, everything inside was dead. But you could have gone across town, to the wrong side of the tracks, and there was an old livery stable there, where they'd kept horses. This funny looking 'cheese box' of a building that badly needed paint. And there was power inside, because they had found an old road, and they decided to follow it. Oh, it didn't look like the rich churches. It didn't look like the powerful churches. It didn't look like anybody wanted it to look. But the minute those people set foot on that road, they knew it was the right one. Because no other road had ever had the power this one had. No other road could ever change anything inside. No other road that they'd ever walked on, could they find a way to heal their broken hearts. And there's no other road that leads to eternal life. Oh, there's so many ways you can follow. There's so many different religions. There's one religion, that if you translate the name of it, it means The Way... but the way to what?

Jesus didn't say he was "a" way. He said he was THE way. He's the way to eternal life. Yeah, it's a dusty old, unpaved road, but it's a beautiful road. And as Sister Mickey Mangun sings, "Someday this road will turn to gold. For some, this road's already turned to gold!" I won't trade this old, narrow way for any big, beautiful, paved highway. Brother Lewis and I have talked many times about the fact that the churches grow so slowly, that all our churches are so small. And we both knew the truth, that if we were to compromise what we teach, we could have huge churches. We could be packing them in by the hundreds, if we just stopped standing on the original foundation, if we'd just be willing to compromise a little, and let people believe anything they wanted, if we'd just be willing to let them make their own rules and laws and regulations on how to get to heaven. But how could we do that? None of those other ways will get them where they want to go. In all honesty, how could I call myself a minister of the Gospel if I didn't tell the truth, If I didn't stand on the original foundation?

You see, the only record Jesus ever left was what the apostles wrote down. He didn't write a book Himself. So the only way we know what He taught is by what they said. And if we decide that we don't need parts of what they wrote, and how do we know which parts we can and cannot trust? We might as well throw the whole thing away. It's not a pick and choose affair: It's all or nothing. All the stones of the old altar, of the old foundation, or none of them. I want them all. And I'm going to dig till I find every one. And not until I'm sure we've got this foundation right will I begin to build on it. And each one of you needs to do the same thing in your life. Check the foundation, not just once. Check it often. I've been building this foundation for more than twenty years, and I still find things in there that aren't supposed to be there and I pull them out. And I imagine till the day God calls me home, I'll still be finding things that I need to change because they're not quite right. But if Christianity is worth living, then it's worth living right.

Build your foundation, with the apostles, the prophets, with Jesus being the chief cornerstone, and then anything you put on top of it is going to stand for eternity. *Stand for eternity!* We're a group of people who've been told that we couldn't build on this foundation, that we couldn't have any part of it. Like I said, I've been working on this foundation, or building this foundation, more than twenty years, and God's never chased me away from it. *Hallelujah!* He's never once denied me the things that I need. He's never turned me away. And in fact, He said he wouldn't. *"He that cometh to me, I will in no wise cast out."* Not under any circumstances! God doesn't throw people away. We're not disposable to him.

This whole world thinks people are disposable: Use them and throw them away. But God knows people aren't disposable. And He doesn't throw us away. The love God has for us is absolutely unconditional. No matter what. No matter what, and nobody can take it away from us. Nobody can block our entrance to the kingdom. They can try all they want. Oh, you'll hear them: They'll stand in their pulpits. They'll pound them, and they'll scream and holler, and say that we can't go to heaven. But you know what? It's not their decision! It's not their decision to make. Only one Person gets to make that decision, and He already made it: "Whosoever will, let him come and take the water of life freely." Whosoever will may come! Anybody who wants to! You don't need a ticket to get in the ship. Just walk in. He's waiting at the door. And anything that you need from him, you can get.

He said to the Jewish people one time, "Would you, if your child asked you for a fish, would you give him a serpent? If he asked for a piece of bread, would you give him a scorpion?" Of course not! And if we, as flawed human beings, know how to give good things to our children, how much more will He give us? The things that we need are exactly what is He giving us. He said,

"It's your Father's good pleasure to give you the kingdom." A kingdom! Now, the world can try and promise you things like that. But how many of us are going to get a kingdom from the world? But He has given us the kingdom, His kingdom. A kingdom where the sun never sets. Because He's the sun. A kingdom where He wipes away tears from off all faces. There are no more broken hearts. There's no more pain. There's no more trouble or sadness. All the troubles of this life are gone. They're gone! I'm looking for that. I'm looking for that and believing. I'm looking for a city whose builder and maker is God. The invitation is out there to whosoever will. Admission? It's a strange price you have to pay, because it's nothing... And it's everything. I could take all the money in the world and I couldn't buy my way into the kingdom. But the price is me: everything I have, everything I am, everything I do. It all belongs to Him, because I was a slave. And He bought me and set me free. And now I belong to Him.

That's the first thing that God ever told me in my life, was that I was not my own. I was only seven years old, didn't have a Bible, raised in a church that said I shouldn't have one. I'd never opened the Bible. My family didn't have one. And the Lord spoke to me in the church I attended. And I didn't know it was scripture. I didn't know it was in [the Bible], because I didn't have one. He just said "You're not your own; you're bought with a price." I didn't know what the price was, but it didn't matter. He cared enough about me to pay a price! I guess I belong to Him! I've come a long way through the years. I still belong to Him. But He paid that price, not just for me, but for every one of us. The highest price anyone could pay. He bought our lives with His own. We were under the death penalty. He took our place.

Too many churches just want to present Him as the judge ready to pronounce sentence. And yes, He is the judge, but it's very strange because He's a judge who loves us unconditionally. That left me no choice but to turn and run to him. There was no place I could escape to. You can't fight love. I could fight judgment. I could fight anger. I could fight all that kind of stuff. But I couldn't fight love. What possible weapon could you use against it? Nothing is as powerful as love. The Bible tells us love never fails. Everything else may pass away, but love goes on and on and on. You can't fight it. It won me over. It's won over countless others. It makes it worth every hardship I might have to bear on this narrow, old road. It makes it all worthwhile. And I promise you, the minute we see His face, we won't remember the hard times anymore. We won't remember.

When I was in Bible school, we used to talk about things together, me and the other students, and we talked about what we were going to do when we finally see Jesus. What's the first thing we're going to do? Well, everybody had their own idea of what they were going to do. Some said they would be shouting, and some said they would be clapping. And some said they'd be worshiping and they said to me, "What are you going to do?" I said," I know what I'm going to do. The minute I see Him, I am going to fall down on my knees. I'm going to have my arms around His legs, and I'm just going to cry. Because I'm going to be so glad to be home." And they said "Crying in heaven?" I said, "Well, how can He wipe away the tears from my eyes if there aren't any?" And I'm going to cry until He wipes those tears away. Just so glad to finally be home. And it will be over.

I don't know how much longer. This old world isn't going to go on the way it's going much longer. We're close to the end. There's not a lot of time left. You know, when Noah preached about the flood coming, nobody believed him. But even those who might have thought, maybe he's right, figured there's still time, there's still time. Then God shut the door of the ark, and the water started to fall, and people started knocking on the door of the ark: Let us in! Let us in! Noah couldn't let them in. God had shut the door. When God shuts, nobody opens. This is the day of salvation. This is the day to get into the church, which is the ark today. Because once God shuts the door and takes his church out of this world, there's no more getting into it then. It's a dangerous thing to put it off, to wait to wait for a more convenient season. We may find out just how convenient this season was. It's gonna get worse. Today's the day of salvation. And whatever we need from Him, we've got it. All we have to do is ask. He promised that. One of the few things He cannot do is lie. God can't lie. He **is** the truth. He doesn't change or vary. He said, "I am God; I change not." Just the way He was 2000 years ago, the way He moved in the first century church with all the power, with all the miracles, with all the wonders, with lives being changed: He's exactly the same today. He hasn't changed. And we will see exactly what the first century church saw, and even more, when we build on the proper foundation.

Do you need something from God tonight? Whatever it might be, it's here. All you have to do is ask for it. He doesn't turn people away empty. Read about His ministry when He walked on this earth: He never sent anybody away without, even people who didn't deserve what He was offering. They got it anyway. All they had to do was ask. The Syro-Phoenician woman, not a Jewish woman, a Gentile, she had no business asking Him for anything. And He tried to tell her that, but she wouldn't give up. And she got what she came for. We're of the household of faith, and we have the right to ask anything in His name. What do we need? Healing? Salvation? The Holy Ghost? A new touch? That's something I need all the time, like that Lanny Wolfe song: "Lord, I need a brand new touch. My touch from yesterday is gone." I want another one! I need the strength to go on another day. Whatever you need, it's here tonight. We want to turn these seats into a makeshift altar. Anybody who wants to, pray. Just make yourselves comfortable. If you need somebody to pray with you, grab somebody, buttonhole them and ask them. Whatever you want is available. He sends no one away empty handed. All you have to do is ask. I'm not going to do a real dismissal. Just gonna say, stay, pray as long as you need to. When you got what you came for, then you're dismissed.

About the Author

Rev. William H. Carey founded the first LGBT-affirming Apostolic Pentecostal organization in 1980 in the city of Schenectady, New York. Affirming Spirit-filled churches can now be found all over the world. Bro. Carey served as Presbyter of the Apostolic Restoration Mission, an international denomination, as well as Dean of that body's ministerial training school, Apostolic Institute of Ministry.

Born in 1958 in Brooklyn, NY, he graduated from high school in Galway, NY before moving to Schenectady, where he received training for the ministry. Bro. Carey was ordained in 1981 in Omaha, NE, ministered in that city, and also in Houston, TX, before returning to Schenectady, where he served as pastor of Lighthouse Apostolic Church for more than a decade. He was a student of research writing and the humanities at Empire State College (SUNY), and has authored a number of books on theological topics.

Also by William Carey

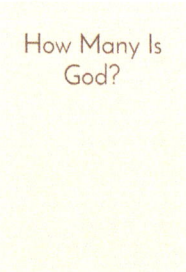

How Many is God?

A comparison of the doctrine of the Trinity with the teaching of the Oneness of the Godhead. Uses scriptural, historical and linguistic evidence to demonstrate that the Bible teaches an undivided Godhead: A single divine Spirit who took on flesh for the purpose of our redemption.

Derailed: How One Man Sabotaged Revival

A true story of how one man's ego and pride destroyed a mighty move of God that had just begun.

Repairing the Apostolic Church

For many years, Apostolic churches have lagged in growth and efficiency. Why? Because they are using the Protestant model of church administration, instead of the Apostolic model taught in the New Testament. It's like trying to drive a car with several important engine parts missing: You might get it to move, but it will never do what it was originally intended to do. This book shows the errors of trying to build an Apostolic church using a Protestant model, and demonstrates the original Apostolic model, explaining how and why it works.

www.ingramcontent.com/pod-product-compliance
Lightning Source LLC
Chambersburg PA
CBHW051509120626
46551CB00012B/845